What Time Are We On?

Published under licence by Brown Dog Books and
The Self-Publishing Partnership Ltd, 10b Greenway Farm, Bath Rd,
Wick, nr. Bath BS30 5RL

www.selfpublishingpartnership.co.uk

ISBN printed book: 978-1-83952-395-3
ISBN e-book: 978-1-83952-396-0

Cover design by Kevin Rylands
Internal design by Andrew Easton

Printed and bound in the UK

This book is printed on FSC certified paper

What Time Are We On?

**An Oral History of The London Jazz Scene from
The Early 1940s To 1965, Told By The Musicians
Who Were There**

Matt Haskins

BROWN
DOG
BOOKS

For my partner Hilary and son Max, without whom this book couldn't have been written

My eternal gratitude to my father Chris, and interviewees; Chris Barber, Don Rendell, Eddie Harvey, Tony Kinsey, Wally Houser, John Critchinson, Harold Pendleton, Paul Jones and Tony Pitt. Their willingness to be involved left me amazed. I very much extend this to their wives as well.

Contents

WHAT TIME ARE WE ON?

INTRODUCTION

So this is the tale of a time long forgotten. Of an era that maybe shouldn't have gathered dust, and been left to rust. But I'm not interested in giving you large histrionics, why would I want to give you what you've heard before? Oh how dull! So let us not dwell.

Since The Beatles and The Rolling Stones the time I'm talking of has been left behind, when so many love the music since, why do so few have a clue about what happened before? Stories of someone called Chris Barber as the grandfather of British blues, a gent by the name of Ronnie Scott as the father of jazz over here. I wonder, I wonder, I wonder, I wonder? Well wonder not much longer, I intend to put the record straight without scratching it.

After the Second World War music in the UK had its own major rebellion.

Long before Rock 'n' Roll, Beatlemania, the Swinging Sixties, Cool and Psychedelia. The people behind It? Your parents, Gran and Grandad. The full story not properly told, so this is my greatest effort to convey the saga. If you want the finer detail then I'm sure it's out there.

What Time Are We On?

Well I've got out my cloth and polish and tried to buff up what I can find. I can't say it's been easy given that many of the fine people involved are no longer with us. Though some of them are, and over the last 11 years a number of them have been happy to talk, to recount their tales, express hard upbringings, share the jokes, tell of fashion mistakes and of very humble dwellings. Seedy Soho, London Clubs, villains, characters, filthy streets and drugs.

So what did the young music lover have to get so worked up about in the mid-1940s? Why would they want to get so agitated when the war had just finished, we were finally victorious, celebrations were over and let's face it, I'm only talking about music? It's hardly the end of the civilised world. It has a lot to do with the big band and the Lyons Corner House, amongst other things. Firstly, I'm sure there's many of you out there thinking, 'how on earth can you get worked up about big bands?' But also, 'what on earth is a Lyons Corner House?' I hope in the following pages you'll allow me to enlighten you.

To complete this book I've also used the words of those that aren't here. Visited the sites and places talked about and frequented by the following, to help take you back to a time very different from now. What I've also brought to the table is I hope another perspective. I'm a jazz musician (having started out as an alternative/indie guitarist) and my dad was a professional for well over 50 years, and as a result I grew up with all of this in the mix and lurking in the background. So I see the music from both sides, fan being the other, which is pretty rare even now it seems. The people involved here don't always frequent the same circles, bars or clubs. Depending on which side of 'divides' they fall.

In these pages you'll find the words of the people that mattered, whether you've heard of them or not. They include Chris Barber, Ronnie Scott, Eddie Harvey, Don Rendell, Tony Kinsey, John Critchinson. Harold Pendleton, Wally Houser, Paul Jones, Humphrey Lyttelton, Jack Bruce and others. It's taken several years to complete and has been a real labour of love, in which time many of them have since passed on.

The broader point of my tale is not just to give you an account of jazz in London and the UK, but also of the rhythm 'n' blues scene here too. Of how it grew up and out of jazz then became so big that it brushed it aside. For better or for worse, forever and after, that's that. Then I'll leave you in the 60s where I guess you might know what comes next. What I also want to achieve is to bring all of you who read this, whether you're a highly trained jazz musician, a dedicated record collector, Traditional Stomper, bebop aficionado, skiffle lover or know virtually nothing about this music at all, an insight into a highly significant time before it's lost forever. So if you're ready then hold on to your trilby or service hat, let me lead you back to a time when life was a little more tricky, and definitely more dirty.

CHAPTER 1

Britain was a bleak and dangerous place during the early 1940s, London even more so. This is a familiar story I'm sure. Music in the UK, like the rest of the western world at the time, revolved around the Classical variety and then everything else. The latter was dominated by the dance orchestra and the big band, by the swing music of America.

A significant inconvenience for those who wanted to listen to, and play jazz, was the falling out between the Musicians' Union (MU) and the American Federation of Musicians (AFM). The storm broke in 1937/38, when they banned each other's members from performing in their respective countries. The agreement they had was called 'The Exchange System'. It was just that, if a band went over from the UK, then a US group had to come over here in return. The Unions felt that these imported players were 'stealing' the work of their hard-pressed resident compatriots. For the UK, the ban meant that the bands that contained the most talented and virtuoso American players, like Duke Ellington, Louis Armstrong, Coleman Hawkins, Count Basie, Benny Goodman, Fats Waller and Benny Carter, stayed in the USA, instead of touring here. Also, before the ban many would happily go to a jazz club after their show, sink a few beers, and play for and with the fans and players who wanted to be in the know. This event was called a 'Jam Session'. Some jazz clubs disappeared with the talent. The ban stayed in place until 1956, and we'll come to that later.

Out beyond the Smoke in Kent, a young Eddie Harvey was having his own first-hand experience of the war. Eddie is a well-known musician, arranger and educator. As a trombone player he was in the Johnny Dankworth Seven during the 1950s, as well as with other groups of the time. 'When I left school at 16 I worked on a farm, during the Battle of Britain. I saw all that. I lived in Sidcup so I was on the right track for that, it was all thrilling stuff. I started playing at seven, when I was a kid I was in the choir, my mother was a singer, I learned the piano from seven 'til 12 'til my family broke up. Anyway, I had a background in music. Having played the piano and stopping at 12 I'd started improvising anyway, although in a very crude kind of way.' He says this with a broad smile across his face.

I'll let the gent continue. 'It really started at school for me, I left when I was 16. I had a mutual friend at school in Wally Fawkes (alias Trog, the well-known satirical cartoonist employed by the *Daily Mail* amongst others) who was at art school at the time. He'd discovered jazz there and this mutual friend of ours had one of those houses where all the kids meet round there. I met Wally round there and he lent me my first jazz record. It was Muggsy Spanier, Johnny Hodges, one of the Duke Ellington small groups, but I remember I was so excited by it that I never slept for a week. It was like falling in love, I mean literally, if you fall for a girl. It was just like that. It would have been 1941. Anyway, Wally and I got on very well so I really got into this stuff, y'know?' I do, exactly.

What Time Are We On?

For those of you who may have only ever got your music on a CD or through your iPod we come to a substance called Shellac. 'What on earth's that?' I hear you cry. It is a resin secreted by the female Lac bug to form a cocoon, on trees in the forests of Thailand and India. At this time records were made out of Shellac, until the late 1940s when it was replaced by vinyl. It was also used in electrical applications as it had good insulation properties. Very useful for the military.

For Eddie and many others like him throughout the UK, this was a very BIG problem. 'In those days, because Shellac was a "strategic material", as they called it, only a few records were issued, only one jazz record a month called "Billy Elliott's choice", who was a critic. This record came out and of course we all bought it, so by the time we'd had it for a week we could actually sing it! We used to talk about phrases of Louis Armstrong's and all that kind of thing, and I realised some years later of course, when I became a tutor at university, that this was how we learned the music. By having a very small amount of information and learning it. Nowadays there's a problem because there's so much information, guys buy an album of John Coltrane and all that and they can't remember any of it. In those days you actually took in information straight off the music.' Given that Eddie's a music lecturer, and seeing it myself as a former student, I didn't think I'd witness one saying that you can have too much to listen to. This goes against the grain of all the usual advice you get which is to 'play, play, play!' regardless of what the tune is. But being able to perform something backwards is no bad thing. Honest.

Eddie continues, 'After that I became an apprentice at Vickers which was an armaments factory. I fell in love with one solo in particular,

I remember which one it was. It was Glenn Miller's trombone solo on either *Hello Lola* or *One Hour* which is a famous record now by McKenzie's Blue Blowers. So I wanted to play the trombone, it seemed like that was the instrument I was interested in, I saw this one [shows it to me] in an antique shop and I bought it for about 12 quid, which was a lot of money in those days. So at 16 I was ready to get into the real thing. Prior to that I'd been buying song copies and trying to play them and stuff like that, and I liked dance band music really, it's what we all liked was on the BBC, Geraldo and all that those bands. So I was ready for this move from that into jazz proper.' While Eddie Harvey is gearing himself up for the next step, a young Chris Barber was evacuated from London like thousands of other kids like him.

Chris is now a very well-known jazz musician and bandleader and is a central figure in this story, a stalwart of the scene for over 60 years. He starts to explain his own like this. 'It's very funny, I had been keen on music when I was a child. My father played the violin, as an amateur. He was at Christ's Hospital School and was Leader of the Orchestra. He must have been a good player, you can't do that without being an able performer yourself. I never heard him play the violin or the viola. He gave me a little violin when I was seven. I didn't want to know, I didn't bother with it at all. When the War was on and I was going to boarding school in the country there wasn't much to do there. The school I'd been in at Golders Green had moved itself to a farm, by one of the teacher's families in Royston. My father in the meantime had been separated from us during the War 'cos he was living in London, working all the time, and my mother was away with my sister and me in the country. My father gave me a full-size violin and he said you can get some lessons. The nearest place to get a lesson every week was at Cambridge. I was at Royston which was 14 miles away.' A difficult predicament to resolve. But how?

Chris continues his tale. 'This was about 1942/1943 when I first went to the school there. We listened to the American Forces Network, I had a radio. Another thing, people didn't really have radios, kids in those days. I had a little Bakelite radio, valve of course, so I'd listen to the AFN all the time, and they played jazz records a bit, not a lot but some. I heard some jazz on the radio. A bit on the BBC, but not much, and then I was looking for it. I read about it, not difficult and having been brought up in quite a left-wing household we were naturally all aware of what slavery was and why, and how it went and what happened and all those different things. It's part of what makes people become left wing. So, my mother's father was a Rural Dean in the Church of England and his first parish as a young vicar was in Mile End, London. So he became a Socialist right away. So I was politically minded to jazz and the idea of it.' Good to know it.

Down in Kent Eddie moves on, using his initiative. He and his mate trying to make something count. 'I went to Vickers and Wally and I continued playing. We used to hire the Liberal Hall, Sidcup, for 1/6d (less than ten pence) a night, Tuesday night, and the pair of us, trombone and clarinet went there and played together, and got complaints from the neighbours! In no time at all other guys were saying "we hear you're having a play." We got a guitar player and a drummer, we had a little terrible band y'know, but that's how it's done. So, we did that for a while, but that was the start of it. Anyway, I went to lunch one day when I was at Vickers at Crayford and I heard these two guys on the other table talking about Bix Beiderbecke. Now up until this time I thought Wal and I were the only people who liked jazz in the whole world, 'course nobody else liked it y'know, still a bit like that isn't it [laughs]? The result of it was that I spoke to George Webb and another guy. So we started talking about jazz and all the rest of it and they ran a jazz club at the place called The Red Barn, in Barnehurst. So I said to George, who played the piano, "well I've got this clarinet player and he's keen on Sidney Bechet, and I play a bit of trombone," and all that and he had a trumpet player, Owen Bryce, so we had the nucleus of a band. This club that they were running at Barnehurst, near the station, they weren't pulling the people in, or something like that, so we decided to form a band.' They started gigging there in 1943, and things started to move along.

He elaborates further. 'In fact, George became a kind of surrogate parent for me when I left home. I moved nearer the factory, as a "paying guest" as they used to call it. The result of that was that I was only earning £1.50 a week and that's all the dough that I had. I used to go over to George's place, they were an Elephant and Castle cockney family, a very warm group of people. One of those cockney families that used to play cards at the weekend, friends round for drinks and all of that. But George was into this early jazz y'know? So I went over there and we rehearsed at his house every weekend, we'd go through this music and learn it by heart. King Oliver's [1920s/30s American Traditional trumpet player] music, early Louis Armstrong [his protégé], and after about a year and a half of rehearsing with the band round at George's house, and playing in this club, somebody, I don't know who it was, found out about it. This is 1943. The result of that was they'd never heard this music played live, not like that. There were professional bands, the players were in actual fact too good to be able to play this music. They were schooled players. There was a feeling against early jazz at that particular time. Swing was the King, and all the people, Harry Parry and all these professional musicians they weren't interested, and quite right too! So the music that they were playing was really based on Benny Goodman and people like that, whereas we wanted to go back to this earlier stuff. The nights at the Red Barn also started with a record recital, and then we'd go on. People would bring their own and play this early jazz to each other.' To me that's starting off with a DJ set from audience. Keep the crowd happy until the band's due to tread the boards!

Humphrey Lyttelton, the well-known jazz musician and broadcaster, describes in his book *I Play as I Please*, the impact he first experienced of George Webb's Dixielanders in 1944, and the authentic traditional jazz that they played. 'At the beginning of the Revival, there was a danger that amateur jazz would become a cult, a sort of stuffy, introspective mutual admiration society between the musicians and the "initiated students". At the Red Barn, where George Webb's Dixielanders played, the band played at the seated rows of listeners, who drank the music in and digested it and regurgitated their views and analyses of it all with the greatest solemnity. This was the atmosphere in which all amateur jazz was played then. It had no function other than to provide food for thought to the brotherhood of serious critics and enthusiasts. No wonder then that it showed signs, after a time, of being stifled by its own self-consciousness. It would not have survived as long as it did had not the musicians been sustained by the sheer enjoyment of playing.' It's always good to have a first-hand account, and I'm sure he's not wrong on that last statement.

Confirming the point he says, 'it created a whole Revivalist movement. For a lot of people it was revolutionary at the time. It was validated by the fact that it was being performed by self-taught amateurs, who in turn started to form groups of their own. What also mattered to these musicians and enthusiasts was that this music was being played in the UK. To many the music of Swing was fake, just like the big bands and professionals that made their living from it. They felt it was hardly creative to use the same written parts, from the same written pads, night after night. Their aim was to break the firm grip that these musicians had on the work, the airwaves and the recording industry.' A creative Punk, based on a handful of chords. It's what you do with them that counts.

George Webb's Dixielanders. Eddie Harvey left, George Webb right.

What Time Are We On?

Going back to initiative, Chris Barber is about to make the most of his. A vital quality at any age, and in any year. 'Anyway, I had to go to a fiddle lesson in Cambridge every Saturday. So I got the bus fare which was about 5 shillings (25p) return. A 78 record cost 5/4d ha'penny (27p) at the time with 'purchase ex' (Purchase Excise Duty – a tax) on it. So what I did was, I got on my bike. Hitched on the back of a lorry and got a free ride to Cambridge and back the same way. I bought a 78 every week, a single every week for three to four years!' The fact that Chris was able to do this was a piece of great fortune, and foresight.

The brass player goes on. 'The thing was, the one reason it worked was that it was Cambridge. If you had looked into where you could buy a jazz record, or a blues record for that matter as there were some about, in Britain from the stock of a shop it would have been London, Oxford or Cambridge. They were the only colleges there were then. That's where there had always been a following for jazz and blues music. In London, because there are more people here, the law of averages says there's more of them. I went into the record shop in Cambridge and said "have you got any jazz records?" "I don't know what you want" was the reply. I bored them to tears and they gave me the catalogue. Then I got behind the counter and started looking at them, all these records. They had to stop buying them in when the War broke out because they had patrons/students, new ones, coming every year of course, who are probably gonna buy that stuff. But, the only thing is that generation of patrons went because of the War. If they were old enough they got called up. So, there was all this stuff in the record shop. HMV had an export series, catalogue numbers began with an 'X'. 'JF' was another one. They produced them in England because there was a market for them in France and Switzerland. You could buy them in England if you ordered them especially. But at that shop in Cambridge they were there all the time, they knew which ones to get, they had someone to advise them, right. I bought those. I got King Oliver, and Duke Ellington, Louis Armstrong's Hot Seven, some even obscur-ish ones. Fats Waller, so on and so forth. So I knew what they sounded like and what the players sounded like. This wasn't messing about, it was really good playing. When the War finished and I came back from Royston I had 50 78s already!' In 1945 Chris was 15. It's an admirable achievement; some of the collection still exists.

Although Eddie Harvey is beginning to have doubts about playing what is called 'traditional jazz,' during my first interview with him he sets the record straight with regard to the start of our musical story. 'I wasn't totally convinced about early jazz, I was really quite interested in people like Jack Teagarden [American trombonist and bandleader] who I was a particular fan of. I was already looking at a broader field than George and the other guys who were really interested in recreating King Oliver [1920s/30s American traditional trumpet player]'s music. Anyway, we had this band, which was the first band that really started doing that. There were other bands about but they weren't actually trying to do that. There's a blue plaque on The Red Barn now. It says 'This is where the traditional jazz revival started' [Eddie smiles broadly through his thick, grey beard]. There's no doubt about it.

He continues, 'anyway, the result of that was "the critics". You see the situation in those days was that there were not American musicians here. We never heard live jazz. There were some of the Glenn Miller guys evidently in Artie Shaw's band who used to play in the West End. But we weren't part of that, we were suburban people y'know. The result of that, was that we started to get a repertoire together of this early stuff. The power, what we called the "Jazz Police", were the critics. Because they were well informed about all the recordings and the music and stuff like that. So they had this sort of superior attitude. Y'know, if you were a musician these people would almost tell you what to do. I mean a case in point was you could see the way things were going then. I became interested in a more advanced school of trombone players. I tried playing like that in George's band and I was hauled before a "Kangaroo Court". In those days you had what were called Swing clubs, where people gathered in rooms in pubs and had record recitals. They would play records to each other. There was a group of university guys, they were Oxbridge people, these were the founts of all jazz knowledge. I was hauled before a Kangaroo Court 'cos I was "playing out of context". I wasn't supposed to be JC Higginbotham, I was supposed to be Kid Ory [both American musicians], y'know what I mean, as a trombone player? It was LIKE THAT! Looking back on it, it was absolutely stupid [laughs]. Anyway, the result of that was we made a couple of records.' When critics start giving advice like that I'd suggest playing out of context even more! Musicians often don't take kindly to being told how to play, by people who aren't musicians themselves.

So where did matters take him next, the Capital surely? 'The next thing that happened to me was that I was called up in 1944 when I was 19. So I was in the Air Force and all that, and eventually I went to India. So I was off the scene for a short while, not for long but a guy "depped" [deputised] for me [in the band]. So I came back and the band seemed to have raced sharply backwards, I did concerts with them. We played at Birmingham Town Hall, to 2,000 people, I mean the band got quite big y'know, quite popular and we were drawing quite a lot of audiences for these concerts that we did. We did some concerts up at Kingsway in London, and all that. There was a whole society. And the fervour, you look back on it now and it all seems a bit daft but at the time we were totally sincere about it y'know. So professional musicians were sort of off limits to us [laughs]. There was all kinds of silly stuff.' They were dedicated.

One of the only venues where you could hear 'live jazz', at the end of hostilities, was in the West End of London. The Nuthouse on Regent Street still had the easy, dark and vibrant atmosphere of the clubs that had existed prior to the war. One regular visitor was Humphrey Lyttelton, who was at the start of his trumpet-playing career. For the record, he's also known by musicians, colleagues and many fans alike as 'Humph'. He'd left Eton by this time and was now a Captain in the Grenadier Guards, posted to Chelsea Barracks.

I'll leave him to explain what he found on a good night out here. 'The clientele was a mixed one. There were plenty of GIs, quite a number of Guards and Cavalry Officers on a slumming kick and the usual floating population of night owls – men and women of doubtful occupation who only appear at large after dark.' Occasionally fights would break out between the soldiers, often escalated by the GIs who were quite happy to get stuck in, regardless of the whys and wherefores. Humph's first course of action was to get onto the stage with the band as fast as possible, trumpet in hand, and one night played *Who's Sorry Now?* flat out for half an hour in self-defence. There was an unwritten rule that said if the band kept playing it was left alone. His brave colleagues from the Grenadiers would hide under the tables, shielding their bottles of gin from the fray. Another witness to the melee was Don Rendell, a young tenor saxophone player, who was at the front of the modern jazz scene that isn't so far off (and who we meet a little later).

One of the attractions for the clientele was that one of the Yanks might be a familiar name they'd know. From say the Glenn Miller Orchestra or Sam Donahue's US Navy Band, who were in London at the time. The group that played there regularly had the classic line-up. Each musician a solid and sound performer. They were fronted by the drummer Carlo Krahmer. A real musical driving force. The 'horn' section was made up of a trumpet, an alto saxophone and two tenor saxophones (or tenor and trombone). The 'rhythm' section was made up of piano, double bass and Carlo himself on drums. He was also a man of many talents, as a piano and vibes (vibraphone) player. Having played in jazz groups and orchestras in the 1930s, at the many clubs and halls in London prior to the war, he was unique as a performer, and fountain of knowledge. In his flat, at Bedford Avenue, W1, he had assembled an enormous collection of jazz on record. He was happy to have fans, from all ages and backgrounds, of this great music come to sessions where they could hear it played, and meet each other. This at a time when, as I've already illustrated, obtaining records was not without serious obstacles.

Carlo Krahmer was also very astute when it came to bringing on fresh performing talent. In jazz the method for doing this is the same as for recognised players. It's called 'sitting in', and Humphrey Lyttelton certainly benefitted from it, as did countless others. If the band (in Carlo's case), or venue (in a jam session) encourage musicians from the audience to perform with them, usually given the nod by the band leader, they will play a couple of 'standard' jazz tunes, then return to the crowd. It's a great way of getting experience, learning the ropes and making the mistakes! On your arrival to the stand you often get looks of grudging mistrust from your new colleagues, like you're invading their territory. If you screw it up you can get the filthiest looks from the other players. I've seen both sides of it myself, but as a method it's invaluable in a profession where there's no apprenticeship, or training scheme when you start out. You learn how. Carlo's enthusiasm for recorded jazz was exemplified in 1947 when he launched the record label 'Esquire' in 1947, with Peter Newbrook.

The only jazz club in London, where you could hear 'live' bands in 1945, that resembled anything that was about in the 1950s, was the Feldman Swing Club at 100 Oxford Street. Humph explains, 'a friendly Jewish couple, used to preside over jam sessions featuring the avant-garde of London's jazz musicians,' on a Sunday night. Carlo Krahmer was its unofficial musical director. It still stands today as the well-known 100 Club. It was owned by Mr and Mrs Joe Feldman, who provided jazz for dancing between the practical hours of 7 and 10.30 pm.

The result of VE Day, and the end of the War means that Chris Barber is leaving Royston. In 1945 he buys the disc that changes his life, and most of us have been there even if it wasn't jazz. 'It was in that year that I got George Lewis' (American traditional clarinettist) *Pretty Baby*, it was the one that convinced me to play jazz.' As a consequence of the record collection he's assembling, the level of initiative that's needed remains high in order to keep it going. 'From 1946, we moved back to London. So then my mother and my sister and me lived in a house in Hampstead Gardens, a suburb, which is near Golders Green. What you do have in Hampstead Gardens is a lot of Jewish people. In the centre of the Gardens you have this house designed by Lutyens. It was complicated, odd shape. However, we were there. For a long time after the War there were no dollars to be had, right. In fact, if you went abroad you were allowed to take two pounds with you. That was the maximum you could take with you. You had to rely upon people giving you money over there or whatever, that sort of thing you see. One of the neighbours, they said "we get these dollars from our family in New York, they send us money every month." I said, "you're getting dollars?" I said, "would you get them to buy something for me with it and I'll give you the money here?" "Yes of course," they said. So I ordered all that was current on the Major American (Record) Labels of current blues material, and they sent them over (something else for the iPod generation to think about!), so I had those in 1947 you see, 1948.' Well my jaw hit the floor when I heard that.

He then does the obvious. 'Anyway, I started looking for jazz. I went into a couple of record shops. In there, there was a leaflet on the side for a Jazz concert, which was George Webb's Dixielanders. They did a concert every three weeks in the King George's Hall, which is in Adeline Place. It's a big concert hall with 300 seats, behind the YMCA at the bottom of Tottenham Court Rd. This was when I was 16, in September 1946. So I went there, and the first time you hear a traditional band, even if they're not very good, it's overwhelming compared to records. The records now, they give you BIG overpowering sound. You didn't get that from 78s on a wind-up gramophone, even an electric one really, it wasn't like that. George Webb's Dixielanders were overpowering

George Webb's Dixielanders, Recording Studio

totally, to hear. I think I walked right down the aisle to the front like that [Chris leans forward holding his hand to his ear] y'know? That was the George (Webb) way of Dixieland, Georgia yeah? I know George very well. Lovely guy, can't play the piano very much but doesn't pretend to be able to, 'cos he enjoys himself playing. And his band? The two trumpets are Humphrey Lyttelton, Owen Bryce, and Wally Fawkes on clarinet, the best guy in the band. So I went down to see them in Barnehurst 'cos that's where they played all the time, down at The Red Barn pub.' The King George's Hall gigs were part of a larger series of concerts the group were involved in, called The Hot Club of London.

What Time Are We On?

Humph puts an enlightening view on the new audience for jazz. Aside from the Feldman Club he says, 'there were countless small Rhythm-and-Hot clubs meeting in pubs and back rooms all over London, sometimes with a live band, sometimes relying entirely on gramophone records.' It's a very lively, hands-on and active scene.

By 1946, a new, 'hardcore' revivalist had started to appear. The purists. Think the original Human League or Killing Joke after the Buzzcocks and Stiff Little Fingers. To them the early jazz of the 1920s was the only true definition of the music. The commercial music of the big bands, the established music press and the major record companies was sacrilege. These Revivalists were very much influenced by two American musicians from New Orleans, called Bunk Johnson and George Lewis. When their colleagues King Oliver and Louis Armstrong left that southern city, and set themselves up in Chicago in 1920/21, they were branded as traitors. They had sold out to play slick jazz for the wealthy city elite; rather than keep the jazz that they loved at home in its roots. The music wasn't the real deal, being as it was full of smooth solos, clever harmony and dressed up in smart suits. In the UK the purists began to ape and mock the professionals. They'd turn up on the bandstand with their jackets off, and shirts hanging out of their trousers. One might take his trombone apart and stare down the pipework, looking for a problem that didn't exist, while the trumpet player took a solo. They might turn the PA and amps up to make the microphones scream with feedback (this will take some of you right back to the 100 Club Punk Festival in 1976!). If any of them went as a group to a concert, or radio performance, with both Revivalist and Professional bands on it, they would applaud the former and keep quiet for the latter. With the educated critics, the 'Jazz Police' as Eddie Harvey called them, they made for a significant challenge to the established order. The Professional bands, the music business and the BBC though, could handle themselves as well.

At the same time the jazz scene is proving particularly trying for Eddie Harvey, but he's determined not to let it get in the way of his own musical ambitions. 'Even at that time I went and sat in with some of the local big bands that were playing in town halls, for dances and stuff like that. Free. I would sit on the end on 4th trombone and watch the parts 'fly by' 'cos I wanted to read properly, and I was castigated for that because they [the critics and others] said, "if you want to read music it'll ruin your jazz." Another bloody myth! This kind of stuff went on all the time, it was really weird.' As a means to an end, the reading? Perfect!

What happened when you completed your commission? 'So one of the lucky things that happened when I came back, they always ask you in the Air Force, "where would you like to be posted?" And so I said Uxbridge, Hendon, Biggin Hill y'know. So they posted me to a place called Silloth. It's 20 miles west of Carlisle on the Cumbrian coast (laughs). There's two trains a day to get there, nothing of a weekend. I think it's what they [the Air Force] used to do to find out where you wanted to be, and post you somewhere else so you weren't near your family, or liable to skate off y'know, that kind of thing. But the great thing about it was I didn't have a job there 'cos the job I did was as an engineer by then, having worked at Vickers, and I worked on aeroplanes and all that stuff in the Air Force which I quite enjoyed. I mean I could have actually done music, I was what they called a voluntary bandsman in the Air Force, you played in station bands but you weren't a bona fide musician. So anyway, at this place all I had to do was open the Sports Store for about an hour a week. The rest of the time was mine so I practised, and I practised. Right for that last

George Webb's Dixielanders, group photo.

six months I was in the Air Force, I practised my arse off! I really did [laughs].' What can I say? A committed gentleman.

In 1947 Humphrey Lyttelton joined George Webb's Dixielanders, in a two-cornet line-up. His first real break as a musician, it was good going, though. This band, and some of their smaller contemporaries, had started to gig outside of London. Playing at jazz festivals that had booked them, and privately organised shows put on by amateur clubs. As a working musician myself it's worth noting, through my interviews and research, that getting to gigs still involves you driving there or climbing into the back of a van with the gear. Nothing's changed in over 70 years!

ACKNOWLEDGEMENTS:

I Play as I Please: The memoirs of an Old Etonian trumpeter. With drawings by the author. [With plates, including portraits.] Humphrey Lyttelton, 1921–2008. London: MacGibbon & Kee, 1954. – (P. 189/190), (P. 104), (P. 100), (P. 101)

CHAPTER 2

It's late afternoon, on an autumn evening in 1948. It's grim, foggy and damp. The street lights attempt to brighten up the gloom. On the gentle slope that is Charing Cross Road, in the heart of Central London, the motorcars run up and down. A red number 24 STL double decker bus, with an advert for Watneys Pale Ale stuck to its side, heading for Pimlico, Grosvenor Road, chugs south over Cambridge Circus. A passenger gets up from his seat and pulls on the cord in front of him. 'Ching, ching' rings the bell, the bus pulls up at the stop and the young man alights. He straightens his light brown trench coat. On his left is 77, Charing Cross Road, the premises of Dobell's Book Shop. It's one of the first of its kind in the country to sell a limited number of jazz and blues records, but then go over entirely to this trade. When this had happened in 1950 its slogan became, 'every true Jazz fan is born within the sound of Dobell's.' Our traveller pushes the brass doorknob and enters. Abruptly he stands in surprise. The face of the customer in front of him is very familiar. They grin at each other and shake hands, astounded by the coincidence. We'll find out who these characters are a little later in the chapter.

What Time Are We On?

Humphrey Lyttelton was in George Webb's band for eight months. Wally Fawkes left at the same time and The Dixielanders folded. At the beginning of 1948 Humph decided it was time to put together his own outfit, the Humphrey Lyttelton Band. Wally, and Harry Brown on trombone, joined from his previous group, as well as John Robinson, a 17-year-old drummer, found at the *Daily Mail*. Pat Hawes on piano and guitarist Nevil Skrimshire both came in from a group that had recently split up, Les Rawlings played double bass and sometimes they'd have Pip Gaskell on clarinet. They rehearsed in a room in Great Windmill Street, Soho, called The Cave. Occasionally it was used as a nightclub, 'The walls were painted green and rust coloured slime, and hessian stalactites hung from the ceiling,' says Humph. For their first gig, at a north London club, they were paid £10.25 shillings each plus the same to the band account to pay for expenses (this is still standard practice today). Lyn Dutton became the p/t manager of his band in 1948 as well.

Despite the ever-growing amateur club scene, and growth and popularity of revivalist and purist jazz, the 'live' club scene still came to not much more than the Feldman Club in London. A band from 'Down Under' was soon to arrive on a boat from abroad, and through their performing style become the catalyst to moving this situation on.

Graham Bell's Australian Jazz Band were the Antipodean answer to George Webb's Dixielanders. At the beginning of 1948, in the small circle that was Revivalist jazz, they made a big impact. The Aussie group went for a less formal, more expressive and entertaining style of performance. With the assistance of a few interested parties, including the Leicester Square Jazz Club, they created a new venue for jazz dance. It was called the Leicester Square Dance Club. Chris Barber knew it well. 'This club was on the north side of Leicester Square. On the little side turn leading up to the Prince's Theatre, or cinema. It leads up to Lisle Street. On the right-hand side there, it was called the Café de l'Europe. It was a building that backed onto the YMCA. They had an upstairs hall as a jazz club. They couldn't have admission on the door (licensing), so therefore they had to go to an office round the corner, meet someone, and buy a ticket, then go over with the ticket. It was like a ballroom, with a stage and round the wall there were seats you see. Not like a concert hall, people had to be able to dance there.' A very different layout.

It kicked off here! The purists went mad. The committing of a deadly sin had taken place. 'Dancing to jazz? How dare they?!' The dancers themselves were Art students, shop and office workers, solicitors and the low waged. They were wearing colourful and striking clothes. Some of them dyed their hair. Sound like Punks, the New Romantics that came later? Humph's group had its initial breakthrough into the London jazz scene in March 1948, at the LSDC when Graham Bell's band were otherwise engaged. The dancers led by the enthusiastic art school crowd throw themselves around trying to 'jive'. This is for three very good reasons. There's no set 'technique' or 'method', no knowledge of how it was done originally in New Orleans. Also, they were very purist when it came to the music, so the jiving and jitterbugging of the ballrooms and swing was right out. Because of this they simply made it up. THEY WENT WILD! It must have been a sight to see. Throwing themselves around, swinging each other about, skirts and jackets swirling through the air. The parallels with the 100 Club in 1976 seem marked here too. But, eventually their dislike of the orthodox style of ballroom jive receded, and they settled into the groove of jazz swing.

Seeing the Lyttelton band made a real impression on Chris Barber as he explained. 'Humph was a big influence in one way. I used to go and see Humph every week when they played at the Leicester Square Dance Club. By this time I was really keen on the music being played (live). I didn't know about playing it, I hadn't thought about it. So I was the keenest fan. I sat on the edge of the stage. But I went to watch Humph, instinctively just in Humph. Alright, I loved Louis Armstrong particularly [he smiles]. You couldn't sit in front of Humph or he'd be behind you, so I sat in front of the trombonist so I could see Humph and Wally Fawkes you see. The two best players.' Soon came an opportunity that he couldn't refuse. 'At one of the sessions Harry Brown the trombonist said, "Chris, do you want to buy a trombone?" I said, "well, er ... how much is it? Oh, I don': think I will today, [pauses] how much does it cost?" "6 pound 10, 6 pound 50." I had that much in my pocket. I could think of no reason not to buy it [pauses again]. So I bought it. That was it. That was September 1948. I had a record of it, of the George Webb band before Humph joined it. But it wasn't worth two quid, I mean all the joints coming unbrazed, held together with string.' Doesn't sound like the best deal.

After a few months the Leicester Square Jazz Club closed down. The dancers moved to a new venue called the London Jazz Club, which was under Jack Solomon's Gym, at Mac's Rehearsal Rooms off Great Windmill Street in Ham Yard, Soho.

At this new venue, the Lyttelton band soon started to play Saturday and Monday every week to crowds in the hundreds. They were made up of the ones who were there for the music, as well as those who were there to dance. Bert and Stan Wilcox ran the club itself.

Humph's group were a collection of varied players, from other areas of the jazz scene as well as the Revivalist. A divide that was regularly bridged at the time. His good fortune continued with an invitation to play at an International Jazz Festival in Nice, France, the same year. At this event he saw the great American traditional jazz trumpeter Louis Armstrong for the first time. It blew him away. Lyttelton's first radio broadcast for the BBC, also from the London Jazz Club, was made in 1948. The amount of airtime given to live jazz on the radio (which WAS the BBC then) grew steadily during the late 1940s.

By 1948 the two biggest record companies in the UK were EMI and Decca-Brunswick. After the war and by this time, several independent record companies, started by ambitious amateurs, had begun to appear. They were committed to bringing Revivalist jazz to a bigger audience. Esquire (co-owned by Carlo Krahmer), Vogue and Melodisc were the most successful of these. When they began they also started putting out jazz records that weren't on the 'majors' catalogues. This also nurtured a market for new pressings of old 'standards' independent re-releases were later taken up by the likes of Decca-Brunswick and HMV. Lyttelton's band first recorded in 1948 for the Tempo label. Subsequently, having turned down better offers, they set up their own label called London Jazz. They recorded at a private studio in Glasshouse St, Soho, just north of Piccadilly Circus, where they also pressed the discs.

I went to secondary school listening to the records from independent record companies like Rough Trade, Stiff, Island and 2 Tone, like many of my contemporaries. These labels came to life from the mid 1970s and out of the punk scene that followed. I was very surprised to find that the resourceful music entrepreneur of the 1940s pre-dated the Andrew Oldhams and Joe Meeks of the 1960s.

The next central character in our tale of music and fact, who met Chris the record collector in Dobell's Book Shop, is the late Alexis Korner, who passed away in 1984. A blues guitarist/singer and BBC broadcaster, who I remember seeing pictures of, and hearing on Radio 2 when I was a kid. He often wore flamboyant clothes, seriously colourful shirts with big lapels, crushed velvet jackets, had sideburns like laser-cut Brillo Pads, and had the voice you can only get from smoking 40 a day. His style in the late 1940s, early 1950s, was more of a smart/formal cut though, with a very smart moustache. His friendship with Chris Barber would change the direction of British traditional jazz, blues, and rock and popular music for good.

I asked Chris, 'So you knew Alexis from very early on then?' 'Yes, I was at school with him. What amused me was when I heard someone say that Alexis Korner was the father of British blues and Chris Barber was the grandfather, Alexis is two years older than me! At public school he was two forms above me so I never knew him. You wouldn't dare know anyone two years above you in a school like that. They wouldn't deign to speak to you either.' Given this was the case, for a period after the war they went their separate ways. Despite confusion with the family tree, when it came to the music one thing was clear. 'We were both exactly equal in our experience of it. We met in Dobell's shop in 1948, looking for blues 78s and I got two Robert Johnson ones and he didn't [laughs]. Which I sold recently, they're worth so much money I thought it best to get rid of them. I've got them on CD. Anyway they were seven and sixpence each. Not bad really. I didn't look after them and of course record players weren't so gentle on records then.' He's right there.

A highly significant player in this tale is Harold Pendleton. He has had a long and successful career in music, starting, with Chris Barber, one of the most well-known live venues in the country, London's Marquee Club. His leading role in the creation of the National Jazz and Blues Festival, which is now known as the Reading and Leeds Festival, should be given wider recognition. Especially given what it is now, one of the world's leading outdoor live music events. Even I went to it in 1982. Harold said, 'I was born in Southport, Lancashire, and I only came to London in 1948. I had qualified as a Chartered Accountant and I wanted a job in London. Because, I felt having become interested in jazz, and having collected a few records, that that was where the English jazz scene was. Although there was in Southport a Dixieland band playing the music of Muggsy Spanier, which I'd listened to, which people forget. They talk about George Webb's Dixielanders as being the first jazz band, but I can tell you that, same time in Lancashire we had the Dave Wilson Dixielanders playing all the Spanier numbers, which people don't know about.' Good to know.

He continued by describing his first day in the capital city. 'I wanted to seek "new horizons", I arrived at Euston Station, crossed the road, got on a bus, said to the conductor "take me to the action", and he dropped me at the Dominion Theatre on Tottenham Court Road. I walked down Charing Cross Road 'til I got to the lower part, and … (pauses), as I walked past the old bookshops I saw one with a record sleeve in the window, a 78 cardboard record sleeve. This was 1948, October. It said

What Time Are We On?

"Jazz Records" written on it. So I entered and in the middle of all these dusty old books, there was a chap in a raincoat going through a sort of a crate of records, looking for a record. I tapped him on the shoulder and said, "Excuse me, do you know where the London Jazz Club is?" He turned round and said, "III ... mma ... ggggoing there tttttonight. I'll show you". Tremendous stammer. If anyone ever told me that he'd be a performer I'd have never have believed them. So anyway this was Chris (Barber). The second person I spoke to after I arrived in London, the first being the bus conductor [laughs]. And we went to the London Jazz Club together.' I asked which shop he met him in? 'Dobell's, and it later turned from an old bookshop into a jazz record shop. A very famous one. And that was my first meeting with Chris. We got on and we became friends, and ah, I used to go to his house and play records. And he had an encyclopaedic knowledge of records, more than me.' These early memories can be enormously enlightening.

It was around this time that the London Jazz Club, run by the Wilcox brothers, took the significant step of moving to the basement of 100 Oxford Street, to hold its nights on Mondays and Saturdays, in October 1948. At this time, jazz dance was a large part of the club's makeup. By day it was Mack's, just another restaurant in a very big city. Humph then made a shrewd move and took it on for several nights a week as the Humphrey Lyttelton Club. In the end it was the London Jazz Club, who got the lease from the old lady who owned Mack's. There's still a vibrant scene for the Jivers and swing dance crowd in London, and in other parts of the country now. There has been a permanent home at the 100 Club for jazz and dance ever since. On a different note, behind the club there is the musicians' pub, every live venue has one! In this case it's The Blue Posts on Eastcastle Street, north of Oxford Street.

Returning to Chris and his new purchase, with good humour Harold Pendleton told me how he first encountered it . 'He came in one day with a trombone. I said "that's nice, what's that?" he said, "I've just bought this off Harry Brown". I said, "good lord, what are you going to do with it? Paint it? Hang it on the wall? Or what?" "No, I'm going to play it," was the reply. I said, 'You're going to play it?" And blow me he did. He learnt the trombone and before long he had his first band. The two trumpet, "King Oliver" style of band. I remember it well. And cutting a long story short, I was a friend and went along and listened to them but I wasn't in any way involved in this, I was just a fan if you like.' Complicit by association maybe?

When talking to Chris he really poured a floodlight on his career, and thoughts at the time of entering the live jazz scene as a performer. In particular, the first couple of years. I asked him whether he was completely self-taught on the trombone? 'I wasn't self-taught about music but I had no trombone lessons at all. I had to teach myself entirely which is a great shame. I wish I had [had lessons]. You see, by the time I formed the amateur band in 48 I was still at school, just doing A-levels. I wasn't thinking of being a professional musician at all, I was just thinking "I've got an amateur band that plays". And then I was a mathematician. My father was definitely a good mathematician; he got a double first at Trinity College, Cambridge [University], in Maths and Economics. John Maynard Keynes taught him. In fact, I used to go to sleep when I was four years old on this lovely armchair Keynes gave my parents when they got married! My parents met at the Cambridge University Labour Club, around 1928. I'm good at mental arithmetic, but higher maths, algebra, not. I got away with it. I got a distinction in A-Level Higher Mathematics. How? I've no idea. I'm a good examinee, I get through exams. That's what you need playing traditional jazz, improvising. Someone who comes out in front somehow anyway, they've got to have the confidence to do that. Look at a musician, playing with a virtuoso and bandleader, who's waiting for a gap [in the music], but there isn't one. You've got to get in there and play! Ain'tcha? It's like playing the double bass [one of my instruments], you can't wait 'til they've stopped to start playing [yourself]. You've got to start playing with them! You've got to be able to listen to them while you play yours. So with the "front line" (the brass section), same thing.' He's not wrong here, it was the same with me.

He returned to the forming of his first band. 'So I met some other guys who had the same sort of view to me, again in 1948, at Dobell's. When they found out that I had a trombone it turned out there were two or three of them that had instruments. I got together with them. Alex Revell played clarinet, and Ben Cohen played the trumpet and Ferdy Hubage played the banjo. They used to go to the same school in Ilford, Gants Hill, and that's where we went to rehearse. We carried on there and by 1949 it was a band. We had two trumpets, we got another guy playing the trumpet who was also good and found a piano player, and so on and so forth, and Alexis joined me on guitar as well. So we had, right away, a band in the sense like I've got now. The interesting part was, I didn't think about it until many years later. I mean I just knew we did these songs, we had a love for the music and that was that. I realised I had no idea aural, in my ear, of what Alexis sounded like. I looked at the picture, and I suddenly thought … 30 years later, and thought he didn't have an amplifier, and he was playing a semi-acoustic Höfner. It was a Höfner copy of a 335 Gibson, you see. He'd go slash/slash/slash/slash/slash. Crunch/crunch [laughs]. You know, there was no noise. You didn't get anything out of it. I mean, if only he had, he wasn't a natural musician Alexis. If you said to him, "play me the tune of *Stardust*?" he couldn't, by ear. I don't mean the chords, the notes. Not even the tune. I mean some jazz people, rhythm people, are hopeless at doing that anyway. He did know good music when he heard it and he could make an atmosphere. Create an atmosphere. I mean very much like Brownie McGhee played [a blues guitarist and singer from Knoxville, Tennessee], only Brownie McGhee played much better than that. But the way Brownie McGhee plays, you've got Sonny Terry [a jaw harp player from North Carolina] playing all these things, and harmonica stuff, and Brownie playing nice. It's rhythm patterns, it's setting up grooves, and that sort of stuff and just sticking to them and happily doing it. Which Alexis was happy to do 'cos he couldn't play much else. But he was doing it. Obviously he was trying to do that when we were playing with him so I couldn't hear it [laughs].' It's a great shame Alexis wasn't around to interview for the book.

Chris went on, 'the thing is it was inevitable 'cos if you look at America it happened there. The same way. People played one thing and they carried on. And went on playing, and new ideas, you know, other things came along and they follow it as night follows day. And they did it too. The difference being when my band started off trying to do the King Oliver things, which were much more technical than the things that his band was playing, where three notes of silence was all they could manage. We knew where the music had been and where it had got to. I mean my record collection had in it the earliest records of jazz ever made. Otis JB made in 1916. The King Oliver's, Louis Armstrong's, the Hot Seven's [Louis' band], the Duke Ellington's, so on, and so forth right up to Charlie Parker's *Cool Blues* [Parker, the alto saxophonist, being one of THE modern jazz icons in America in the late 1940s], one of my favourite records, always has been and was then. And if I could've played it I'd have played it. We did a bit and it was OK. It's the way you try and learn. We knew already because at the same time as having that (musical knowledge), Alexis Korner played guitar in the band and we had a blues band in it. Guitar, me on bass and singing along with Alexis, and a piano player called Roy Sturgess, a good traditional ragtime piano player, and also a very good 'boogie-woogie' player, and Brian Laws on drums. So my band was big 'cos I had two trumpets. Normally, I had guitar, banjo, bass, piano and drums. five rhythm section. Four horns in front, including Monty Sunshine on clarinet. So anyway it was a nine-piece band but big, in general there were six. What we did, we played blues numbers, which were current. We weren't playing 1928 records of the blues, we were playing the records I've got 'cos I was very fortunate, you know. They were the ones that were almost new when I got them sent over from America, which we played too. So that's what Alexis and I were doing with the blues part of my band. My New Orleans band in 1948/49.' He's very sure.

'That's the first music that you started playing in your band?' I asked. 'Yeah. I mean it didn't reach a big audience because we weren't playing to the audience. You know we did them, and the fans didn't complain about them. Well fair enough but they weren't the first thing they asked for. Played *When the Saints* [a very common New Orleans, traditional jazz standard] even then really. So it did start then. Absolutely, for sure, in 1949. I mean people who came to hear my band would've heard the same blues numbers that Eric Clapton still to this day happens to like best. Which are the ones by Tampa Red [a Chicago blues guitarist and singer], Big Maceo Merriweather [a blues pianist and singer from the same city] and people like that from 1945, 44/45.' Chris' knowledge of the music at this time, and the instrumentation of his band, would definitely have put him ahead as far as playing authentic American jazz and blues music is concerned. Recognising that he had a 'Band within a Band', and performing with it in the interval, was another great advantage towards developing the music in the UK.

Our early starter has never got the full recognition for his understanding. 'I told that *Blues Britannia* [a BBC TV documentary shown in 2009 that Chris was interviewed for]. They kept talking about the blues thing starting in 1959 or something because we [Chris and colleagues] got Muddy Waters [a famous and influential Mississippi blues guitarist, singer and harmonica player] over. No. More people tried, but Alexis and I had been doing it since 1948. It all started up with the skiffle and blues thing, Alexis and myself really. Members of my band, they liked it but I mean they weren't as keen. It's 'cos it's the singing as well to me, that AND the playing. I loved the records and had a lot of them. I suppose by 1948 I must have had about 200 or 300 78s which is quite a lot really.' The point is, the skiffle and blues music Chris and Alexis performed here, and in the years ahead had a profound effect on British jazz and blues musicians, contemporary, to appear, and on the next generation's new music to come. By far the majority of the many musicians, managers and fans who experienced this time, who I interviewed for this book corroborated this statement. The modern jazz fraternity would have a different take on this but, their story I'll come to shortly.

In 1948 the majority of English cities had their own jazz venues and organisations. A touring circuit for the bands began to develop that included Manchester's Houldsworth Hall, Sheffield's City Hall and the Picton Hall in Liverpool and the Town Hall in Birmingham. At this time the jazz scene here was growing steadily. Humph had originally taken more of a purist stance when he started out, but given his ever-growing experience of jazz, and of live performance, this was beginning to change. Also, just like Eddie Harvey before him Lyttelton found himself in a Kangaroo Court thanks to purists. Much to his consternation and embarrassment, he was accused of being a Louis Armstrong impersonator, the most famous and respected traditional jazz trumpeter of all time.

In August 1948 Humph's band played festivals in Brussels and then Nice. By 1949, the amount of gigs that the Lyttelton group were getting simply meant that they had to take a far more professional approach to the running of the band, as well as the music. They were also getting a lot more press coverage. Humph explains where he focused his attention from here. 'For some years, Lyn Dutton had been working as our full-time manager, and the operation of the band eventually became, in effect, a business concern operated from our permanent office in Denmark St, and later in Newman St,' running their eight-piece, two-clarinet, line-up. The quality in the performance of jazz is at the top of the list, for most of the musicians who play it.

Ensuring that this was the case now was becoming a much higher priority for a band leader.

The next player of importance in our story makes a brief but significant entrance. Ken Colyer was a young, and very purist trumpeter, originally from Great Yarmouth. He was self-taught and wanted to be gigging, having left the Merchant Navy at the end of 1948. Shortly after he had his first encounter with Chris Barber, as he explained to me. 'Funnily enough I had tried Alex Revell, my clarinet-playing friend inside the first band off with me in 1948. He and I tried to get together with Ken Colyer, in 49, we'd been practising and that, but we said, "it's silly to have two armed camps" in the "Bunk Johnson's versus the King Oliver or Louis Armstrong" sense y'know? And we actually rehearsed twice with Ken Colyer and Sonny Morris (on second trumpet), myself and Alex Revell, Ben Marshall on the banjo and Ron Bowden on drums, and Dave Stevens on piano, at a pub in Goodge St. It was very nice, in fact, I taught Ken a couple of the King Oliver numbers and he still played exactly the same as I taught him. Because he had a great ear for doing things like that. He couldn't improvise very much, he didn't know enough music. Still had a great ear though, so he could still play what he'd learnt. Ten years later, I sat in with him somewhere and we played one of them. So, we almost got together with Ken Colyer in 1949, but we didn't. I wrote him a letter, I've got a copy of the letter somewhere saying, "it's not going to work, I'm terribly sorry but all the best", y'know?' From here Ken Colyer went off to form the Crane River Jazz Band, a very purist outfit who'll we'll meet later.

One break that any group like Chris' needs when it first starts out, is what's known as a Residency. This is where you get a regular gig at the same venue. I'm sure you just know it from clubbing, a good night out or both. It's a great help when you're trying to make a name for yourself, you get experience and put a bit of cash in your pocket. 'When I had my first amateur band and we used to play Studio 51, before when it was a ballroom dancing club, lessons place (it got its name from the year of its formal opening). We were the first jazz band to play there of any kind. We ended up playing Tuesday nights there, and that was in 1949 I suppose, and we did Sunday afternoons, and then Sunday evenings they had Kenny Graham and his Afro-Cubists as they were called,' Chris says. The club itself was in the basement of 12, Great Newport St, round the corner from Leicester Square tube station, on Charing Cross Rd. The pub frequented by the bands here, and the theatre musicians nearby was the Porcupine, a good old fashioned Victorian boozer, at the Charing Cross Rd end of the street.

At this time Chris, like Lyttelton, decided that he wanted a more dedicated and professional band. Changes were needed. 'By this time I realised by watching Humph, let me put it this way. With the George Webb Dixielanders, they were playing under the amateur rules. It's like tennis before pros came into it. It doesn't matter what you do so long as you are polite to the referee, and wear the proper clothing, and own a racket. That's all. In this case you've got an instrument that is featured on all the jazz records you like, and they play all these nice tunes, and that's what you gotta do. HOW you play on them is not the major consideration, but you play how you feel. So Humph suddenly played it with 'musical standards' [a requirement of classical music]. Humph immediately gave one the feeling, "well you can actually play this music right". You've got to. So Humph was the person who inspired me to be a professional musician, really. It was worth playing the music for that. If it wasn't for that then I'd 'ave happily gone on collecting, and not bothered with trying to play it. Because until then it was questionable whether it was worthwhile trying to play this stuff. If you couldn't play it better than that then it's going to be nothing but a waste of time. Or just fun!' With any genre of music it always takes a figurehead/frontrunner to step up to the plate, stand out, and take it to another level.

Chris, keen to explain about the musician he admires in this case, continues, 'so Humph was playing it right. Especially when I heard him playing alongside one or two American guys who dropped by and sat in, not officially playing there (avoiding the MU/AFM ban) y'know. I saw him playing with Rex Stewart and Jimmy McPartland (both well-known and influential cornet players) for example, and he didn't play the same style as them but, then they weren't the same as each other anyway.' Lyttelton had just got stuck in despite differences.

After this it became apparent that some tough decisions might be necessary. 'So that [band line-up] we tried and it was perfectly obvious that some of them really weren't good enough players. They weren't even interested in being good enough players you see. You know Sonny Morris, and Ben the banjo player that was the basic thing of it. My first amateur band started up, you know, with an awful lot of good intentions, with the idea of getting onto one of the more complicated bands which was the King Oliver Band. Because it was a … very technical band, largely because the players were all virtuoso, and didn't tend to play as if, as if they were part of the three-chord trick [just playing the blues] you know [laughs]. And, there were bands you know, taking it quite seriously, trying to play the music right, um, but not really being willing to give up their home life or whatever to play all the time, which you need to.' With regard to the music he clarified his thoughts at the time for me. 'I mean partly, it's the very thing that's also improved music nowadays because so many, many people actually learn the guitar. At the end of the day you've got to make chords. You learn how hard it is to play.' Put simply, chords are made from scales. In jazz, like most music, if you play the wrong scale over a chord, or vice versa, it can sound awful. If, as a musician you hear it, in some circumstances it can make your teeth grind! I kid you not.

In November 1949, Humph managed to get himself into deep water with the law. Bert and Stan Wilcox, of the London Jazz Club arranged for the well-known soprano saxophone player Sidney Bechet, to visit from America and record and perform here. Despite the tight restrictions imposed by the MU and AFM I talked about in Chapter 1. The concert was put on at the Winter Garden Theatre, in Covent Garden. It stood on the corner of Drury Lane and Parker St, where the New London Theatre now stands (it closed in 1959). That night there was a full house. Lyttelton got a hard slap on the wrist from Scotland Yard after the gig; the contracts were full of holes, they were illegal. This occasion showed just how popular traditional jazz was becoming, and the lengths people were prepared to go to in order to work with American jazz 'Greats'.

Decisions about Chris Barber's professional future were quickly honing into view for him. 'I wanted to study Mathematics, I was intending to go to Cambridge (University) as my father had. Then a chap from the Life Insurance Offices Association came round to my school in St Pauls and said "well you're going to go to university, we'd like to interest you in a possibility. If you go to college you'll be there for three years, it'll cost you a lot of money. You won't earn any money, at all. You could try and become an actuary". Actuaries are people who, in very simplistic terms, can work out from statistics, how much an insurance company is going to charge you for life insurance, in order to make money when you finally die. Not too much, it has to be competitive, you see. It's all statistics. My father was in fact a statistician. They said (the LIOA) if you work for a life insurance company you'll get to study three afternoons a week, get paid ten quid a week right away and you'll take one exam a year. There's five parts, that will take you five years. At the end of the day you'll make a £1,000 a year. Well that in 1949/50 sounded like wealth, you know. My father sent me up to see the CEO of the Prudential who he'd been at Cambridge with, who he knew, to tell me all about it. But unfortunately I was only interested in jazz, you see. I remember the Actuarial Tuition Service; their offices were in Holborn, it's almost opposite the one that comes out in King's Cross. On the right-hand side, in that old building there. In that library they had a complete, bound copy of *Punch* [the British satirical magazine]!' It's worth bringing to your attention that the money you'd get for a gig at this time, particularly if you weren't in a dance or big band (where the Musicians' Union ensured slightly better pay) wouldn't have been good. To a lot of traditional jazz players, who were self-taught, and probably couldn't read music or were not very musically proficient, playing full time could have been financial suicide.

While the music of the traditional jazz movement had been growing in popularity, differences between revivalists and purists continued to be problematic. Also, since the War another form of the music had been simmering away on a small stove in the USA. It was being embraced in London and the UK by a young, and equally passionate group of musicians and fans alike who'd been listening to the mainstream genre. There was great music and more thrilling times ahead!

ACKNOWLEDGEMENTS:

A History of Jazz in Britain 1950–1970. Jim Godbolt, 1922–2013. London: Quartet, 1989 (P. 263), (P. 6), (P. 54), (P. 4), (P. 7), (P. 8), (P.51)

I Play as I Please: The memoirs of an Old Etonian trumpeter. With drawings by the author. [With plates, including portraits.] Humphrey Lyttelton, 1921–2008. London: MacGibbon & Kee, 1954 (P. 148/149), (P. 150 – 152), (P. 161), (P. 163), (P. 124), (P. 167), (P. 170), (P. 171), (P. 166), (P. 178), (P. 174)

52

CHAPTER 3

One place where you'd have no problem finding musicians in London, in say 1946, would be on a stretch of Soho, at the south-western end behind the Windmill Theatre (which faces onto Shaftesbury Avenue) and Piccadilly Circus, called Archer Street. During the 1930s, 1940s and 1950s it was the professions unofficial Jobcentre. On that backstreet, in offices contained within a big old Victorian building, were the offices of the London Orchestral Association. If an agent, or bandleader needed musicians to complete a group, dance bar.d or orchestra, then that's where he'd go, on a Monday, also known as Fixing Day in the trade. Straight musicians (classical players) on one side of the street, dance band on the other. It was particularly useful for booking at short notice. It could be for one gig, it could be for five, maybe a tour with three days of rehearsals. From lunchtime through the afternoon, the street would fill, from a handful at first to a couple of hundred, London's music labour exchange came to life. Sharply turned out in Italian suit and tie, or scruffily shambolic jacket and trousers from a late night before, musicians would gather. Mostly there with their instruments to show what they played. The odd one with the wife, a girl here and there checking out who's familiar. They'd stand out in the street, maybe one hand in a trouser pocket, the other with a cigarette on the go, keeping an eye out for the faces they know. Catching up with the latest amongst their mates, checking out the agents down there, who's looking for a tenor saxophone player, all of this out in the open of the long, cobbled space that is Archer Street.

For a good three or four hours the banter, the chat would continue apace. Also, let us not forget that there was no such thing as a mobile phone at this time. The only way to stay in touch with your colleagues, the business and the scene all in the same place, was here. Often moving from the Street into the local pubs – first port of call The Red Lion on the corner of Great Windmill St – bars and cafés. You wouldn't carry out the finer points of your trade in the open now would you? So that's where you'd go with the face(s) that's interested, to get your diary out, making sure no one can get a crafty look at your arrangements. To get the gigs in the book. This Soho backwater plays an ongoing role from here on in.

The next of our highly influential characters, was learning his trade on alto sax, at London's Royal Academy of Music in 1946. John Dankworth was a regular face on the Street. 'It was there that I met, directly or indirectly, such contemporaries who, like me, were in love with jazz and determined to make a livelihood out of it. There was Ronnie Scott, himself the son of a well-known sax player, who played the tenor sax with great promise – as indeed did Don Rendell, who was later to become a close friend, and Leon Calvert, whose fluent trumpet playing attracted my attention. Pianist Tommy Pollard, drummers Laurie Morgan, Cecil 'Flash' Winstone and Tony Crombie, bassist Lennie Bush and trombonist

What Time Are We On?

Ed Harvey were all typical of the youngsters who went to the "street" in search of work and communion with fellow musicians.' Having just gained his Performer's Diploma at the Royal Academy of Music, in the summer of 1946 John was conscripted, and joined a Royal Army Service Corps based just outside Cirencester in Gloucestershire. You'd think that was a rough stroke of luck. But there he found they had a ten-piece band that played the music at their dances, and that needed an alto sax player. If you haven't gathered already, there's nothing better for a musician than to Practise! Practise! Practise! That's just what John did. One of the best places for this of course, was at a jam session. The main one for the young players like John and all the other likeminded above, was Carlo Krahmer's on a Sunday night at the Feldman Swing Club. A venue already being frequented by young Traditionalists. Or just a couple of small clubs in Soho.

You found musicians with the highest and more restricted musicianship on Archer St. Don Rendell, in the higher bracket, on the other hand, is another gent kind enough to give me his time when it came to this book. His tale from an early age is packed with much detail and incident, as he explained. 'City of London School where I studied, was evacuated to Marlborough in Wiltshire during the War. I came from a very musical family; my father was a church organist and choir master. he was also musical director at the D'Oyly Carte Opera Company. I was taught the piano from five to nine and I convinced my dad I was never gonna be a musician because, I wasn't interested [he laughs]. So, it was at the school concert, end of year, about 1941 and it was like a light went on in my head. As soon as I heard it [an alto saxophone] I had to have one. I went back to London and said, "Dad

I got to have one, | so he hired one, and within a couple of weeks I started playing.' For the light to switch on in his head so early on, Don was a very lucky lad.

He was still keen not to hang around. 'Anyway, at 15 I left school. So, I did three months in Barclays Bank, and then I left. I think the staff were very glad when I left 'cos I was never any good at maths [laughs]. But I had met young guys in this area, and three particular ones. Laurie Morgan, who was the drummer, Stan Watson who was the guitar player and Denny Turner the pianist. Denny Turner's uncle, a violinist, who had a show band, was playing in variety theatres on the road. Doing a week at Scarborough, week at Newcastle, a week in Liverpool, a week in Bolton. I turned professional.' Don now moved onto tenor sax. 'I got in a show and it was around this time I started playing nightclubs. I'd do the 3 till 6, and 7 till 11, and go down to Soho, to the Blue Lagoon [on Carnaby St] and the Kit Kat [under the Capitol Theatre on the Haymarket]. What you'd do is join the band and play. This was 1943.' Urgency was the key here. This is how it worked. If you were young, jazz was what you wanted to play and traditional wasn't enough, then you did like Don, and all his contemporaries. There wasn't really any choice, and money was short, times were tough.

Well one hard fact about 1943 that's got lost over the years, has been the cost of living, the realities of life. This is another gap that Don was able to fill in, something else that young musicians had to deal with. 'In those days the money was ridiculous. You got four quid a week, and out of four quid a week we paid full-board, sleeping three in a bed. We then worked with Peggy, a singer in the show, and we formed a group. We got another job playing second rate shows, not third rate shows, and that was "South American Way". And we were the "Gay Cuban Serenaders", We wore sombreros. And then I was called up.' At which point he laughed like a drain.

His time in uniform was short-lived due to ill health, but empty pockets produced pressing problems, and fresh starts. 'After that, when we [the British Army] went back into Europe for D-Day [1944], I found myself out of a job. I think the next thing that happened was going down Archer St, and it was somewhere where work was handed out mouth to mouth, hand to hand. Cecil 'Flash' Winston the drummer, was fixing a band for Duncan Whyte at the Astoria Theatre, Charing Cross Rd. I guess this would have been 44/45. So then I joined Oscar Rabin's band, and with that band you just travelled everywhere, like Scotland, but don't forget there's no motorways. It was long journeys. Meeting the coach at Baker St at 8 o'clock in the morning, and playing in Sunderland at 7.30 at night, y'know, and it was a life on the road which was quite a life. I'd have been 18,19.' I then asked him when he first met the tenor sax player Ronnie Scott. 'Well in those days, when I was in Duncan Whyte's band [at the Astoria], and I used to play nightclubs, I played The Fullado Club.' This venue which was in the grubby basement of 6, New Compton St, was becoming the meeting place of choice for the young guns. The ones who'd started to hear the bebop records from America, who were taking in the sounds of Charlie Parker, Dizzy Gillespie, Thelonious Monk and alike. This included some of the Archer St crowd. Bebop was played using new, challenging chord sequences and scales that made jazz sound very different from big band, and traditional forms of the music. It was a real smack in the face, for different reasons, to those who heard it for the first time.

One thing any new music needs is a way of getting the sound out there, as well as a way of hearing it. Regardless of whether it's good or bad. In his book Jim Godbolt reminds us of a jazz impresario who seems to have had a lot more interests and influence in the music at the time, than Richard Branson in his Virgin Records day. 'Once past the Customs (along with a few other items not easily found in post-war Britain) the records found their way to an address in literary Bloomsbury, 39, Bedford Court Mansions, Bedford Avenue, the flat of drummer/bandleader/collector and record producer Carlo Krahmer. He was an extraordinary man. Only partially sighted, a jazz-record collector from the early thirties (he once owned over a hundred versions of *Tiger Rag*), he, unlike most others of the late forties, displayed unusually catholic taste. He was also the first to record British bop musicians on his Esquire label, the first independent to issue American bop records. Understanding of the new idiom owed much to Carlo Krahmer. Every Sunday afternoon at his flat he held record sessions, attended by young musicians keen to hear the new jazz.' His acquiring of all that three to four minute Shellac seems quite extraordinary, but he is clearly the right man, in the right place, at the right time. Someone not to be forgotten.

Ronnie Scott is a name that will be familiar to most inside, and many outside, the world of jazz. Like John said, he was born into the trade, came from a working class background, and was undoubtedly a great character, musician and club owner. His sense of humour very much entertained as well. Again sadly, like John he is no longer with us, his autobiography is a great record. The following story from it, I think is a great way to introduce him to the tale. Ronnie was Londoner, born and bred. Son of a well-known tenor player, Joseph. 'I was with Johnny

(Claes' Band) for about 18 months; then in 1946 I got a job with the Ted Heath Band – and that was really the big time because Ted's band boasted some of the finest musicians in the country – it was an excellent band (13-piece) and, to be honest, I was a bit out my depth in that company. Still, it took me a full nine months to get fired. Jack Parnell (the drummer from that band) was planning to form his own band and he asked me if I'd be interested in joining him. I said I would – and later, when Ted came to me when we were playing at the Hammersmith Palais and asked me if I was going to join Jack's band, I, like an idiot, said "Yes". That was a tactical error which was compounded after we played a gig in Liverpool. When it was over all the other guys in the band went back to London on the night train because we had a West End engagement the next day. But I was still intoxicated by the heady experience of being a big-time musician – so I decided to book into a top hotel and fly back in the morning. That night Liverpool had its worst snowstorm in 20 years – and the next day, by the time all possibility of a flight back had been ruled out, it was too late to catch a train to make the gig. I think Tommy Whittle was brought in to dep for me and a few days later I received a letter from Ted Heath saying that my services were no longer required.' Remember Ronnie throughout my book, in the variety of roles I've described. From talking to many people over the years who knew him well, I think it's the best way to do the great man justice.

John Dankworth was certainly happy to see the bright lights of Civvy Street when they came, as he testifies in his book. 'My period of Army conscription came to an end. I was given eight weeks "Demob Leave" and an outfit of clothing including, I remember, a pork-pie hat.

I donned the lot and made for Archer St at the very first opportunity. The first person I saw was Ronnie Scott [in 1947]. "Just the bloke we were looking for," said Ronnie. "I hear you're out of the Army. Are you interested in a job on the Queen Mary? It sails for New York in July – first time since the war ended – and they're auditioning bands. Not much money in it … but then, we'd be able to hear Bird [Charlie Parker] …"' For young British musicians looking to hear AND see bebop, the newest and hottest form of jazz on the planet, was the equivalent of the mountain coming to Mohammed. Huge and exciting, this chance burned like a comet re-entering the Earth's atmosphere. Parker, also an alto player, with trumpeter Dizzy Gillespie, had the impact in jazz of the new music of The Beatles and The Rolling Stones, or the new broom of Sex Pistols and The Clash. In New York they could also see the likes of young pianists Thelonious Monk, and Bud Powell, bassist Rickie Laird and drummer Max Roach. All of them playing in the sweaty dives that were the jazz clubs of 52nd St, New York City, USA. John Dankworth and Ronnie Scott took it with both hands, in the company of others, and went.

The Queen Mary docked at virtually the end of 52nd Street in Manhattan. The first person John met and saw was Dizzy Gillespie, then with his big band. He saw Charlie Parker whenever, then with Miles Davis in his most formative years. But he and the others saw the Beboppers on the street during every trip. John, Ronnie and the other Brits who made the sailings, soon became known as Geraldo's Navy, named after the canny London agent Geraldo Bright, and Navy for the fleet of Cunard Liners for who he was musical director.

Having left Eddie Harvey in 1946 with the RAF in Cumbria,

he didn't regain his own freedom until 1948. Like his colleagues he needed some cash pretty quick, when he found himself back in a suit. 'Then I was offered a job, I didn't know what a professional musician was at that stage of the game 'cos during the war they were all called up. You never met any, you see what I mean? The result of that was I got a professional job with Freddy Randall's band, its what's called a Chicago-style band [very traditional] y'know Eddie Condon, Muggsy Spanier. I went into that with a few faces, people like "Bruce" Turner who's a famous, eccentric clarinet [and alto sax] player, marvellous man. This would have been about 1948'. But Eddie was soon clock-watching again as he explains. 'I played with them for a year and a half, and then I got fed up with it. I got fed up with playing in Bb, Eb and Ab all the time, I knew the repertoire backwards and I was more interested in more tunes which were ... nicer. I was playing them on the piano you know. Playing more exotic tunes, like Nat King Cole's. I remember playing *Sweet Lorraine* and all these lovely tunes, and I just got fed up of it [the Chicago-style] really. So I left the band and I did what all musicians did in those days, I went down to Archer Street. Well, I got a bit of a name so I did get a few gigs and stuff like that. But the important thing that happened to me down there, I met John Dankworth. He was a traditional clarinet player with a band called Freddy Mirfield's and His Garbage Men (a great name). I did a dep for them while I was with George's (Webb) band, for the trombone player Danny Croker. Because there weren't very many people who could play in that style in those days. Probably two or three people, so they were a very small circle y'know. So I got this gig with the band, and John and I got on very well. He doesn't remember it funnily enough but I do.' At this point Eddie just folded his arms and grinned from ear to ear. The appreciation for Mr Dankworth, and the fondness for the time just shone through.

Archer St from here starts to hold another special significance. It becomes the hub for the modern jazz players to meet. There are two particular reasons for this. Firstly, because they can read music. The young musicians, like Eddie Harvey, who are starting to look a little further 'beyond the horizon', in some cases, are in dance bands and show bands by 1948. So they're using Archer St. Secondly, you'll notice that I didn't mention the Traditionalists here. This is mainly because a significant number of them are self-taught, and have decided they're in it for the enjoyment of playing, and don't want to read dots, crotchets and quavers. They've no time for three in the bar, flattened 9ths! They like to get the joint jumping! They're ceasing to mix with the Modernists and doing their own thing. Starting clubs in which they can play, jam, dance and make merry without being disturbed, thank you very much! Believe you me, there's a storm brewing and trouble ahead.

Tony Kinsey was also good with time for me. Very much a key member of the early John Dankworth groups, as a drummer. A member of many bands, as well as leading his own, the years ahead will be full of opportunity for him. Born in Sutton Coldfield, the son of musicians, 1948 was when he finally flew the roost. Not by himself, as Tony explained. 'He [Ronnie Ball] was a great pianist, and we became great friends. We eventually came to London together, so we stood on the corner of Archer St, with 30 quid each in our pockets, which lasted about three or four weeks, but started to get some work. We all used to go into that café on Archer St, the Harmony Inn. It wasn't about lots of boozing, not in them days. It was the café for the jazz musicians.' He continued. 'Ah, I got some work on drums, in some nightclubs. I worked with Art Thompson, who was married to Kathy Stobart (a very well-known sax player from South Shields) who was working down the Embassy Club, and was 18 by then. Mind you, I hated nightclub work, because for a drummer it's like death. All you've gotta do is play below the level of the conversation (a drummer wants to whack the hell out of it from time to time!). But it's what we had and it was money. We needed money.' The story of most musicians' lives, and not just them, I would dare to suggest dear reader.

He ploughed on and good fortune smiled. 'Then eventually I got the job everyone wanted, the job [playing] on the Queen Mary, and that's going backwards and forwards to New York. And I got, I was lucky to have the job fall in my lap, about 17 trips backwards and forwards, which was a fantastic experience, we were still on [State] Rationing at the time. And to go on the Queen Mary as a cabin class passenger, was to have fantastic long menus shoved in front of you every meal of the day. For breakfast, lunch and dinner, every day, y'know, was absolutely extraordinary. Because we hadn't had food like that at all, as a consequence I was constipated for three weeks, but as a young man it didn't bother me (laughs). Whilst in New York I took the opportunity to study with Cozy Cole, had a few lessons from him. Some lessons with Bill West, that sort of thing.' Tony continues to recount. 'But, um, Ronnie Ball also being on the boats, when we were in London and shared a flat, in fact we had a double wedding together. We ended up getting this flat in Grafton Way, and I couldn't believe it. It cost us about £10 a week at the time, it be about 50, 60 quid a week now. But it was just a room with two beds in it, and a wash basin. And I couldn't believe it, it had a piano in there.' A dream come true for these two gents. 'So Ronnie shared the room with me, and we used to play in there a lot y'know, with me playing on the brushes on the telephone directory, and a lot of banging on the floor of course. But we were also lucky to have a landlord who approved of what we were doing.' Residential law would make that very difficult now.

Finally, at the end of 1948, the Modernists start a club of their own. Soho is where it's based. Frustrated by the lack of progress on this front, a group of them take matters into their own hands, as Ronnie Scott explains. 'The incorrigible jazz men among us would congregate whenever the opportunity arose and play unadulterated, unrelenting jazz. To make this easier, a group of us got together in January 1949 and rented (Mac's) rehearsal rooms at 41, Great Windmill St, which we ran co-operatively as the Club 11. There were ten musicians – Leon Calvert, Hank Shaw, Lennie Bush, Joe Muddel, Bernie Fenton, Tommy Pollard, Tony Crombie, Laurie Morgan, Johnny Rogers and myself – and a manager, Harry Morris; hence the Club 11.' Clearly very driven players.

Also digging his hand in his pocket with the others in this bold venture, was John Dankworth. 'Fortunately for all of them the room had been a club in a past life, with fixtures and fittings still there, which made things much simpler. On a Saturday night the club started up, with two resident bands. I was elected leader of the quartet with pianist Bernie Fenton, bassist Joe Muddel and drummer Laurie Morgan. Ronnie's six-piece with Denis Rose on trumpet, Johnny Rogers alto sax, Tommy Pollard on piano, Lennie Bush on double bass and Tony Crombie on the drums.' This is how he explains it in his own book.

What Time Are We On?

So now they had what the Traditionalists had at the 100 Club. A place to gather, a place to play and a place to hang out. This just starts to move things on. By this time John Dankworth started his own group too. Don Rendell remembers the time, and connections. 'Coming on to 48/49, and Club 11 was going, and I'd go down the Club 11. Again it's such a small world 'cos Stan Watson the guitarist, who was with me in Duncan Whyte's band, when I went with him to Club 11 we'd see Laurie Morgan, who was on drums with the John Dankworth Quartet, and Ronnie Scott's got his own group. So I was around in those days and I knew Ronnie, and we used to go to the Stepney Girls' Club, and Stepney Boys' Club, a kind of Jewish connection. Because Ronnie and Harry Morris, and Tony Crombie did so ... a very Jewish connection to jazz.' But when Ronnie Scott went back on the boats, 'that left a gap in the Club 11.' You can guess who filled his shoes. Meanwhile, Eddie was finding life a little tricky at this time, he wanted to get over to the States and New York City like his contemporaries. 'I was screaming to get on the boats, but they didn't have trombone players, because they didn't have bands that were big enough to warrant them in those days.' By the sound of his voice he was very exasperated by this. 'So that's all I could do.' So learn it from this side of the 'Pond' if you like, I asked? 'Yeah, I had to, no option, you know? It was called Club 11. I went down there, I became a sort of "country member" of Club 11, as a trombone player. There were two groups there, Ronnie's and John's, and they were playing all the Charlie Parker tunes, and stuff like that. I got into bebop in a heavy way.' So as you can see, Club 11 very quickly became a big draw to a small but youthful, talented and dedicated group of musicians.

A man of great significance, but rarely ever mentioned when you're watching jazz on TV, or even in a lot of relevant 'reads', is Denis Rose. At 26, he was several years older than the musicians we've met so far. As a result he'd been on the circuit a little longer, this made him just a tad more experienced. A man who virtually lived in Archer St, and that's everyone's account! His gift? Despite not being a musician filled with the virtuoso talent of Ronnie Scott or John Dankworth, it has the ability to pass 'the knowledge' on to those who didn't get it. This is how Eddie Harvey puts it. 'Denis Rose, he was an "éminence grise" of British bebop. He was a Jewish guy from the East End, he had fantastic ears, and he taught us all the changes of these tunes (having learnt them without an instrument!) So, if you wanted to find out the changes of *Confirmation* [a tune by Charlie Parker], you go and ask Denis and he had 'em written up here [Eddie points to his head]. He was a "Deserter" Denis. He used to live down in this basement, we used to take food down to him. He never came out 'cos he was afraid of getting arrested, and whipped off into the army again [laughs]. He was a real character, lovely man. So Denis, with these great ears, knew all these great tunes. He showed them to us, and to Tony Crombie, and all the people that were contemporaries.' Jim Godbolt in his book very much adds to these sentiments. Those who also knew him paid him these compliments. 'I got most of my [bebop music] theory [its mechanics] from Denis, but then so did everyone else,' Ronnie Scott; 'A brilliant mind,' John Dankworth; 'Socially, Denis was reticent, aloof. But when it came to music he was the most generous and outgoing man I have ever known. If he was teaching you something you would have to plead with him to let you go – he was that much of a perfectionist,'

What Time Are We On?

Laurie Morgan (drums, vibes and piano). All these years later they seem like very genuine tributes, from people who could see how well he could lead the uninitiated in the music, in the right direction. Denis Rose shouldn't be forgotten.

The other feature that always goes with music in a big way is fashion. From The Beatles to David Bowie, punk to Britpop to grime. Obviously with us musicians, the first thing we want to talk about is the music, the significance of what we're doing, and our inspirations for doing it. Well, when it came to the sometimes thorny issue of couture, Eddie was more than happy to give us some insight and perspective. 'It's funny, I had an interview with a guy. He wrote a book on fashion, it wasn't about music at all. We were talking about that period. I remember it well because as a "Trad" I wore corduroys, a tweed jacket and a big knitted tie. I had to completely change for that. I suddenly had to wear a black barathea suit and dark glasses at night [laughs]. And you had your hair cut short, with a "flat-top", which was a very contemporary, American way. It was funny! But it was all part of the "milieu" of that period. So that's why I had this interview with that guy. I've got it [the book] somewhere, I'd never really thought about it before. He was just interested in dress style, and that was the period when all this was going on. Some of the guys even wanted to go as far as looking like Dizzy Gillespie, wear dark glasses and berets. I think I had a beret at one time. That would be 49, 1950.' Then Eddie smiled broadly.

The clothing was great and I wouldn't mind a bespoke Italian suit myself, if the coffers in my wallet start to swell. With the right cut, and a well-patterned piece of cloth, the clothing can make you look very sharp indeed. This is where cheaper, yet fashionable items to wear start to become more everyday, and available. Funnily enough though, where jazz was divided in fashion that's also the case in music. Sadly, that was about to get a lot wider, deeper and become much more of a chasm. Very few musicians could get beyond it, and relations between the two genres will continue to deteriorate from here.

What Time Are We On?

ACKNOWLEDGEMENTS:

Jazz in Revolution. John Dankworth, 1927–2010. London: Constable, 1998 (P.40–41), (P. 50, p.3), (P.61.p.3)

A History of Jazz in Britain 1950–1970. Jim Godbolt, 1922–2013. London: Quartet, 1989 (P. 31 p. 3), (P. 29 p.1), (P. 32 p. 2)

Some of My Best Friends Are Blues. Ronnie Scott; with Mike Hennessey; preface by Pete King. Ronnie Scott, 1927–1996. London: Northway, 2004 (P. 36 p. 2)

CHAPTER 4

The next significant premises in our tale is a club that put on traditional and modern jazz. The site is off Charing Cross Road, near the busy Cambridge Circus in a quiet cut-through named Great Newport Street. I visited the site of Studio 51 myself about eight years ago with my father and son, it's now the former storeroom of a defunct stationers. From the front, on the left-hand side there is a sandstone, portico entrance with a black fire door. To the right the larger glass frontage of the shop. Once inside we descended a central staircase to the basement.

We entered the first of two small, vaulted cellars; facing towards the road above to my right the stage. The band swung hard to the feverish crowd, as they threw themselves and each other around. The steamy, sweat-soaked air clinging to the walls. Crossing the room from left to right, ahead you see a small room under the pavement, dark and gloomy. In the corner of the right hand wall is the entrance to the second room, where you find the crowd talking and laughing, smoking and drinking. The girls and the guys hanging out, while the older ones have a seat and take in the sounds. Ahead on the right is the bar, where the blonde-haired and tight-dressed owner surveys the vibrant, if murky scene of her club. Making sure the soft drinks cross the bar with care, but content that the booze of her clientele sits in paper bags around the wall. To the left of the bar in the corner is another small entrance and the bottom of a stairwell. There sits a woman taking the money from the eager punters coming down from the dark street above. She hasn't had a chance to stop since the doors first opened.

So as we enter the 1950s even some of those in traditional jazz are well aware that if the music's worth doing, it's worth doing properly. Humph knows that if he plays it right the audience go wild, and the buzz that comes is a real high. Having seen the man at work, Chris Barber's come to the same significant conclusion.

While at this time jazz clubs were opening up, many of them still maintained the Great Divide, are you into Modern or Traditional? A musical Berlin Wall. But there were some that were more than happy just to put on a good time. This is where the great, in mine and many others opinion, Vi Hyland strides into the tale. I'd love to enlighten you with the story of her background, where she grew up and why she came to London's West End but this would prove more than a little difficult, if nigh on impossible. All we know and that I've found out is here in my book, unless you know more. What we can be sure of is, that as the owner and proprietor of Studio 51, she was remarkable inasmuch as she was a woman, and in putting on all genres of jazz. She was unique for her decade.

Chris Barber was the first to play the club, when it was originally playing ballroom dance music, as he explains, but 'then Vi Hyland, and Pat obviously got together [1951], so they got in quite short order John

Dankworth Seven on a Saturday nights, and Kenny Graham's Afro-Cubists on Sunday nights, we had Tuesday nights and then we took Sunday afternoon as well.' Chris' club night was originally called the Lincoln Gardens.

Another of my interviewees, Tony Kinsey, who after a while managed to get his own band booked at Studio 51, is also able to shed more light on Vi. I asked if he found her a very easy-going woman, a character. 'Yeah. Anything I asked her she'd say yes to, y'know? Never any problem. Tony don't do this, Tony don't do that. "What do you want to do?", "yeah fine no problem." Sweet in that sense, relaxed about it I suppose, she wasn't on my back at all, ever, and I worked there for quite a while. Actually I must find out how long it was one day [laughs].' He definitely talks of that time and of her venue with a fondness, something he has in common with several other people in this book.

She certainly knew, just like some of her male counterparts, that looking the part and being seen as the woman in charge was part of the requisite for the job. I also said to someone we'll meet later, was she quite glamorous do you think? I always understood she was blonde, always very well dressed, and he replied, 'yes, she was a smart woman. Yes, and glamorous in the sense of she exuded glamour, I don't think she was a raving beauty.'

These qualities are something that stand out in all the photos I've seen of our subject. A shapely blonde, in dark, tight, knee-length dresses. Our drummer was right about the smart. Throughout the book, bear in mind that her venue is running as a constant centre for jazz.

Something that you wouldn't have seen in these smaller clubs – traditional or modern – that were appearing at this time, given the more 'street'/'working class' background of the musicians and their audience, were dance bands and big bands. Chris said to me, 'they wouldn't have wanted to play in the 51, Studio 51 as it was called. They wouldn't have wanted to play on Eel Pie Island [another club], they wouldn't. They want to play somewhere comfortable.' Like American jazz, and the blues it came from, this music was being created by people with an ordinary background, and being started up in a similar fashion to punk, or the rave scene. The significance of this is enormous and can't be understated during this time.

While getting this break with his band at the 51, another piece of good fortune given the MU/AFM ban fell into Chris' lap. Something that a lot of music buffs would try for, but he came up trumps with, is a blues great. He recounts the tale. 'Yeah, ther. we were fortunate enough to see Big Bill Broonzy at a concert in 1951 with "Mayday" Mahalia Jackson, a strange concert at the Royal Albert Hall, the opening band was Charlie Gabway's band, with Jim Thomas on piano who was very funny, then Big Bill, then top of the bill Mayday Jackson. It's funny 'cos Big Bill, y'know, we went backstage to see if we could meet him, I'd brought records, and he was pretty upset. He said "he shouldn't have a singer like me on the bill," y'know, Mayday Jackson, "It's sacrilegious to see my music on this (the bill). But I've got to do it because I'm being paid to do it." She wasn't playing his music! He was complaining that his music shouldn't be put on with her mother's music. It's funny isn't it? Rather nice in a way. He'd been fished out of America by these two French-speaking Belgians. They'd been over to America which was easy to do. But Belgians didn't have the same problems we had (with regard to the ban), and they brought him cver to Europe and he did a very nice album for Phillips while he was over, I know.' In modern times it's hard to believe that such important musicians, who in some cases people have never heard of, have been able to fill a venue that today seats over 5,000. It was also lucky for Chris that this wasn't the last time he'd meet Big Bill.

With Chris now doing well with a regular series of gigs, Humph, at the forefront of the traditional jazz movement, is having to get more organised even if underneath it all he'd like to keep things a little more straightforward. He explains in his memoir, 'with regular (radio) broadcasts, regular recordings on a major label and regular tours into the provinces at weekends, the band started to increase its following to a degree that was far beyond our wildest dreams in the old days.' It's now all about becoming more organised.

But with suitable humour he goes on to explain where his small band stands now, at the beginning of the 1950s. 'As a result of the increased demand for our service, we became more ambitious in our activities. Lyn Dutton abandoned his daytime job and to take up residence as full-time manager. We remained spare-time musicians, however, and at one time he had on our strength George Hopkinson, Income Tax man and drummer; Wally Fawkes, cartoonist and clarinettist; Ian Christie, photography student and clarinettist; Keith Christie, RAF 'erk' and trombonist; George Webb, engineer and pianist; Buddy Vallis, insurance agent and banjoist and Mickey Ashman, aircraft-factory clerk and bass player. We continued to treat our music seriously and our band engagements with levity. The advantage of remaining semi-professional was that we could afford to remain specialists in the music we enjoyed. And although there were ups and downs, music remained a source of enjoyment instead of becoming routine work. There was a freshness about every job on which we met which kept our spirits high –sometimes too high.' Behind the scenes the band was happy to have a good time, whether that was a drink or two too many and a 'play fight' within the band, or just for the hell of it.

Despite the increasing desire by the musicians to want to perform the music to a higher standard, there's also a 'Jack the Lad' attitude and humour pervading the culture of traditional jazz, that is also embedded in the modern genre as well. Something that I think is still important now. Wouldn't life be dull without it, no matter what the profession? If you think those in jazz are a bunch of chin scratchers you couldn't be more wrong.

With managers, as we all know, and to some our dismay, comes responsibility. As Humph says, 'But it wasn't all high jinks. As time went on, the reputation of the band increased, and our responsibilities with it. Lyn Dutton and I became partners in the administration of the band. If the difficulties of co-operating with someone who had remained, in spirit, an incorrigible amateur have caused him any private irritation, he has never betrayed it.' So praise and honesty indeed, though the amateur could very much be a professional if need be. If you watch the man presenting music shows on TV in the 1960s, or hear him on BBC Radio 4 in the 1970s and beyond, you'll see what I mean.

Like Vi Hyland, Humph happened to decide it was time to start his own night out, given the bands ability to draw in a large crowd. 'Our Club activities were simple enough. In 1951 we parted company with the London Jazz Club and started our own "jazz for dancing" club in the same Oxford Street premises on a different night of the week. Apart from the necessity of taking on a secretary to cope with the administration of the club, there was no great difficulty about it.' The growth in the popularity of traditional just continues to expand, so as things stand the snowball continues to roll, and it seems every kind of character wants to get involved in whatever way they can. Harold Pendleton told me, 'there were some very good dancers including Chris Barber, who was a brilliant jive dancer and he danced a lot with my wife, who was also a good jazz dancer, this was before he was a performer, he was just a punter. The 100 Club was a focal point for what we were doing.' The names and faces of the people who are well-known now, or that you may never have even heard of, like George Melly, Spike Milligan, George Chisholm … are down at this hot nightspot!

It was around this time that Chris Barber decided to make the obvious move to jazz musician at this time, he wanted to take his playing up to the next level, even if they weren't into classical music. Formal training. 'When I first got to the Guildhall School of Music [which he attended between 1951 and 1954] there were no other brass players studying at all. They did in the orchestra, they had one trumpeter who came along who was in the [Guards] band, who played like he was awful, and me on trombone. So I got Eddie Harvey and Keith Christie to come and join as well, which was quite nice.' He seemed very pleased and chipper about this. Can't blame him.

His good friend Harold had resolved to move things on as well. For him, being a Chartered Accountant wasn't enough given his other interest. He explains. 'I started on the career of launching clubs, 52, when I left the City. I played with the Doug Whitton band for a couple of years. Then off went Chris to the Guildhall School of Music, the band broke up. But I tried to salvage some of the musicians and I needed a club for them, so I found one in Little Newport St, Soho (depending on your boundaries). Which was in the evenings a nightclub. I called the band the Gallion Jazz Band, based on a Sidney Bechet number called *Out of the Gallion.'* The Gallion was where they kept slaves, not slaves. He's talking about out of the slave compound. 'So I thought it seemed a nice name so I launched "The Gallion Club"'. I'm happier for the clarification.

So for any of you out there dear reader, who'd like to be more familiar with how to run a nightclub in the early 1950s this is how Harold did it. 'This somewhat dusty nightclub opened at 11 o'clock, so we only had it from 7.30 'til 10.30 and we'd play until we were chucked out at 10.30, and we managed to attract 20, 30 people for a few shillings, and it was great fun. I did it to pay the rent on the club so the whole thing was a self-financing operation. You took a few bob on the door, paid the landlord and you had a club, and therefore you had a place to play. But effectively it was one step up from playing in someone's front room. Because it was in those early days it became desirable to play to somebody, as we had played at home for oneself.' To be honest it's not so different now though the licensing situation is a little more tricky, as a result you may want to be a little more circumspect. But I certainly wouldn't advise against starting a club.

If you wanted to move a little further up the ladder in terms of venue and distance, then Humph explains the practicalities in a positive and hardy light, especially when you consider the physical consequences. He explains, 'In addition to weekly meetings, we started putting on our own weekly promotions at places like the Birmingham and Leeds Town Halls. Ever since the start of the Revival it had been the ambition of the musicians taking part to be self-supporting and to run their own activities. To run a concert in a big hall you need enough capital to pay for it in advance and to pay the Entertainments Tax (then fill in forms for the unsold seats to get your money refunded). With publicity and all the other paraphernalia thrown in, it takes quite a bit of capital to get a concert going. Building up capital was not as easy for us as it might appear, because although we had more offers of work than we could accept, we could only travel out of London at weekends, being semi-professional musicians with careers to pursue to during the week (jazz musicians are much more likely to take the risk these days I can assure you, given the lack of work). We made money by working at weekends, and lost a great deal of it by not working during the week. To build up our finances we had to work hard, travelling out of London almost every weekend.' To a large extent it's the same now when it comes to building up finance, in order to pay for the things you need to promote yourself with. Studio recordings, CD pressings and sleeves, photos and promotional brochures. That's also before you've got a record deal. It's still a costly business, I guess you must be mad to get involved! There we are.

In 1951 Ian Christie, and later that year Keith, left his band due to dissatisfaction with its musical direction. Lyttelton was enjoying playing outside the purist form of the music, and the siblings had been gigging together for a while doing just that as The Christie Brothers Stompers. Recording 18-sides with Ken Colyer on trumpet. Humph replaced Keith with Bruce Turner, on clarinet and saxes a year later, and this got the goat of purists even more.

Given the workload and pressures that Humph's band found itself with, the gigs and the increasing fame and commercial recognition, really matters needed resolving before the mirror cracked. He says, 'the decision was not eventually a difficult one. Several members of the band were firmly fixed in their careers and which they felt disinclined to abandon for a chancy venture into professional music; and I on my part was unwilling to break up a band which had been together, virtually intact, for the past two years. Furthermore, there was the strain, which I felt very keenly.' Eventually though, when you work in these circumstances the situation takes its toll, as he confirms, 'In the winter of 1953, the final decision was made. We reverted to a completely semi-professional status, confining our work chiefly to the Club on two weekday evenings a week and to an occasional weekend jaunt out of town.' Humph very much made the sensible decision here, what he had was just too good and don't want to do too much, too soon. Break up. What's the point of that?

While Lyttelton had been contending with ramifications of the 'Revivalist' uprising in British jazz, Chris Barber was still running his own band which included Alexis Korner, in the early 1950s. He explained, 'so I carried on with my Louis Armstrong (Chicago) Hot Five type thing through until 1952. We got to the point where to get any better we'd all need a lot more technique. We weren't going to get it playing the amount of time we played, we could (really) get playing.' They wanted to take it up to the next level.

As ever with Chris what can't be underestimated is the depth of his passion for the music, and what he's doing. Continuing, he says, 'if you couldn't feel it (jazz/swing) you wouldn't be able to do it anyway, and if you could feel it you'd be able to do it. You know what I mean? [Laughs].'

'Yeah, absolutely. I mean the reason I ended up doing it [double bass] was because I started off playing traditional jazz self-taught,' I replied. 'It helped me feel it too,' responded the trombone player.

But then on the subject of 'where I went from here', Chris, illuminating his story further said, 'so August 52 we got the 4th, "Professional" band together. It was Monty [Sunshine] and me, and then Lonnie Donegan joined in and, he lied about everything. Well 20 years later he changed it all. He came and joined us 'cos he was doing National Service stationed in Woolwich. He managed to wriggle out of it one day and came to see us, so we sat and had a cup of tea in a restaurant called the Rec's in Old Compton St, Soho, one day for hours. We thought we'd find nobody that would want to be professional at first, we did find some. Monty found Ron Bowden who was playing drums in the last Crane River Band [Ken Colyer's group], I mean he was living at home on one gig a week for six quid. Lonnie had Jim Bray on the bass. Jim could have had any count, he was so clever. He had a job at that time, 52, working at Shell researching flamethrower fuels, and he was getting marched to the safe with his notebook by two coppers every night. Well it was a state secret y'know. But he didn't really want to go on doing that. 'Cos he was a lot older than us, he'd been to college and had spent the war years in Texas. He'd speak out of the side of his mouth like a Texan, had degrees in Chemistry, I expect. He was a typical, high IQ, highly intelligent person whose common sense was nil. Funny.' All of this just shows regardless of the profession, music, finance or the building, there's little that a good session of 'brainstorming' won't put right.

Like a lot of founders, regardless of their field, Chris' sense of where his music stood amongst the wider movement around him, was particularly perceptive. As a result, he felt able in hindsight to explain this to me, though some may see it in another light. 'But the sounds of jazz was played by the amateurs, would-be players, but was improving but I don't think it really improved until ... really my band, my "power band", co-operative band it was, started up with Ken [Colyer] on trumpet because Pat Halcox chickened out, but we had Pat in already, all set to, then he promised his parents he'd get qualifications before he did anything stupid like playing music.' As a father myself I can't think of any better advice in this day and age. To be clear about the who, what and why I made a point of asking, is the band with Ken Colyer? 'Yes, Ken joined it. 'Cos Ken went to New Orleans. He knew what he had to do. They (the business in the UK) weren't going to give you any more time than once a week to it, but he wanted to go and get there and play it all the time.' Out of curiosity, and to set the record straight, I then put the obvious to him, 'so did you go to the States?' 'No. I just got records. I suppose my team were more interested in the [pauses] ... the more virtuoso music of the New Orleans players who went up north to play with King Oliver and all those sort of people like that, in Chicago, rather than the ones who stayed at home who put the philosophy and social life of New Orleans above the chance to play really good music, but they weren't such good players. You can't doubt that, you can hear them playing and they weren't so good. They were very charismatic, lovely music, in point of fact they got a time later on. One of the reasons that I was happy to start up the band with Monty, he had the same trouble with his amateur band, as did Lornie and I, playing once a week. The ones who wouldn't play more than that were holding them back, they wanted to get it done better.' So you can easily appreciate all their motivation, Ken Colyer included. The traditional purist who has to take his music to the ultimate conclusion. But for a while it means that one of the most rebellious and determined characters on the scene has dropped off the radar. You can also argue it's for the best, but the silence isn't for so long.

Back with his enterprise in Soho, Harold Pendleton has been getting to grips with club life. The fact that it was relatively new to him certainly didn't seem to be colouring his ambitions. 'I was stumbling about with my Gallion Club and then I launched another club called the Club Creole, which some people rudely called the "Pee Hole Club", which I supposed I asked for. It was in Gerrard St in what had been rehearsal rooms, and at night time they took down the partitions and then we had a club down there, that was my first club, 44, Gerrard St. This is 52.' Funnily enough, a year or so later someone else opened a club at number 48.

In the meantime, Chris picks up the tale of his new band. 'So we met, decided to get a trumpet player. We met Pat [Halcox]. It's funny Pat started playing trombone with that band. Ever since then he played the trumpet. It was called the North West London Stompers, something like that. He was really keen on the idea [Chris' band].' So finally he has a line-up that he feels will play to the professional standard that he's been striving for, that'll get across the sound and musicianship he wants to get out there.

Harold picks it up. 'I remember one night Chris came in having now finished at the Guildhall, and he said, "Harold, can I bring my new band down here to get some practice, play to an audience, and try some things out?" I said, "of course Chris, y'know, we're best friends."'

Very quickly he found himself with some dates.

The trombonist goes on. 'We actually started off with two live sessions for the band, before Pat had changed his mind, it was Christmas Eve and New Year's Eve 52, at a jazz club in Gerrard St. It was called Club Creole and run by Harold Pendleton. And we played down there, and I thought the band was very good with Pat down there. Funnily enough, when Dick Smith, who joined Ken Colyer and then later joined us, said he was there both nights and he was, said it was just as good as the Ken Colyer Band, which was nice.' Good as it was to get that kind of confirmation, a quality performance on the day makes all the difference, as in any job, and that's what clicked with Harold. 'They had a little play down there and I was very intrigued, I said to Chris, "That's jolly interesting, what are you going to do?" He said, "Well I've got this idea for a band, and would you like to manage it, as you're an accountant you know, good with numbers?" I said, "sure love to."' Harold became manager but this didn't last long for those involved, this initial partnership was brief.

For Chris, though his grapevine was coming to a very vibrant life, there was a definitive course of action he felt he had to take. 'Then, as it happens, I then that week heard that Ken Colyer was coming back from New Orleans. So I wrote a letter to him saying, "We've got a nice band going, a co-operative band, why don't you come and join it? We'd like to call it your band really, because people want to know what you found in New Orleans, you see?" Well, Ken came back and we met him and he came to a rehearsal, appeared to enjoy it very much indeed, thought it was very good, so that was it, the Ken Colyer Jazz Band happened.' The jazz of the East Coast southern States brought back to the UK.

Harold had a sense at the time of what he wanted to do and opted to let matters take the following course, as far as his own interests were concerned, he goes on. 'Ken Colyer came back from New Orleans and there was a "jazz club" broadcast, it could have been called *BBC Rhythm Club*. And Ken was going to talk about his "goings on" in New Orleans, they [the BBC] wanted a band to back it. So Chris took this band along, and they played a couple of numbers while Ken talked along. At the end of it, Bill Colyer [Ken's brother], came over to Chris and said, "Look, you've got a band, I've got Ken. Ken is famous [in traditional jazz circles], your band's unknown, why don't we merge and your trumpet player, Pat Halcox, still has a job? I've talked to him and he's a bit uncertain as to whether to give it up or not for an uncertain life. Why not have Ken on 'lead' trumpet and cash in on Ken's fame?" So Chris said, "Well that seems a good idea." And Bill said, "well why don't I manage the band?"

Chris said to me, "well what do you think?" I said, "Sounds like a good idea."

So the Ken Colyer Jazz Band was born so off they went.' Well it seems like an ideal start to an ideal marriage. Harold, given his own professional concerns with clubs and jazz, and the practicalities of just 'finding the time', he's decided to stay in control of what he's already built up. Very astute.

But then with no small piece of wisdom makes his next sharp business move, he tells me, 'I now move from the Club Creole to the London Jazz Centre at 14, Greek St, which was my most successful club up till then, and it had two floors. It was a club called the Latin Quarter during the day, and was the London Jazz Centre during the evening.

What Time Are We On?

I dug in there and developed the Ken Colyer Band.' More than one venue in the same premises, a shrewd move.

Chris is in the middle of a young, busy time and this was what it meant for him. 'Where it felt good as against not, where you wanna play is, somewhere where actually the facilities can give you a chance to play and not hinder your playing by being, whatever gets in the way, y'know. When we started out the band, in 53 with Ken Colyer on trumpet. It could be done, I mean you can count, if the jazz club's full you get enough money to live on. When we started out in, y'know, when we actually started out. I think it was about maybe three or four jobs a week, but by the end of the year, the 12 months which was spring 54, We then had six gigs a week. We actually, for the time, we earned about twelve quid a week. Which at that time was very good really. I mean, it was above the National Average I would have said probably, at the time. We worked bloody hard for it, but then we were playing the music we loved, what more could you ask?' The group's success also included a tour in Denmark.

So with Chris now set on a new course the person we want to catch up with now is his friend Alexis Korner, now that Lonnie Donegan is sat in his chair in the new band. In 1951 he joined Dick Hawdon's band as well, a trumpet player from Leeds who had moved to London and subsequently joined Chris' band at the time. With Ken Colyer's return to the UK in March 53 Alexis took the chance to join his skiffle group, and recorded with them on mandolin and guitar. It must be said that by now it's not unusual for musicians to be quite incestuous when it comes to the variety of bands their involved in, and who's in them.

Humph at this time is keeping his affairs pretty much as they were.

In traditional jazz things remain the same with two name acts, and a bunch of more amateurish outfits performing on the side. The titles of which I refer to from time to time.

Chris Barber though gives a deeper insight into the entanglements with which he was slowly getting snared up in, they can make slightly awkward reading, but he's a frank man. 'We didn't have nothing 'til Ken Colyer joined, so no, he was a great player, a very good player. Just his brother 'cos he'd been shot. Awful. You haven't had to deal with it. Ah, well we had to deal him. Well we knew that when Ken joined the band, that Bill would want to be the band manager you see and we didn't want Bill to have anything to do with it at all. We didn't trust him an inch. We said to Ken we don't want Bill and he said OK. By six months later Bill (who played washboard) had wheeled himself in past Ken by manipulating him you see, so Ken couldn't turn him down.' He continues, 'Ken had an absurdly enlarged sense of family responsibility. All from the fact that he'd been left protecting his mother from his drunken father, while Bill and his other brother Bob went off to fight in the war. 'Cos he blamed them you see, they walked out and left him protecting the mother when he was younger. That was a psychological prison, perfectly normal. But he wouldn't turn his brother down.' So from here on the situation in the band would only degenerate.

On the plus side though, he was keeping his skiffle enterprise alive and well down in Greenwich, south-east London. This would prove very rewarding over the next couple of years. Playing with Lonnie Donegan and Dickie Bishop (a banjo and guitar player) down in Woolwich at a club called The Shakespeare, on Powis Street. I asked the brass player, so working for Denis Preston, it was kind of that area? 'Yeah, [he reflects] well … of course, … the world has of course changed. Totally. In certain ways, and certainly in regards to the music business and the entertainment business. For example, Denis Preston was an enthusiast, loved music and had got into recording things more or less, in about 53 or so. He got interested in the first place by, in those days there were three big record companies and they didn't deal with anyone but artists who hired at scandalous fees or, or for no fee at all, and that's how they became rich. Denis was one of the first persons in England to do what they'd done in America after they'd had those strikes with the Musicians' Union [referring to the American Federation of Musicians] sometimes, and then it was the composers who wouldn't let them use their stuff on record, because they weren't getting the right deal. They still don't, I mean records. Having your composition on record in America does not bring you any money, much. Not unless it's played on the radio. Here it's automatic. If you get your song on the B-side you get the same amount of money as the A-side gets. It's simply a proportionate thing.' This is standard practice with the record industry in the UK via the PRS for Music (formerly MCPS–PRS Alliance).

So at this juncture Denis Preston (born Sidney Denis Prechner in Stoke Newington, London in 1916), who is also the business partner of Lyn Dutton, Humph's manager, has started his own record production company 'Record Supervision Ltd'. He's a kind of Dave Robinson/ Jake Riviera character (who started Stiff Records). Known as a smooth operator it has been said, by some, he was the first independent record producer in the UK, maybe even Europe. Denis often works by recording the band first, and then licencing the recording out to a major company like Pye to press and distribute to the record shops. As a result retaining the control of it, and potentially making more money. Not a disagreeable way of going about it, and this is not the last we hear of Mr Preston.

The Ken Colyer Jazz Band is unique and offering a different prospect to Humph's Band, particularly with two such virtuoso horn players fronting it. Hugely popular on the traditional scene. Sadly though, there are dark cracks beginning to appear in its thoroughly engaging woodwork. For Chris he's performing in the most exhilarating environment to date. He can't get enough of what he's doing, and also opens right up and emotionally tells me, 'When in May 54, after a year playing with Ken you see, and playing in this band a lot was a marvellous band, unbelievable! I mean to hear him now it makes me cry. It was so good and so away, all because of Bill Colyer. We could've kept Ken going alright. He used to get drunk a bit, but we could've kept going. We used to play *Bernie's Tune* (a track famously recorded by the American Modern trumpeter Chet Baker with baritone saxophonist Gerry Mulligan). Can you imagine Ken playing *Bernie's Tune*?' 'No, not from what I've heard,' I said. 'We played it as was it written originally, not bebop, who would've thought? We played things you've never had thought. He'd deliberately play tunes that weren't the real thing.' His passion for their music is undeniable.

But it's here that what they have just shatters. 'And then when Bill Colyer decided to fire Lonnie and Ron, and Jim, and to condescend to tell Monty and me we were getting quite fast so we could stay. Then I said I just felt quite abandoned, it's five to one, we're giving you your notice, go, you've got two weeks. Not having any idea that Pat would change his mind.' Quite a change of events. Not expecting to get caught out.

Chris explains further the complexities and juxtapositions that causes a very bitter break. 'Bill Colyer wanted to sack the rhythm section. Ken didn't say a word. He never said anything, only grumble if he was drunk. Bill was the "Rasputin". He was a stupid man that was the trouble, he loved the limelight but he didn't deserve it. It was a shame, his brother, but he was so reticent. Whether it was his lack of language or whatever, sometimes people are embarrassed at their inability to talk, when they're talking to people who are educated, like me (joke), ha! But he knew the music perfectly, but people would often be asking him, "But I'm not quite playing that bit quite right, can you tell me?", and he'd go "Oh, 'ruh 'ruh." You know, as if to say "what you bothering me for?" Well, because he bloody well knew it you see? He just couldn't say it. If you played it wrong he'd echo it on the trumpet on stage, y'know. As if to say "can't you understand?" But you weren't sure if he was doing it because someone in the audience had thrown something at him, or because it was too hot to play or whatever, or because you weren't playing it right. You couldn't tell. But you asked him he wouldn't tell you. The only way you could find out what Ken Colyer was like was what Bill Colyer would tell you.' 'That clearly doesn't help does it,' I said. 'The way he played things I could understand exactly what he was doing. The thing that's unique to this sort of "New Orleans" style of ensemble improvisation is that you don't have that improvised contrapuntal way of playing in between melody instruments, anywhere.' Chris now says with deep sincerity, 'I've played with a lot of trumpet players, y'know from great famous

Black (American) ones to English ones, all kinda ones, He Played That Role The Best! Simple as that.' 'That's great,' I responded, astonished. I didn't expect to hear that as his conclusion.

Explaining the falling out between Ken Colyer and Lonnie Donegan, which took place at the London Jazz Centre. 'He [Lonnie] fancied himself as a "cheeky chappie" y'see, and of course that didn't suit Ken. The one person in the world who hated "cheeky chappies" was Ken Colyer, and Lonnie was one of the "cheekiest chappies" you'd ever meet, not a very good one but,' to which he shrugs. To be absolutely clear, and to not end up with my neck in a noose, I asked was it quite a clash of personalities? 'Oh yeah, I mean, Lonnie was easy to be with. But when Ken was playing he [Ken] was sort of alright, he didn't say anything ridiculous, they sang the skiffle things together y'know. No problem. Until Bill Colyer said Ken's "gonna sack the rhythm section." We said, "Why? Jim Bray doesn't swing". I said, "no, he doesn't have to. Well he just has to play the right notes and we swing," you see. "Ron Bowden's too modern, I think he played the (drum) brushes once," Ken said' [Chris laughs]. "And he [Ken] hates Lonnie's guts. They've gotta go." Well I don't think anybody hated Lonnie's guts, and I don't think Ken was that bothered about it really. If asked he didn't think that much of him, but that's alright y'know.' Good to hear this from another perspective, connected within the band. Relationships can get very fragile in these scenarios.

At the very least I should provide a second, if not third opinion on all of this as you'll appreciate I'd be dead in the water, face down, if I didn't so here we go. It's been intimated that Harold Pendleton, being he's a good mate of Chris', would tell me what I want to hear, but he's his own man I think. 'I was there at the famous bust-up. Donegan,' he says with dismay and dissatisfaction.

'Lonnie Donegan was a bloke rather given to shooting his mouth off, and causing trouble.' But during the row the 'trigger point' seems obvious, 'and on this night he made a remark about Ken Colyer's wife Delphine, which was not very complementary. So Ken, quite rightly, decided to throttle him, and chased him throughout the club upstairs, got him in a corner, and proceeded to throttle him. 'Cos Ken was quite taciturn, not given to talk, but given to punching, and the rest of the band pulled Ken off, which I think was a shame.' What Harold says from here is very candid, "'Cos I was never a great fan of Lonnie's. 'Cos Lonnie was nothing but trouble, always. Ken was in a terrible rage and said, "Right! He's sacked." And Chris, ever the democrat, said, "b … b … but Ken, it's a co-operative band. We all have to." He said, "Rubbish! It's my band, my name, and not only is he sacked but that fucking bop drummer Ron Bowden goes as well." So Chris says, "well we must discuss this."' A very diplomatic response in the circumstances I suggest.

With tensions running high and maybe a sense of diplomacy he tells me, 'to cut a long story short it's Ken that went, and Chris turned to me, 'cos it's my club that this is happening. "Harold," he said, "what shall I do?" "Well ring Pat Halcox, see if Pat's had another year of doing what he's doing, and whether he'd rather play jazz?" Of course he was playing as an amateur with the Albemarle Jazz Band, but is he willing now to risk becoming a professional, because that's what the Ken Colyer Band was, and toured and made money, and was a proper band? There were about three bands making a living. Lyttelton's, Freddy Randall's, which was my favourite and the Ken Colyer Band.'

The managers recount of the tale is detailed, as well as fascinating. Hard to find these days.

So from here Chris picks up the crisis, 'there used to be a pay phone in the corner of "The Blue Posts", a pub still on Berwick Street, Soho, just to the north of our current location. 'I went in there and rang Pat, and said 'Ken's going, would you like to do it?' He said. 'Yes! Yes! I don't wanna be a chemist, I wanna be a trumpeter.' That was it, so he joined two weeks later. That was it 54, May 31st.' As Harold reiterated, 'we rang Pat and he said he'd take the gamble. Oh he'd pack in whatever he was doing and play trumpet,' and then his smile became very broad, content at the outcome. It seems a very happy end to a frantic and turbulent evening.

Well you've heard it twice, and a visceral row as intense as this has no other route to take except to explode. Maybe the only bright light in this is Pat Halcox's belated second chance? For another view on Ken I'd like to quote you a short piece by Jim Godbolt, the jazz writer who was an expert and around during this era, and knew the musicians. 'Colyer, however, had ideas incompatible with a co-operative set-up and it was not long before he was imposing his dominant personality on the band, or attempting to do so. There was bitter discord on and off the stand. It was pointed out to him that he was part of a co-operative, and he had no right to sack anyone. His dissatisfaction with the situation affected his playing, he was drinking heavily, and the event, left the band in May 1954.' He paraphrases the night in Harold's club, you can find a copy if you want it. He also refers to Ken Colyer's 'Intransigence and blunt demeanour making him a cult figure.' It was clearly quite a dramatic evening, and a lot of anger and burning aggression was brought to the surface as a consequence. Rightly or wrongly, the same band members were threatened and told they were history, whether they liked it or not. It's for you to interpret the above and make of it what you will, I'm keeping my counsel from this distance. This is a very significant night in traditional jazz and for its future.

I said to Chris, 'what's your next step from this?' 'So I rang all the owners of the clubs. George Renfrew who had the Woolwich Club, Art Solomons from Wood Green, the guy who ran the Southall Club, Harold Pendleton who had the jazz in Greek St. Oh the 100 Club we played on Mondays. Oh yeah Ken hasn't got a band at all now.' Also in the 'mix' is the album that the Ken Colyer Band had recorded for the Decca Record label prior to its demise, with a great deal of deceit in some quarters. Chris explains, 'so all Bill had to do was ring up Decca, about the lovely LP we made for them. Not telling the Decca guy that we'd all left. But we wanted to get playing together, and learning how to play the bloody stuff better.' In the circumstances a remarkably determined man indeed.

At this time despite the ructions and rows of the tale just told, traditional jazz is in a healthy state and growing in popularity at a fair pace. In 1954 you've a large, solid group of amateur bands with a loyal hardcore following. On top of that you've Humphrey Lyttelton's successful band as well as the above. Out of the Barber/Colyer bust-up of course two bands are born. I think we can guarantee they'll go their own separate ways. Harold recalls, 'so in he comes, now it's the Chris Barber Band. The residency at the London Jazz Centre I immediately turn over to Chris, and I ring all the other promoters saying, "Ken's out, it's now the Chris Barber Band", which I'm managing, they've got a residency at the London Jazz Centre, I have a concert at the Royal Festival Hall coming up, 'cos by now I'd started promoting (putting on, and providing the publicity of concerts) as the National Jazz Federation, all big concerts and so on in the Royal Festival Hall (on London's Southbank), that's another story, that's about me.' But we shouldn't underestimate the significance of Harold in the music industry, at this time. He's no minor league player anymore.

As he illustrates here, 'I controlled these concerts. I said to Chris, "right you're top of the bill with your brand new band nobody's ever heard of." Immediately all the clubs changed their bookings from "Ken Colyer Band" to "Chris Barber Band", so that got Chris off to a good start and we had an enormously successful Royal Festival Hall concert, and he was on his way, and was now managing them, and that is really the beginning of the 12 years that I managed the band. And that is the story of the launch of the Chris Barber Band, which has occupied the next 12 years of my life. That's roughly the 12 years from the mid-50s to the mid-60s. Which is the period of the great success of traditional jazz.' Of that there is no doubt.

Ken Colyer soon put together his new line-up in the September, and in retrospect it gives cause to raise a very high eyebrow. He recruited Eddie O'Donnell, trombone, William 'Diz' Disley, banjo, from the Yorkshire Jazz Band; Stan Greig, drums, Dick Smith, double bass, from Sandy Brown's Edinburgh band and a young clarinet player from Pensford, Somerset called Bernard 'Acker' Bilk. That name may just ring a bell. Ken's band played regularly at Studio 51 and Vi Hyland even gave him a spell where it became the Ken Colyer Club on certain nights. She knows his name carries a certain amount of kudos given his abilities. I wish I'd had the chance to meet Vi, she sounds amazing, a real character.

Another challenge which faced jazz at this time was a growing misconception about Soho, created by the press, which was making it out to be the seediest and most lurid area you could imagine. As a consequence parents were being very wary of letting their 'young adults' – terrible term but you get the picture – venture into W1. In Humphrey Lyttelton's first book he gets the issue across well. 'Only a day or two ago, an anxious mother telephoned me at my home with an enquiry on behalf of her daughter, who had expressed a wish to visit our club in Oxford Street. There was no doubt, from her comments, that mum had the gravest misgivings. When I said the club was in Oxford Street, – "oh yes, that's Soho, isn't it!" I said it was not, but she didn't believe me. "I'm not keen on my daughter visiting a jazz club!" she said frankly, and when she rang off, I knew that the daughter's chances of coming to see us were small. In vain, I protested that our members were just ordinary human beings keen on a lively night out. In vain, I pointed out that, in six years, we have never had the smallest fight or disturbance. The newspaper stories of drug-ridden Soho jazz clubs had sunk in, and we were clearly suspect. One point which the anxious mother raised is an interesting one.' Very illuminating I feel.

I'm sure that if you looked hard enough you'd find vice and depravity, but all my interviewees first came to Soho in their youth. If you visited the lesser-known boozers and clubs on your back doorstep in the mid-1950s, I'd venture you'd have found the same. But like now, at 17, 18, 19 we all find our way and most of us keep our noses clean. The public's misconceptions about Central London's most colourful district must've been tricky for musicians and artists alike at the time.

Chris Barber certainly didn't hang around, he couldn't afford to. Finances and people's loyalties wouldn't allow. He didn't drink or smoke. His will to succeed was noted by many at the time, George Melly and Jim Godbolt. It soon made the band's name. 'We just carried on from there, just tried to get as near to the music as we possibly could, and we were very fortunate, within a month of taking the band over we recorded our own first LP which of course had *Rock Island Line* on it.' No rest taken.

The album was released by the Chris Barber Jazz Band in July 1954, the song in question credited as the Lonnie Donegan Skiffle Group, with Chris on double bass, Lonnie Donegan, Ron Bowden and Beryl Bryden on washboard. In 1956 it was released as a single in the UK and US. The album sold around 10,000 whereas the single was a massive seller here and abroad. Donegan eventually collected a Gold Disc for sales into seven figures, I'll take that. Sadly, Chris had other issues. 'Apart from anything else it sold a lot, I don't know what the sales were, I never found out. But I didn't get a royalty (payment based on sales) on it at the time, I had no right to demand it, I could have found out in the end if I'd realised 'cos of the MCPS (now the PRS for Music Ltd who collect royalties on behalf of musicians), or the copyright I owned. I could tell from that because all the figures go to the copyright of the composer, so we can tell what the sales are. It's the best way possible 'cos it's impossible to cheat the composers, it's still a matter whether to cheat the artists or not [laughs]. It's not against the law.' Decca records originally paid the musicians two pounds and ten shillings each for both discs, I must admit I'd feel a little miffed in the circumstances!

What Time Are We On?

Like Alexis, Chris was remaining true to his love of skiffle and blues, especially on the live circuit by maintaining his residency in south-east London. It was his lucky day when an old American acquaintance rolled into town. 'Then Big Bill Broonzy was in England, and then we had a chance to work with him at a few gigs, and of course we even had the skiffle group which was doing tunes of Big Bill's. Lonnie had even got off singing My Old Man's a Dustman, I don't blame him because for the Variety stage you've got to do something the audience will accept. Some of the time at least, you see? And he enjoyed them. Lonnie's all-time ideal performer was Max Miller [he laughs], which I liked. So we actually played several gigs, at the club at Woolwich, The Shakespeare, with our skiffle group, which was Lonnie, Dickie Bishop and me, and Big Bill.' It must've been a great piece of fortune for them all.

I asked if at that time they'd been able to get into the studio with Big Bill Broonzy on this visit, 'the sad thing is that we recorded … basically, the thing is we were under a recording contract with the company of Denis Preston, who was the business partner of Lyn Dutton who had the agency that all the trad bands worked for. Anyway, Denis Preston was a bit of a phoney, he drank a lot apparently, he wasn't a record producer, he wasn't any good at it, he didn't have much idea of what would and wouldn't sell, 'cos he never picked anything up. Anything of ours that did well he opposed us doing it, when we started doing it. "Son," I said, "we should record that, that sounds fantastic. We should record the records, I know what Big Bill's done. It's terrific stuff y'know." "Ha," he said. "You should be playing with people of the other calibre in America, he doesn't play with banjos, he plays with saxophones."' Certainly keen to express his opinion.

If anything though, it would appear Mr Preston was quite happy to have the courage of his convictions when it came to giving an original idea a whirl in the recording studio. 'He did this awful EP of Big Bill with a band including Kenny Graham, Ronnie Ross, Ronnie Scott and people like that. The arrangement sound was just so unsuitable. But you can't believe it was ever done, seriously by anyone. Awful. I reckon with Lonnie we could have made Big Bill a hit record. He was so lovely, so entertaining, so nice, so good, and all he liked doing [Chris thinks], he'd sing an hour. He'd be singing *When did you leave heaven?*, *I'm falling over a four-leafed clover*, *Glory of love*, songs like that. That's what he loved doing. I mean Roger Whittaker eat your heart out, all that plus charisma.' On a personal note, I have never been able to get the bearded crooner, maybe that's down to an upbringing from musically educated parents. Apologies to those offended.

Chris makes his point well, 'but of course he didn't get to record any of that, and could have had enough money to get his stroke cancer treated properly, instead of dying.' 'This was in 1954 we're talking about?' I asked. 'Yeah, 54/55.' Chris recalls quite an experience.

The traditional musicians were as happy to travel to a gig as anyone else. Mike Daniels who had his own band and ran a business as well, travelling with his employee and clarinettist John Barnes, would meet up outside the Rex Restaurant in Old Compton Street at around 10.30 am, and make their way by road up to Manchester.

By now there were several well-known singers on the scene. George Melly received the greatest recognition for the men. There's a lot to be said I think for the number of female singers that had names for themselves. At this time you had Rosina Scudder, Joan Roberts, Beryl

What Time Are We On?

Bryden (who my father later played with), Jackie Lynn (with Dick Charlesworth's City Gents), Neva Raphaello and Doreen Beatty (the Mike Daniels Band).

Humph, like Chris and Ken Colyer, has a definite idea of what their jazz in the mid-1950s was about. It also seems to be an aesthetic for him that was consistently evolving. Maybe not so for many others. In his own words, 'to me the whole joy of jazz music is not in reproducing a set pattern, but in getting together a workable group of compatible musicians and allowing the style to emerge. This a dangerous policy for a revivalist, since the purist notion of jazz is that the New Orleans style, because it is the prototype, is therefore the most "real", "pure" and "authentic" style and anything which deviates from it is a move away from jazz.' I think it also helps explain the internal conflict and dilemma in which traditional jazz has found itself. also, out of punk came Public Image, Siouxsie and the Banshees, Joy Division, Killing Joke, alternative music and the New Romantics. Meanwhile the Anti-Nowhere League, the Exploited and others, carried on as before. Same events do come around don't they? It's all very enlightening when looking back.

On the subject of different genres and factions Chris Barber recounted to me a very revealing story on how different sides can just get together, have a good social, and play. Yet you'd never know it happens. 'So most of the Modernists, I knew some of them and I enjoyed what they played. I remember from about 1954, 55. I had my own bass in town, there was this Social Club off Denmark St we used to go to. There's a mews off Denmark St that curves and comes back onto Charing Cross Rd by the theatre, what's it called?' The Phoenix Theatre

I suspect. 'There was a Greek Social Club there, which was generally inhabited by the Greek, or Cypriot guys there, who worked terribly long hours in tailoring shops making suits that sort of stuff you know, and night cab drivers. But this building, called the A and A Club. A and A being two Greeks per each among names starting with an A. There was nothing on the ground floor at all, just at that same little alleyway there's a store for theatrical costume, and flats for the theatre.' Whether they're still there I just couldn't say, but you could find out.

Chris continued, 'anyway, on the first floor there was a room you could have dances, parties and so on. The next floor was a restaurant, and the top floor was a billiard hall. But the restaurant was open all night you see. So we used to go there and eat after the concert. After working club nights whatever, and then Monty and I used to then go upstairs and play snooker on the top floor. But there was going to be a session on at this first floor place, and it must have been about 55 'cos Ronnie Scott told me, I used to see him quite often. He said the Woody Herman Band [from America] was in Europe and they did a concert in Dublin because they couldn't come to England 'cos of the Union thing [the Ban], and people went over from here actually. Then they were coming back here to England to go home to America or something, to go home by boat you had to see.' This diversion certainly makes a get-together a lot more likely, American musicians at a loose end in London before they return to the States.

He continues his tale. 'So they were going to have a jam session, and said would I like to come along and play the bass. So it was Irving Green on the trombone, and there was Dizzy Reece on trumpet who also played the drums, Flash Winston playing the piano which was funny and Tommy Pollard played the piano as well, and I played the bass. I mean I played "walking" parts rather than arpeggios and I hurt my fingers too, but it was quite normal and friendly, and no one was sort of, I got on very well with Tommy I remember and all that lot, because I played music with them quite often. I didn't try and play some kind of weird thing, I just played what I could and I, we got on fine with them.' A great combination of musicians, including British Traditionalists and Modernists.

By 1955 traditional jazz is becoming big and popular. It's playing live and recorded, in clubs all over the country, is creating bands all over, has known names, is selling records in significant quantities for the time. The clubs are filling up and the music is currently spreading in an upward direction. Not bad considering its humble beginnings ten years before.

ACKNOWLEDGEMENTS:

I Play as I Please: The memoirs of an Old Etonian trumpeter. With drawings by the author. [With plates, including portraits.] Humphrey Lyttelton, 1921–2008. London: MacGibbon & Kee, 1954 (P. 178), (P. 179), (P. 180), (P. 181), (P. 192/193)

Second Chorus. Drawings by the author. Humphrey Lyttelton, 1921–2008. London: MacGibbon & Kee, 1958 (P. 76)

A History of Jazz in Britain 1950–1970. Jim Godbolt, 1922–2013. London: Quartet, 1989 (P. 74)

CHAPTER 5

At the turn of the decade for modern jazz, Club 11 is proving to be a big success in modern circles. A venue they can all meet at, play in, exchange ideas, pass around contacts, circulate records and who knows what else. The Metrobopera is proving popular for the same reason too. The growth of the jazz club is about to arrive but we'll approach that often exciting, and dingy subject in a little while. There's also another change appearing on the horizon.

As Eddie Harvey tells, it's not just a good night out that's about to influence the direction and style of what they want to do. 'Out of all of that John Dankworth wanted to form a band. Which was really, very similar to the Miles Davis *Birth of the Cool* band, which was 1948.' His friend and colleague recalls it in his own autobiography. 'It's inspirational effect on me was electric. Why had I not thought of assembling a few friends the same way that Miles had? Heaven knows, they were always popping in and jamming at the club – why not have some music for them to read next time? I nailed Don Rendell one night as he put his tenor away after a jam. He agreed to come to a rehearsal, as did Ed Harvey.' He started putting the band together at the end of

1949. As Don Rendell remembers, 'that was when John was starting the Dankworth Seven, and by then I'd got married and moved to Islington. So John would often stay at our house anyway, I was a kind of … I think John wanted Ronnie Scott. I believe I was second choice.' As it transpired Don was an excellent choice.

Eddie's connection to his new band mate had started earlier than I'd thought. 'Well I knew John when I was 16. Yeah, he went to the Royal Academy quite early, as a 16 year old. I envied John because his mother ran the local choir and the orchestra [laughs], she ran the whole council I think. My mother was the same, the pair of them were very similar of that generation. She [Eddie's] was an "Empire builder", a manageress in NAAFI, in the Army. During the Normandy Landings she fed a 1,000 men three times a day, and sang to them in the evening! She'd find some squaddie who could play the piano, and sing Gracie Fields numbers to them. And John's mother was similar. A very stately woman who you didn't argue with.' Very quickly John Dankworth had got his ideas together and put them into action. He was then fortunate and got a break that really mattered from a man with a very big band, Ted Heath, who offered him the support slot at the London Palladium.

Someone else who gave the Dankworth Seven a chance at this time when it mattered, who we've mentioned already is Vi Hyland. With John having got in Jimmy Deuchar on trumpet, Don Rendell on tenor sax, Eddie Harvey on trombone, Bill Le Sage on piano, Joe Mudele on double bass, and Tony Kinsey on drums as well as vibes [vibraphone]. It's the latter from London who provides the memories. 'The 51 Club was at the bottom of the stairwell on the left-hand side from the street. Vi and/or Pat were behind a hatch on the left with an

What Time Are We On?

Alsatian dog. From there you walked on in to the club. I remember Vi Hyland quite well and her business partner Pat, and she treated me with the utmost respect and kindness. She was, I thought, a very nice lady, I mean the fact that she was running a modern jazz club, three nights a week in London, was fantastic.' 'It's exceptional, there can't have been that many women doing that?' I remarked. 'Yeah, I don't know how much work she put in behind the scenes because it just seemed to happen if you know what I mean, I can't even remember her advertising.' I've seen several advertisements that have come from the music paper *Melody Maker* when I've visited The British Library at Colindale, through my research that's the only 'jazz club' advertising I've come across for the time. But I know what Tony's getting at. What matters is that Vi's putting on jazz from right across the spectrum, for people to dance and have a good time to, and people are turning up. As a consequence she's filling her club on a regular basis, and it's got the reputation and trade of the 100 Club and Club 11. Which may be a little insalubrious but isn't that what rebellious youth needs?

For Eddie it didn't just end with Club 11 and the clothes. What he was involved in excited him the most. 'So we loved that music. John did most of the arrangements. I started doing arrangements, in fact we were all kind of arrangers at that time. Sometimes we didn't even bother putting it on paper. We could actually do an arrangement in our heads, and remember four (instrumental) parts! Sometimes we did two a day. We'd rehearse every day, ten 'til six, and then everybody go off and do gigs. Don Rendell, John and I had an arrangement whereby if one of us got a gig we'd split the money between the three of us. So we'd go to a gig, whatever it was and get half a crown (2 shillings and

An early Club gig and line-up of the John Dankworth 7. The Frontline Brass (l-r) are Don Rendell, Eddie Harvey and John Dankworth.

sixpence/16 pence in old money) or something like that [laughs]. We would share, it was that kind of 'feeling' y'know? It was terrific! John and I went to Paris and hung around the jazz there. It was a terrific, creative period, altogether. I learnt a lot from John Dankworth actually, especially in those early days of writing. He was very helpful to me. This was more like 1950, 1951.' The financial 'understandings' the band has is very useful. With so many fresh ideas in playing as well as in business, it's no wonder the modern jazz scene seems so bright, vibrant and almost intoxicating to this younger crowd. The fact that members of the Dankworth group are more than happy to travel to the

What Time Are We On?

Continent, in order to look for inspiration says a lot in 1950 I think. Not everyone would feel a need to go to another town around this time, never mind journey to a different country, and to Paris.

Another significant change around this time is that Club 11 moves to new premises at 50, Carnaby Street, in April 1950. But this backstreet is a dingy dump at the time. Not the colourful parade and trendy shopping attraction it became in the 1960s, and for perpetuity. Ronnie Scott gives a very humorous account of the venue's final night when it bit the dust. 'On the night of 15 April 1950, I was on stage with my band, eyes tightly closed, blowing the last of nine choruses of Charlie Parker's *Now's The Time*. The club was packed; the joint as Fats Waller used to say, was jumping. I finished my solo, opened my eyes and got the shock of my life. A massive uniformed police sergeant practically filled my entire field of vision. I backed up, looked around and saw the place was full of coppers. Commotion, confusion, consternation. "All right, stop the music and turn out your pockets," barked the sergeant. The music stopped abruptly and the ensuing near silence was only broken by the sound of little packets hitting the floor. We were being raided by the drug squad – and the joints were jumping. Those of us in the band had no time to unload the evidence and we were among a dozen guys who were rounded up by the police and transported by Black Maria to Savile Row police station. We were all pretty naïve, apprentice potheads but the police seemed even more uninitiated in matters cannabis sativa than we were. One of the musicians used to make a hole in a matchbox, put a joint in the hole and then slightly open the box and use it as a pipe. When the desk sergeant at Savile Row took possession of this rude accessory he announced to one of his colleagues with pontifical assurance: "Yes, there you are, you see – they sniff the stuff through that hole."' For most people, even those supposed to be literate in these matters, the finer points of drug use isn't really known except by those using them, at this time.

Don Rendell, who has very clear memories of the machinations within the outfit he's part of, picks up our tale. 'Yeah, the Dankworth Seven was a totally co-operative undertaking. It lost money and John wanted to finish it, but Bill Le Sage talked him in to keeping it.' The leader of the group confirms this in his own work when he says, 'The voice came from Bill Le Sage. "If we went co-operative we might make it. We're jazz musicians, so we all know how to live on a shoestring." Bill Le Sage, the driving force behind the co-operative idea, became the manager. Bill from the start was the mainstay of the group. He fitted perfectly into our social pattern, and was always a sobering influence on us when any among us had a foolish or impracticable idea in mind.' For all of the piano player's great expectations, making it work was proving a harder prospect than any of them anticipated. To make money and still be able to play what they want is a big ask. 'We'd play Ted Heath "Swing Sessions" at the London Palladium. The band was thought of as very "avant-garde", we thought people wouldn't like it. Anyway, we played a few jazz clubs and gigs and stuff like that, but that was it,' Eddie corroborated.

Soon after though, the band has the stroke of luck that we all wish for in life. The kind of good fortune that gets you offered the job you always wanted, the car you had to have or the girl/gent you always wished for. Whatever you hope will happen, in music like many other professions it can make the vital difference. Tony relates the tale for

Marion Williams, early vocalist with the John Dankworth groups.

this group. 'Ronnie got us the job as the first trio to work regularly at Studio 51, the Ronnie Ball Trio. And he wanted me to join him. In fact the Dankworth Band played down there a lot. It was down there that we auditioned Cleo Laine. We did it in the daytime, and we'd been up to Manchester somewhere, and of course travelling's not like it is now y'know? Cold coaches and that sort of thing. But John called us for 11 o'clock in the morning, to audition this new singer, up until this point it had been this girl, Marion Williams, and Linda Ellington (as well as Frank Holder who was originally from Guyana). Anyway, we got there, and in came Cleo with her husband at the time, and she sang a few songs. We were a co-operative band at the time so we went over to the pub opposite, where we had a chat about it and decided that we rather liked her, so she got the job, and the rest is history. I mean it's amazing isn't it? Anyway, we worked regularly with JD. It was whilst we were touring with John that Ronnie had the trio.' Not only did they get the break that mattered but also Tony's working in two bands at once, no mean feat in the summer of 1951.

If you've got the right line-up you can still be a long way from having the magic spark for success. We can still scratch our chins for a long time while we procrastinate over what will light the fire, and then from nowhere it falls into our lap from where we least expect it. Eddie remarked, 'there wasn't a lot of gigs about for a bebop band, and as a result of that there was a band that came from Switzerland, called Hayde Osterweld's Band, they were all good jazz players but they did comedy as well. They also played commercial music and we were so keen to keep the band together, that we agreed to make some efforts to compromise, so we decided to play bebop arrangements of commercial tunes of the day. And we played waltzes, we had a vocal group which was Cleo and John, Don Rendell and me singing in four-part harmony and all that. We did a comedy routine for Sunday concerts and all that, the whole lot you know.' I put it to him that for the kind of vocal numbers and some of the jazz material they were doing, did they get some of the people dancing to that as well? 'Well we used to play Sunday concerts, that was another thing that we did. That opened it up, and we did a lot of work, earned a lot of money, it was great y'know?' So the Dankworth Seven are off. Finally, they find the combination and the inspiration came from central Europe, and that's the direction to take things.

Don Rendell elaborated on the band. 'But we played all over. We played Glasgow, yeah we played the Continent. We played Germany. Kaiserslautern, Osnabrück, Heidelberg, Frankfurt. It must have been for the State Dept, and I met Ute Hip and Hans Kohler. It was a groundbreaking group, the Dankworth Seven.' On top of this Beboppers are still playing in more than one band of course, and plying their trade in the grimy, ration-run, bomb-battered city that is London.

What Time Are We On?

John Dankworth 7 with Frank Holder, vocalist, and Bill Le Sage on piano.

The new music is getting about as the record shops of Bristol, Leeds, Southampton, Birmingham, Coventry, Sheffield, Manchester, Liverpool and beyond are slowly beginning to stock and sell small numbers of this new, innovative American sound. Charlie Parker, Dizzy Gillespie, Thelonious Monk and Bud Powell alongside the traditional and big band. The youngsters are getting hip daddy!

For Eddie, a year or so into the band, he realised he would have to knuckle down even more. That even having this finely tuned performance and show, for him he'd have to set his bar even higher. In this day and age people often think that musicians have it easy, and particularly so in the 1940s and 1950s.

His story is not untypical, so given that they were playing in other bands as well, I beg to differ. 'Well in John's band we rehearsed everything, and being arrangers and everything it was all carefully crafted and all the rest of it, but we didn't actually get a new piece of music stuck in front of us to learn to play, y'know to sight-read. And John and the other guys were pretty good at, but I come from a traditional jazz background and so I hadn't had that experience, and I hadn't really had formal tuition actually. 52 I went to the Guildhall School of Music. But the result of that was that playing in Palais bands. I worked in Eric Laws' Band at Wimbledon Palais, and sometimes you'd say "Oh I've got this band together" and you'd go out on tour and maybe we'd work on numbers for the show … [pauses]. It's one of the things that young guys don't understand is that in those days, if you had a band you used to work and rehearse for, three or four weeks, a lot, for four or five times a week for hours, to get your act together so when you went out you really had a finished product for them, y'know. It was very exciting, and by doing it you learnt a lot from other guys, so that if you're a self-educated musician, there were no educating books on how to play bebop.' I couldn't put it clearer myself. Work hard, it's as competitive now as it was then.

He elaborates further, 'I mean I studied harmony, but what I studied I didn't realise was classical harmony and Bach Chorales and all the rest of it, and that was no good for writing bebop. But later on I realised how it was really handy because I was taught classically for 14 years at a public school. So I had all that background. I was aimed wrongly at one time. But the result of that was I gave myself a music education, which was finished off later on when I did a Degree, a Certificate in Education. When I was 44, at the end of the 60s when jazz had fallen through the floor [yes it did dear reader], my mother said,

"I'm so pleased you've settled down". I was 44 by then [laughs], I'd done two Royal Command Performances [laughing even more], and been in the profession all that time, she was so glad I'd settled down y'know.' Eddie is giggling with joy at this point. I've never seen one of my interviewees laugh more hysterically, lost in a mix of tears and happiness, as this man. The reflections and ruminations of a musician so clearly fond, and proud of his experiences as well his achievements, seeing also the humour in the errors were palpable. To witness those emotions come out of this gent like that made me realise how much his life's experience had meant to him.

However, restlessness is already affecting Tony Kinsey, slap bang in the middle of The Seven's initial success, he takes a risky decision for a bop player. 'So after a couple of years with The Seven I decided to leave to join Ronnie Ball. Well it was during that period that we

John Dankworth 7 with Tony Kinsey on drums.

had this double whammy, after a while he decided to go to the States, and I was going to join him, but for some reason I didn't. Anyway, Vi Hyland asked me to take over leadership of the Trio. I never thought of becoming a band leader, but ever since, I mean I don't do all sorts of work. I've worked with other people and I work in the studio, I'm a composer, I've done orchestral music, but I've been a sort of band leader ever since. Just by chance really, many things happen by chance don't they?' He's not kidding. 'So anyway I took over the Trio. The first groups we had there were The Tony Kinsey Trio with Tommy Whittle [tenor sax, other woodwind, flute/piccolo] and, occasionally Jimmy Skidmore [saxes and flute] and various other people. And after a while, I can't remember how long for, I was very keen to get Bill Le Sage in the group. As I say, touring around in those days wasn't a lot of fun at all. The thought of playing jazz three times a week, even if it was for 30 bob a night, or was it 15 shillings? I can't remember, was very tempting.' Well it must've been enough for the time.

Hitting the highway to earn a living can be quite an exciting experience for those us that have done it. The trains are reasonably comfortable, we rely on our average motors with their onboard computers, if we can trust them, and the hotels are … well maybe we won't go there. Especially when we're nearly always sharing. The point is that things have substantially changed over the years, and a good job too! Particularly now the new jazz of bebop is reaching across the country. It's definitely arrived in Leeds and Manchester, and other points north. 'Oh the adventures with coaches breaking down, and other things there's just a host of 'em. Manchester was a really happening place in those days, you could do a week's work in Manchester every three weeks, so we would all stay up there and stay in the old Exeter Hotel, which was another story.' That wide grin appears across his face, pulling his grey neatly trimmed beard wider, and his eyes roll upwards towards the ceiling. Going on from there, 'in those days we used to have one of those "Dansettes", it was a little record player. But they used to come with a wire, and you'd have an adapter on you to put on to a light socket, and that was it. It was about 3 feet long y'know. In hotels you couldn't use it with a wall plug anyway, they didn't have plugs in the rooms. So I have memories of us all sitting listening to this new Charlie Parker record that had come out, we were all in the dark 'cos we'd had to take the bulb out of the light and plug the Dansette into the light socket. And two guys had to stand in the middle of the bed holding the record player up plugged into the light while we listened to Charlie Parker [both laughing], in the pitch dark! [laughing out loud].' This just leaves us in stitches. 'What year would that have been,' I ask? 'Well it was Jim Deuchar and that lot so it must have been 1951/52.' Ronnie Scott's colleagues to you and me.

Now that modern jazz is reaching out to the provinces it's already influencing the generation coming up behind the likes of Ronnie Scott, Eddie Harvey and John Dankworth. When I spoke to John Critchinson, who worked with Ronnie Scott as piano player towards the latter part of his career from 1979, he told me about a small club in rural Wiltshire that really just came out of the DIY attitude of those that started Club 11, Studio 51 and Punk Rock. To his recollection, 'The Icebox' in Chippenham was the Jack Pennington tie-up with Westinghouse (a local Railway Braking and Signalling company). Jack was here working as a Progress Chaser and I was an apprentice, and I suppose The Icebox started in 1952, it was because Jack found out that I was interested in playing jazz, because we sat together in the work's canteen and talked, at that time that I was living opposite Tony Milsom, a local Bath drummer, he had an amazing record collection. We'd actually done a gig, there was a bass player called Mark Cottell, that became The Tony Modernists as such, and Jack decided that he had a trio that he could back somebody with. I'd never backed anybody. We're talking 1952.' From here I was keen to find out how this new club progressed. Who was the first name they managed to get up from London? 'The first guest to play there was Bill Le Sage, on Vibes, 'cos Jack, while he was doing his RAF Service met quite a lot of these guys, because they came and did the Camps.' There are several Army and Air Force Bases (Camps) in Wiltshire, Somerset and Gloucestershire. He continued, 'So Bill Le Sage, was the first thing I'd ever accompanied y'know? So that was quite an experience, and we were in a community centre in Chippenham.' The early chance to perform with a player of this stature meant a lot, but it wasn't long before more names continued to get booked. 'Thing is that club was set up by Teddy Boys. Jack Pennington, and the other three, were Teddy Boys. And they used to decide who'd they'd have, and I think the second guest was Don Rendell, and he became the President of the Club.' The scene in Chippenham moves on remarkably quickly for such a small market town.

Tony Kinsey is a very knowledgeable fellow. Dark haired, under 6 feet and clean shaven. An earnest, serious man but with a wry sense of humour, again who's done and seen a lot in his life. In more modern phraseology 'respect is due'. His situation with the trio is moving swiftly, and by 1954 is now a quartet with Bill Le Sage and Joe Harriott, a young West Indian, on alto sax. When we got together for the book I was keen to know where he went from here? 'Well I suppose we started to get a lot of publicity from "The 51" in the musical press. Jeff Kruger was opening his Flamingo Club and he asked me whether I'd like to take my quartet over there, maybe three times a week and for three times the money we were was getting down at Vi's place, and a much more salubrious environment. The first Flamingo Club was beneath the Mapleton Hotel, down an alleyway off a side street from Coventry St.' He's certainly starting to make a name for himself on the London jazz scene, and that's no mean feat when you're the drummer. As for The Flamingo, it was a respectable family run operation, a step or two up from Vi's and often packed with dancers and those out for a good time indeed, within 1950s parameters.

Around this time a new, young, dynamic and virtuoso tenor and vibes player is starting to appear on the London modern jazz scene. His name is Edward 'Tubby' Hayes from Raynes Park in London who was born in 1935, the young son of a violinist from the BBC Revue Orchestra. In the early 1950s he's just gigging as a freelancer getting work where he can in other people's groups. I asked Eddie when he first met him. 'Oh yeah, I played with Tubby. I first heard Tubby when he was 14. A terrible little hooligan [laughs a lot], and his mates, a gang. I played with him when he was that age. It must've been early, I remember playing in a pub in Acton. I worked in a quintet with him and it was the last band he had before he went with The Jazz Couriers.' A group we'll get to in time but won't miss out I promise.

When we look at Tubby Hayes we encounter someone who becomes arguably the greatest tenor sax player of his day in the UK, if not of all.

I'll leave you to make your own minds up there or just to check him out. In the early 1950s he was still a relatively thin young man, unlike five or six years later, with a cheeky smile on his face, rounded chops, smart dark hair with a small quiff on top and partial to a pint. He had the standard suited attire, for which I have a great regard, and was getting his first regular work.

When it comes to his talent Jim Godbolt explains it as well as anyone in his book. 'His playing was characterised by phenomenally fast fingering, a supercharged ferocity of attack, and extensive technical command. He also played flute and vibraphone and was a first-class arranger – a truly remarkable talent'. This has been a sentiment reflected by everyone who I've spoken to.

If you look at his personality that opinion is expressed by all I've talked to who knew him, John Critchinson gives a good example. 'Tubby would quite often come down and stay with Jack, who was still at home then, and he lived in a place called "No Notion", which is on the way between Chippenham and Melksham, Tubby loved it there in the country staying in this old thatched cottage. The thing with Tubby was that he was a natural nice guy. He never had a streak of "big time" about him, or anything like that at all, he was just one of those people.' I'm sure there are a few of us who would like to have met him, I know I would.

In the south, modern jazz is making its way west and east, Bristol, Bath, Plymouth, Southampton, Ipswich and all points in between. In the north the same's beginning to happen at a similar kind of pace. People are hearing the music on imported discs from the US of A on battered old records players, by going to the occasional local gig or getting on a train and making the long, long journey to London. Even in the big metropolises of Bradford, Leeds, Liverpool, Sheffield and Birmingham of course they have artistic areas and ballrooms. In the case of Manchester it's no exception. Like elsewhere, dance bands are regular visitors.

For Ronnie Scott and Tubby Hayes, including the lesser-known modern jazz musicians, their careers continue to move in a gradually upward direction as their scene goes from strength to strength. John Dankworth is having no shortage of success at the end of 1953. Touring all over the UK, parts of Europe, and able by now to adapt to a crisis as well. As Eddie recalled, 'There were clubs all over, we did do "one nighters" but a lot of the work in those days was for Dances', with The Seven we played in Ireland. Although that was another story that was really funny 'cos, we had all these slick routines. Stand up, sit down, wave your instrument about, all that kind of stuff. We went to Ireland to start all this. We had a snappy first number, *I hear music* right up here [snaps fingers in a fast tempo, sings the intro], 'Da dada da da da daaa', played it and nobody got on the floor, nobody at all. So we thought, and then John says, "hold on a minute they won't dance to that, they want to dance. So let's try something else. Let's try a slow one." So we played a slow one and nobody got on the floor. And there was a little cloakroom next to the bandstand and this voice from it said, [affects Irish accent] "you'll never get on the floor with that"'. That's unexpected.

'Where did it go from there,' I said? 'So we said (to him) "well what do you reckon?"'. 'What did he make of that?' '"Well give 'em an old fashioned waltz."' 'That was his reply, how did you respond?' I queried. 'So we played an old fashioned waltz, everybody got on the floor, and then we rumbled it. They all danced, then we said "we got 'em on the floor, let's play a foxtrot." Everybody went off the floor, and then we twigged what it was, they wanted Irish music. The trumpet player in the band Jimmy Deuchar, was brought up on Celtic music, his father was a bandleader up in Scotland and played reels, and strathspeys and stuff like that. So all night Jim played these "Dum dela dum dum dum da dum daa dum, dela da da da da ba dum da dum" [Eddie starts laughing]. Y'know, and we all joined in and all that. Everybody got on the floor [both laughing a lot] and had a wonderful time. It was a really successful gig [laughing still]. And at the end we had a wonderful arrangement that John had done of the Irish national anthem, and everyone was knocked out and thought it was a wonderful band. We never played a note of jazz all night! [We both laugh out loud].' It's amazing what you can do when the chips are down, your life may not depend on it but there's no doubt you can make it count. Mr Deuchar has certainly dug them out of a hole here when it matters.

Modern jazz is making solid, steady progress but as it becomes more popular, like music scenes now, more possibilities and avenues with what's being created, and the business side of the work, become available. For Mr Dankworth events start to take that turn around this time, given the success of the Seven. Like being at the forefront of the British pop scene of the 1960s or the acid jazz movement of the late 1980s, it can fall in your lap when you least expect it but again, the consequences on your compatriots can be far more than they needed or expected. Eddie explained some of the more convoluted background to this surprise tale. 'In October 1953 Harold Davison, a big time agent, backed John to form a big band, 'cos we were doing broadcasts and stuff like that, and our name was getting about by then. And so we did broadcasts and John got this band together in which he offered us places, some guys took it up, some left. We were quite shocked 'cos our band was very successful but John had had this offer so y'know, that was it. [Starts to hurry] Some of the guys stayed, that first band was a very good band but it was VERY good, and in actual fact I didn't like it, it was too commercial for me. It went over the top. It was very clever, it demonstrated all of John's fantastic techniques as a writer, and I don't remember if I wrote something for that band. I wrote for the second band 'cos I left about 55 and began freelancing. I actually went to freelancing in jazz clubs in the West End by then.' That's how it worked for Eddie, but of course it wasn't just Eddie it affected.

As this is a steadily growing scene there's an opportunity for musicians in these bands to freelance. Four or five years before they had to stick it out together as they were as working as a minority, with a gradually increasing number of clubs they can stay in particular groups, branch out with other people or start their own outfit. Players like Eddie, particularly if they're well educated at a good musical establishment can find themselves very busy at this time.

For Don Rendell it had major consequences as well. From his side of the fence this is how the perspective looked, 'Then after The Seven John had a big band but I didn't want anything to do with a big band. I liked the small group feeling, the improvisation, all I've ever been is a jazz musician. Anyway, the Dankworth Seven kind of finished for me in 53. Then I started playing with The Fugitives, it could have been Eddie Taylor, Eddie Harvey and me. But then I found I was getting booked under my own name. And I swore I'd never be a band leader because band leaders were never spoken of kindly, and I remember telling people, "I'll never be a band leader." But I found it was because I kept getting booked as The Don Rendell Quartet or whatever. In those early groups I had Ronnie Ross [baritone then tenor sax] and Damian Robinson [piano]. With my old group we got a gig at the Jazz Centre, with Joanne Brooks singing.'

So then Don showed me some pictures of his time in the business, then held one in particular up to me and remarked, 'Dickie Hawdon on trumpet, Damian Robinson and Pete Elderfield on bass, and little Benny Goodman on drums in 1955.' 'When this photo was taken?' I asked. 'Yes that's right.' I was curious about the club in the picture. 'Well it says Greek St on the back, in which case it's the Jazz Centre Society. Because I had a regular gig there.' So Don then found himself another major step down the road of musicianship, but now as a leader and a name without having even tried. This happens to many in this trade, though I'm afraid to say not all are suited to it. As for this gent he was just the man from those I've spoken to.

Going on the tenor player threw me another line I didn't expect. 'Chris Barber played 1 gig with my band. It was in the Jazz Centre in Greek St., Harold Pendleton ran it, in 1954. And Chris (Barber) played one gig with us playing the bass. Give him my best wishes. The bass player I had was Ashley Kozak, and the drummer was Freddy Manton. Well I'm pretty sure Chris must've played because Ashley couldn't make it. Chris played the bass which was kind of amazing to me. Yeah! Give Chris my best wishes. Cor, boy! Some history isn't it?' Then he smiled. The memories and experiences these musicians share take you back a bit.

In 1954 the kind of break occurred that many of us in music can only dream of, especially in the UK. A piece of good fortune drifted

What Time Are We On?

in from the US of A. Picking up our chat and the significance of 1955 with the photo. 'Well it was 1954 that Billie Holiday came here and we rehearsed at the Jazz Centre Society on Greek St.' I put it to him that it must've been quite something to have played with Billie Holliday? 'Oh amazing! Yeah! Amazing. Ha, her pianist was called Carl Drinkard, and we called him Carl Drunkard 'cos he was totally out of it [laughs]. And the music Billie gave us to play, I had to correct it. I had to correct it because I had bars where it [the number of beats in the bar] didn't add up [we both laugh]. Tony Kinsey's group was also booked, so it was Tony Kinsey's group, and my group, backed her at a concert in Manchester. Because it was Tony's group, he had Tommy Whittle [tenor sax/clarinet]. I think I did some and Tony did some, that's what it was.' If in music we want some good fortune that's the kind of thing we've got in mind.

But what about the musician moving in and out of the venue while the show's on? That is definitely an acquired art. When working in Jack Parnell's Big Band in 1951, with some other young Modernists including drummer Phil Seaman, Ronnie Scott in his memoir had a tale to tell in that, 'It was a fine band, but after you've played exactly the same music twice-nightly, six times a week, for a couple of months, it becomes increasingly difficult to sustain interest in musical proceedings. Musicians in those circumstances are constantly seeking distractions and, in that band, most of the distractions were provided by trumpeter Jimmy Watson. There was a pub opposite the stage door and Jimmy had worked out the places in the score where he had sufficient bars' rest [time where he wasn't playing] to enable him to slip off the stand, hurry to the pub, down a pint and get back on to the stand for his next cue. Whenever he was missing, the saxophone section used to take bets on whether or not he'd miss his cue – but in the six months or so the [current] show ran, he never failed to get back in time.' That's an achievement that many musicians aspire to, but of course the author is a man of high professional standards and would never dream of sinking to such low behaviour.

Things don't stay steady for too long with the tenor player, or the rest of Parnell's band. 'We were all sitting in the Harmony Inn in Archer St one day in January 1953 when we conceived the idea of forming a nine-piece co-operative band – and it turned out to be one of the better ideas we had that year. Derek Humble, Benny Green, Pete King and myself were on saxophones, Jimmy Deuchar on trumpet, Ken Wray on trombone, Norman Stanfeld on piano, Lennie Bush on bass and Tony Crombie on drums. And we had a singer called Johnny Grant. We were managed by Harold Davison, and our public debut was in Manchester in February 1953.' You can't beat a fresh start. Like John Dankworth's they've gone for blue, band uniforms and group music stands, and even check waistcoats. In his memoir he recalls, 'The band had a few personnel changes during its life. Victor Feldman replaced Norman Stanfeld and we'd feature Victor in a drum duet with Tony Crombie and that always brought the house down. Then Tony left and was succeeded by Phil Seaman, and Henry Shaw took over on trumpet from Jimmy Deuchar.' People moving in and out of bands is all part of the musician's progress and the appeal of the 'group'. New faces bring bright ideas.

Also part of a musician's progress is getting more gigs. So part of the journey is playing on the club circuit, whichever city we're in. Two important venues, amongst a growing number, that have opened in the early 1950s are clubs, both called The Flamingo Club. Tony Kinsey knew both of them, 'I played at both of them. The first one I played at which was Jeff Kruger's first Flamingo Club, was in Coventry St, I don't if it's still there, what used to be the big AA building on the left? As you go down Wardour St, across Coventry St, there's the Mapleton Hotel on the right. Well it was beneath there.' You don't forget your first gig.

The other Flamingo Club was run by Rik Gunnell, a man of character by many accounts and I'll leave it there, I know no more. What complicates matters though is the question of, 'where was the other club?' This isn't as straightforward as it should be. 'If you turn left there off Coventry St, and the hotel was on your right when you cross over and, just about 20 yards along there was an alleyway, and you used to go down to there.' 'So you used to go to the club from the alleyway?' I asked. 'Yes.' The venue had done very well attracting the American servicemen who're stationed around London at this time.

'So then that second venue moved further up the road into Soho, by relocating to 33/37, Wardour St?' I ask. 'Yes. We were there for quite a while, in fact that's where Billie Holliday came in and we accompanied her, and went on a tour with her. It would have been 1954.' 'Did she play at the Mapleton?' 'She just came and sang, and then she asked us to play for her.' 'It must've been a great opportunity?' I put it to him. 'Oh yeah. We did a short tour. Mind you, I worked with all those great singers Lena Horne, Ella Fitzgerald, Sarah Vaughan, Annie Ross and ah ... I worked with the top four [we both laugh].'

I put it to him that as a musician, it must have been a fantastic experience? 'Well it was.' Playing with those singers, that was a superb opportunity, the kind many musicians dream of.

Matt Haskins

Originally from Manchester, one of the characters from London I've met has been Wally Houser. A very helpful man of medium height and build, with a very quickfire delivery in his talk and when we met was still fond of a cigarette. He explains his start in life. 'My mother was a pianist, she worked in the cinema from the age of 14. My uncle, her brother, was a bandleader on the Mecca Ballroom circuit among other things, and it was inevitable I'd take up music. I tried the piano, which I can play a little bit still, I moved to the clarinet when I was 12 and then to the saxophone I suppose. And my first paid gig was on "Coronation Night", 1953. I've heard the odd musician's accounts of that night, it being busy if you were based in the capital. You can probably imagine that I'm curious about the provinces, Wally? 'If you owned an instrument you worked that night, [laughs] and I think I got £3 for working from 7.30 'til 3 the following morning. Awful late time like that. I played at a place called the Country Club on Pallatine Road, however I was more interested in playing for jazz than for dancing. Anyway, I learnt my jazz from an inspirational guy, happened to be a chartered accountant, a guy called Eric Ferguson who was the most wonderful bebop piano player this country's ever produced I think. Unfortunately, he was in his early 40s when he died. I went to a jazz club in the summer of 1953 called The Pedega, and that's where I first heard him. Run by a promoter called Paddy McKean who was quite well known in jazz circles in Manchester, particularly for traditional jazz, but put on modern jazz too.' It's fair to say that he had some good fortune in meeting the right person at the right time, which in musical terms is as significant as in any other profession.

Sometimes people's good fortune can arrive in bigger quantities than they might've expected. But I'm nct going to knock it. When it arrives you just have to do your best to make the most of it, even if you don't know what road it's going to lead you down. Wally's answer to this at the time? He sticks with it, 'I got better then ended up playing at the Club 43, on Oxford Rd [Manchester] which was run by a well-known promoter called Eric Scriven. He was the modern jazz promoter, thoroughly hated by all the musicians because he WAS, the promoter. But he was a good guy because he stuck with the jazz and he didn't always make money by any means. So I used to play there with Eric and another pianist called Joe Palin, who's since died. Another wonderful pianist. He and I were very close friends as well. He obviously settled into a musician's lifestyle very easily and it suited him well.' An honest tale.

He continued, 'I met Ronnie Scott through my uncle. He ran a Mecca Ballroom at the High St Baths, which during the winter became a ballroom. And for some curious reason I've never been able to understand he booked Ronnie Scott's eight-piece band there, for a season. I'd heard about Ronnie Scott but never actually "heard him". I was still at school then, and I went along to listen and was absolutely knocked out.' To the point.

From there the occasion swiftly moved on. 'My uncle introduced me to Ronnie. Learning that I played the saxophone he spoke to me like I knew something about it and said [in a deep London accent], "we're gonna have a curry, come and have a curry?" I'd never had a curry, I'd never met all these musicians, and I went and sat with them and it was like being in heaven! I met Jimmy Deuchar, Ken Wray (who was a Manchester trombone player but was with Ronnie's band), Benny

Green, Pete King, Tony Crombie, Norman Stenfalt was the pianist, Derek Humble was the alto player and the double bass player was Lennie Bush. This was 53, it might have been 54. But it was no later and no earlier [we'll return to the formation of Ronnie Scott's band a little later].' For a young man like Wally with such a desire to play and become involved in this new music, it must be like having all his birthdays come at once. Not just an evening out to see some great music that blows you away, but the rest of the night out with the band and have dinner as well! I know I'm not the only one, from a variety of circles who'd be knocked out by the prospect of this. Jazz musicians, and probably most others, are very partial to a trip to a spice house.

But once a friendship is struck it can remain there for a long time. Maybe it does suit Ronnie to be in with Wally's uncle, but again being a musician, like a lot of professions is about connections, and you do the gigs because you love what you do but to quote John Lydon [Sex Pistols/Public Image Limited vocalist], 'let's face it, we do need the money.' Ronnie's former friend recalls, 'from this time on I was friendly with all these guys, particularly Ronnie Scott and Pete King. So then I played various clubs and came to London for a six-month course to take my Law Society finals then I went back to Manchester after the course, to finish my articles – my apprenticeship – intending to return to London.' For the time being though he decides that one of the conurbations of the north is where he's staying for time being.

What we shouldn't underestimate either is how busy London's West End was in the mid-1950s. Eddie has vivid memories of those times, 'So this was prior to television of course. Television was only just starting 1955/56 so people with those funny little old sets. The pavements of the West End were thronged every night of the week, it was packed with people. We sometimes played two or three clubs, jazz clubs like, ah, and there were other places that were, ah, rooms where jazz players would play, they were really not thought of as jazz clubs more like kinda nightclubs. So there were lots of places to play, and to jam with people, an extremely exciting time.' A very vibrant scene by all accounts, and all this despite the fact it is hard for clubs to get licences to sell alcohol. A huge number are still doing their best to quietly bring in as much booze, from the off licence, as possible and hide it in a brown paper bag.

Tony in the meantime is leading an equally busy life himself. Playing small clubs and much, much bigger, and getting a real variety of work as a result. 'I sometimes have nightmares about drums down the stairs into places like that [laughs while referring to basement clubs]. It's a long way to go down in those days but when you're young you don't think about that sort of thing do you? You wanna get your drums and start playing [laughs].' There are still venues now that meet those requirements, and I've definitely slipped on my fair share of wrought iron staircases.

Some of those clubs are still there, they've either just changed their names or their purpose. Clubs have become wine bars, restaurants or clothes shops. Continuing on the topic of Rik Gunnell's nightspot he reflects, 'anyway The Flamingo Club, well when we moved up to Wardour St, and the entrance was opposite Gerrard St, and again it was right down in the basement, and it was murder to park and get your drums in there on a Saturday evening, 'cos they didn't have any kind of "Assisted" scheme in those days. Or power steering. I have nightmares about getting fined in the West End. That was a much bigger place than the 51. So this was the quartet with Joe Harriott [alto sax] and Bill Le Sage.' 'When did this start?' I asked him. 'From about 52. Did you know Bill stayed with me for eight years?' Of course, with Tony having more than one string to his bow, having the confidence to make his group larger, and early on in his career is no surprise. It's very much the 'Do-it-yourself' attitude that was an integral part of punk in the late 1970s. The only difference being that the jazz musicians at this time are better trained and more adept. I don't think there's too much doubt about that. When new musical movements start there's often this kind of situation. An initial kick-start given by those who are there form the beginning.

Continuing on the subject of his own work at this time he said, 'I remember doing a club in Coconut Grove, I think I was politely asked to leave after a while for falling asleep at the piano, because we used to get into these foxtrot tempos and all drummers had to do was "Schee da. Ta schee da". We used to go to sleep [both laugh]. So I was glad to get out of there, but then I got the job at The Palladium as Lena Horne's drummer. I think it was Chico Hamilton, Joe Benjamin on double bass and Arnold Ross on piano and the drummer couldn't make it so they asked me to do it. And it was probably the first time I'd really played with any heavyweight Americans, Joe Benjamin was the bass player with [Duke] Ellington for some time. We were on stage and Lennie Hayton, who was also her husband, used to come on, and conduct in an evening dress and a yachting cap [he laughs] which was highly amusing. But she was great, Sarah was great, but Ella was fantastic. Anyway, I'm digressing.' 'No, that's OK,' I said, 'it's the kind of thing

What Time Are We On?

I was going to ask you about after the Flamingo Club, so it's fine.' The subject of nightclubs we'll return to in a little while, with the assistance of Tony Kinsey.

Something that was simmering under the surface in UK jazz throughout the 1950s and 60s was drugs. When it comes to understanding the topic and its background at the time, it's very useful to know what that was, as the law was different then, and what street narcotics were for sale are a different matter. I'm very keen to get to the nub of what the music, and the scene of this time is all about. I put it to Eddie that the modern jazz period, particularly during the 1950s is often portrayed as a very glamorous period, was it that? 'Nooo! We had smart band uniforms, but that's all there was to it.' It was the suits as much as anything else then? 'Yeah, we had the suits and all that yeah, but the actual scene itself was about making music, that's what it was about.' For the Modernists it seems crucial, all I talked to.

It was also Soho, it was crime, prostitution? 'There was a bit of crime about, blokes smoked a bit of dope, I smoked a bit of dope at the time and, and then packed it up 'cos you didn't get anything done. That was the worst thing about marijuana [he laughs]. But it wasn't like skunk or anything like that.' A stronger form you could buy in later years.

In wanting to get more tales Eddie does me a great favour in casting his mind back. A man with a great sense of humour and memory, and the fact he wanted to share it with you and I makes us very lucky. Continuing on, 'I remember a couple of Canadian guys turning up with a Morris 1000 and they'd driven all the way from North Africa, and they'd got this stuff that they'd packed inside bags, and the whole car was stuffed with dope. And they'd come through Customs with all this stuff bagged underneath the leather [laughs].' I asked how did they get the car over the Channel, on a ferry? 'They'd just been in North Africa, come over, driven up through France all the way to London to sell all this dope [both laughed like drains]. It was just Keef as it was known, it was just laughter material. It was later when Hash came in, I knew someone who became schizophrenic because of it.' It's for those reasons you can keep those kinds of happy material from me but, hey, each to their own I guess.

There are many tales amongst musicians of mistakes made, fools found and drunks tripped up and over. I've heard many of the modern examples and even witnessed the odd catastrophe. One of our trombonists more entertaining recollections goes like this. 'The famous one was Phil Seaman, he was with Joe Loss for years, famous jazz drummer. Famous character, he was fantastic. The famous one was where he fell asleep, he nodded off of as they do, in the [orchestra] pit of *West Side Story*. So there was some dialogue going on, on stage, he fell asleep, and someone woke up and for some weird reason hit this gong. So there was a hiatus while everybody turned round to see what was going on, and he stood up and said, "Dinner is served". And the whole place erupted of course.' At which point we both laughed like drains. There's rarely a racket more than instrumentalists letting go at another's misfortune, even if we've heard it more than once.

By this time John Dankworth's musical interests have expanded with his popularity and his experience. Much as he still enjoys the Seven he wants to put together an outfit that's more of a challenge, that he extends the arrangements for by putting on shows on a larger scale. It was hard work to do it, as he says though, 'but somehow, like magic, on 23 October 1953 at the Astoria Ballroom in Nottingham, my Big Band was born. We travelled abroad to Europe and to the States, where we had a gigantic success at the world's greatest jazz festival, together with acclaim from the critics. We played the world's most renowned jazz club, and shared the bill in concerts with perhaps the most famous big band of all time.' It seems a common point of view, even if not everyone is a fan of his at the time.

His honesty when reflecting on this period in his career much further down the line, is very laudable. 'And, to be brutally frank, I've decided that no special magic or even wisdom existed. It was all a result of a large slice of sheer luck coupled with a good deal of absolute bloody-mindedness. Nevertheless, one fact came leaping at me – calculation or luck, inspiration or folly, it mattered not which. I'd started something from which there was no going back.' Well said.

The long forgotten and sometimes bitter disagreement between the two trade union organisations from either side of the North Atlantic, had a huge impact on jazz. It had started in the 1930s over a Duke Ellington concert at the Elephant and Castle, and meant that Americans couldn't play in the UK and vice versa. Jim Godbolt in his tome explains, 'the ministry [of Labour's] compliance with the union's demands was justified by the practice of ministry officials accepting the recommendations of experts in industry generally, and in respect of foreign musicians and bands the Musicians' Union were seen as those experts. It was a monumentally stupid prohibition, one that was to deprive jazz lovers of their right to see and hear in the flesh musicians of a kind unique in the whole history of music. Moreover, as later events were to prove, their appearance in Britain could've provided

The John Dankworth Big Band, Tour to Europe, mid 1950s.

British musicians with work, although the union's rigid reinforcement was allegedly to safeguard its members' livelihoods.' Be sure that the American musicians were the ones that were wanted, their country didn't need jazz from anyone else.

It seems absurd in this day and age that the MU could get their members and the specific needs they have, working and playing jazz with Americans, so completely and utterly convoluted and skewed. I say this as a long-standing member myself, who will always advocate membership. I'd like to think the MU sees matters a little more clearly now.

The frustration and anger that was generated amongst musicians and jazz lovers by the ban ran very deep, and was easily generated and expressed by Eddie, who got quickly fired up when he recounted, 'the trouble was with the Musicians' Union and the American Federation of Musicians. The problem was the British just not letting the American musicians in here at all. You had Humph and the Wilcox brothers, they were jazz promoters in those early days. They did a concert with Sidney Bechet [US clarinet player] where he sat in with Humph's band. There were court cases flying about, and the Wilcox Brothers got sued and brought to court for doing it, and of course it was fighting the Musicians' Union. Basically what it was, was that the MU were Glaswegian "Communists" and the AF of M were "Hoods". They were Mafia, and never the twain shall meet of course. They'd had a row about 1934 evidently, and it lasted until the early 50s which was when that got resolved.'

In all my time as a musician and growing up in a jazz household, I'd never heard of this dispute until I interviewed for the book, but I was so delighted to find out that it finally came to an end in late 1955, when a reciprocal arrangement was organised. It was agreed that Oscar Peterson and Ella Fitzgerald would come over and tour in the February of 1956 and yes, Ella had Tony Kinsey on drums. British artists would travel on an exchange visit later that summer.

It can't be underestimated that during the first half of the 1950s, the leap that modern jazz has made in the UK is huge. When the scene started the decade it was technically lagging behind the US, but just like an over-animated adolescent it's focusing hard on the job in hand and is 'woodshedding' like mad. Though still not there yet it just can't get enough. The club scene across the country, and in London in particular, is coming to life to accommodate it. That includes Bristol, Leeds, Manchester, Birmingham, Edinburgh, Bath and even Chippenham. Apologies to the other towns and cities I've missed, I'm not going to get them all in. Jazz fans can be a bit picky about that sort of thing. The music's becoming bedded down and it can only grow from here.

What Time Are We On?

ACKNOWLEDGEMENTS:

Jazz in Revolution. John Dankworth, 1927–2010. London: Constable, 1998

– (P. 71 – P. 72), (P. 75), (P. 97 – JD Big Band, Oct. 1953), (P. 99)

Some of My Best Friends Are Blues. Ronnie Scott; with Mike Hennessey; preface by Pete King. Ronnie Scott, 1927–1996. London: Northway, 2004 (P. 40), (P. 43), (P. 44)

Who's Who of British Jazz. John Chilton. John Chilton, 1932–2016. London: Cassell, 1997. – Re; Ronnie Ball Trio/Studio 51 (P. 16), Tommy Whittle (P. 352)

A History of Jazz in Britain 1950–1970. Jim Godbolt, 1922–2013. London: Quartet, 1989 – (P. 114), (P. 250/252 FOR EXPLANATION), (P. 166)

John Lydon interview – *Rock Family Trees: Banshees and Other Creatures* (1998). BBC recording, broadcast BBC2 on 25 September 1998.

CHAPTER 6

THE CLUBS

By the end of 1955 London is accommodating its developing jazz scene. Regardless of whether you're a Traditionalist or a Modernist, musician or fan, there's a choice of places to perform or just 'hang out'. This chapter provides the best I can give, as the tale of what the club scene is like at the time. For the people at the centre of the music. It's not possible for me to make this comprehensive, you'd have to carry me off to the Funny Farm in the process given the work involved, and therefore it's the best I can do, 60 years after the event.

A large number of these clubs and late night dens were based in the smog-ridden streets of Soho. In the years immediately after the war the jazz scene in the UK was predominantly a traditional and mainstream one. In 1947/48 only the odd 78 would have made its way over the Atlantic with Charlie Parker and Dizzy Gillespie playing blistering bebop solos, or Thelonious Monk's clanking flat nine chords on the ivories like an accident in a china store (love it as I do). A great music trying to gain its first attention. There was a healthy live scene for dance bands. This is where a lot of the Modernists can be found, though some are still with the jumper and pipe fraternity as we know.

The first post-war venue to come to attention, for the traditional crowd is The Red Barn at Barnehurst as we've learnt. Within a couple of years the same people are taking the music they're starting to love into town. The Leicester Square Jazz Club is a traditional home that's playing host to Humphrey Lyttelton's band at the time. It's taking place at the Café De L'Europe in Leicester Square, and it's firmly married to the idea of dancing to jazz. The other club that is quickly coming to prominence is the Feldman Swing Club, situated in the basement of 100, Oxford St (as it still is today). Not least for the same reasons. Its popularity was quick and steady, and is obvious as Harold Pendleton explains. 'It suited dancing, people wanted to dance so your always clearing somewhere for them to jive. Not everyone wanted to dance, not everyone could. Most people have two left feet. Effectively, a really good jazz band makes you want to jump about, more than just tap your feet. So the 100 Club became famous for its dancefloor and its dancing and the dancers. I always remember some of the dancers went on to become quite famous, one of whom was called "Pointed Charlie", because he danced "pointed".' Harold wasn't able to explain any further what he meant by 'pointed.' But when it comes to noise, you're better off underground.

By the time we get to the last legs of the decade Humphrey Lyttelton is running his own, self-titled jazz club at the premises. In future that would run to more than one evening. It was managed by Roger Horton, owned by Joseph Feldman. The musicians' pub to the rear is The Blue Posts, as it is today, I highlight that from personal experience more than once. The area just north of this end of Oxford St, and south towards

Charing Cross Rd is the stamping ground for this genre's followers. At this time the venue is very much the home for Traditionalists, though there are many others starting up in Central London, providing a home. The Nuthouse on Regent St is very much in business, as is the Cy Laurie Club on Great Windmill St. By the end of the 1940s the numbers are 20–30.

Humphrey Lyttelton has strong recollections of his post-war years at The Nuthouse. 'The Nuthouse was a tough little club in which fights were common. These fights usually spread quickly, because the GI population could never let even the smallest outbreak go without joining in, whether they knew what the issue was or not. Consequently, small arguments in distant corners of the room were apt to develop quickly into wholesale rough houses.' Hearing him reflect on a quiet night out fills you full of confidence for the future trans-Atlantic foreign relations. It's also thought this venue was a good example of what nightclubs had been like before the outbreak of hostilities in 1939, in terms of live music and its audience. It included a separate civilian nightlife of dubious employment on top of the musicians and others. Tony Kinsey referred to this as a lively place.

Of course, Chris Barber has vivid memories of this time too. 'I remember the scene when my amateur band started up, at that time the 100 Club was called the Feldman Swing Club. When I went there Joe Daniels' Band was playing, in Drumnastics as it was called. He had Alan Wickham on trumpet who was very good. This was 1947. There's always been clubs. Interestingly, it's never really been mentioned much at all.' You literally have to do a bit of dig Carnaby St. It's significant because you had musicians from the emerging modern jazz, traditional and dance band scenes in it. This made it very rare indeed. It was frequented by the likes of Ronnie Scott, John Dankworth, Eddie Harvey, Don Rendell and Tony Kinsey. They're also frequenting another dingy basement called the Fullado Club, which is more of a home for the young blades listening to the new 78s from the States mentioned before. Tony Crombie, Tommy Pollard and Denis Rose are regulars here too. Situated at 6, New Compton St (which no longer exists) it became The Metropolitan Bopera House in 1948. Then later Metrobopera.

For the modern crowd Club 11 starts up in 1948, followed in 1950 by Vi Hyland's Studio 51. This gives the musicians, and fans, the sounding board they've been looking for. Places the music can be exercised, refined and all being well, 'enjoyed by those involved?' For Ronnie, John, Eddie and the others on each side of the stage, ideal. But as we know Club 11 only makes it to the spring of 1950. Vi always put on traditional acts as well though.

Ronnie Scott's and John Dankworth's motivations for clubs, bands and managing are plain to see. I've always enjoyed the organisational side of the business as well. The other question in the middle of this musical mayhem is, what an earth's motivating an intelligent woman to get into setting up a nightclub? Ronnie had many doubts about 'getting involved' in the venue side of the business over the years. Humph didn't stick with it indefinitely. So I put the question here to all my interviewees. They all had nothing but complimentary things to say about Vi Hyland. Tony Kinsey provides the most illuminating responses of all. I put it to him, how important was the time he gained at her club? 'Y'know, we did our three nights a week and the all-nighter (with the Trio and Tommy Whittle) and it was a fantastic experience really because, there was some great jazz played down there, unfortunately none of it was recorded.' Next I asked, did he think Vi was more of a businesswoman than a jazz fan, or did he think she was both? 'I don't think she was a jazz fan. I don't know why she opened The 51 Club, as a jazz club I don't know what was the motivation behind it or the reason behind it. But I can't ever remember her coming and listening to it too much, she was always occupied "round the back", so I think. I suppose she must've been aware of the music but I wasn't aware of her, being aware of the music. But she must've liked it or she wouldn't have done it. I'm not sure whether she was a jazz fan or not.' I don't think he'd ever thought about it before.

I continued, that I only asked because the notion had crossed my mind from talking to other people, they didn't seem to be so sure either. He replied, 'Well I could put it to you what's the percentage of people running jazz clubs making money from jazz? I'm not wanting to say anything derogatory about her at all, that's the last thing in the world, if it's a business opportunity then fine. Suits both of us.' 'That's the way the business works though isn't it?' I responded. 'Yeah that's right, if you don't draw the people in it's not going to happen.' A basic fact in the entertainment industry, never mind the world of the basement Soho nightclub.

Vi Hyland certainly seems to be a one-off at this time, I've not come across any other woman in the 1950s in a comparable role. Mmmm … maybe one wife at a club a few streets up. She is very ably assisted by her friend Pat who works on the door. She and/or Vi would be behind a hatch on the left at the bottom of the stairwell, with an Alsatian dog for company. 10–11, Great Newport Street, towards the south end of

What Time Are We On?

Charing Cross Road, W1. Our hostess kept a mix of both styles of jazz going for a while. But traditional jazz became increasingly the dominant form at the club, with Ken Colyer the main drive behind this. By the mid-to-late 1950s the traditional nights went under Ken's name. His band plus a support act/acts, at least three nights a week. Modern jazz became obsolete at the club as a consequence, the crowds still came and at times packed it out.

I've heard through interviews Vi kept the club going, putting on various different shows and events, until the early 80s. Not bad at all, and to be admired. She also started nine years before a certain other jazz nightspot, but we'll get there soon.

Again, we mustn't forget that clubs at this time don't have drink licences so alcohol is just smuggled in. But they're so popular by now, as is booze under the jacket. A venue that is several rungs up the ladder from most I've mentioned so far is the Flamingo Club. It's story is very much altered by conjecture and gossip but, through the likes of Tony Kinsey I've straightened out these issues now. 'The first Flamingo Club was beneath the Mapleton Restaurant.' This is well worth establishing as there was more than one in our tale. 'You know where the Swiss Centre is in Leicester Square? You've got that on your right, well going down that's Coventry St, take the first right there and the next road on the right is Panton St, on that first right was The Hotel Mapleton [next to the Prince of Wales Theatre] and The Flamingo started and opened out beneath there.' This venue was below the Mapleton Restaurant, and was owned and run by Jeff Kruger and his father Sam. Wally Houser had connections with both of them. I asked him what could he tell me about the Krugers and Rik Gunnell. 'Well Sam Kruger was a promoter, I think he was a Jewish chap, which I am myself, he was in some kind of business and fancied being in the nightclub business, so he promoted the first Flamingo. I first went there in 55, probably late 54. Sam had a son called Jeff, who I think is still going strong. He was quite a nice guy.' Around the corner was the entrance to Rik Gunnell's Flamingo Club which occupied the basement of the same building.

Jeff Kruger's venue is first created as 'Jazz at the Mapleton' in August 1952. By all accounts it's a smart place to play, and soon runs three nights a week according to Jim Godbolt, and gains it title. Rik Gunnell was a once a Smithfield Meat Market Porter, and is thought to have had some more shadier dealings than his upstairs professional neighbour. But I couldn't possibly comment and will leave that one to others. Prior to the opening of these subterranean premises, he's already opened The Star Club. Tony recalls, 'I remember playing at the Star Club on Wardour St, doing two sessions with some members of the Count Basie Band. It was a drinking club with a bit of jazz.' No mean achievement. One common feature, reported by most of our contributors, about this night-time entrepreneur is that he is more into the kudos and character of jazz than the music. That can contribute to success as we soon see with Vi Hyland, and over the next few years Mr Gunnell opens other establishments, with mixed success.

Of course, as we covered earlier Harold Pendleton has opened two clubs of his own at this point, the Gallion Club and Club Creole. Both more traditional affairs than either of the Flamingos, though he's in the world of club and music promotion for the long-term. Another popular establishment in Soho amongst the American servicemen that are based in and around London, is the Sunset Club. It was quite rough and ready and easier with alcohol, as well as drugs. How much is legit, particularly the latter would be open to question. From after the War, London had thousands of American servicemen based in and around the city as a consequence. Clubs, bars and theatre's catered for the many GIs in town. The entertainment industry was happy to see them, make no mistake.

By the early to mid-fifties traditional jazz in both its forms, revivalist and purist, moved further out into the suburbs of London and beyond. More clubs and jazz nights opened up in the peripheral areas of town.

Well by this time The Flamingo is doing superb business. Tony Kinsey gives a good insight into the kind of premises Mr Kruger is running. 'Well it wasn't a licensed premises at all, and it was just like all those places just soft drinks, and it was all so innocent and lovely y'know. You didn't get any punch-ups, I don't recall ever seeing any punch ups, or anything like that that they get these days. Principally because of the booze. They used to come and listen, and dance, and whatever I was involved in, I never made any concessions to dancing. They danced to the music, you didn't play the music for dancing. No one ever said anything or criticised us, they all enjoyed it and we always had the front row, the first few rows with seats in front of the bandstand. Generally, more often than not it was the same people there every Saturday anyway. The faces, you'd recognise the faces. They all liked it on a Saturday as well, and it was great music played.' In 1957 Jeff Kruger moves to the dark, street environs of 33/37, Wardour St, Soho. He also adopts The Flamingo as its formal title. In 1959 Rik Gunnell, after running his own establishments for a while, becomes the Club Manager, and connections become ever deeper.

For myself I had a 21st-century question for Tony that these days is very relevant if your making your way to a music club, London, Bristol or Leeds. 'Did they do food there at all?' I asked out of curiosity. 'No,' he firmly replied and understandably so. I was doing anything to find another angle.

Moving on, I was keen to know if the venue was just a more upmarket establishment than Studio 51? 'Yes it was, because it was a better place, a bigger place and, I suppose in a sense when The Flamingo first started below The Mapleton, it was slightly more upmarket, but not as big as the place we had in Wardour St. It was a more sophisticated in environment but The Flamingo was a big room.' I think that's a good response to my curiosity. This is where the club now stands in 1957.

A forgotten establishment in this area of London is The Studio Club. It was created after the First World War as a retreat for those from an artistic background. Augustus John was involved in its inception. But I'm reliably informed it became a home for those of any music business profession, from musician to record company executive. The Dankworth drummer tells me, 'there was The Studio Club, in Swallow St. Alan Clare [pianist] used to work there all the time [House piano player 1950/56]. We used to go down and blow sometimes. I don't know if it's still there, the one on Swallow St?' I think it's fair to say given its clientele and its near dead end location, the gloomy backwater off the north side of Piccadilly, but near the Circus suits it well. On a cold night the mist would've rolled up the main road off St James's and Green Parks, a treat.

The modern jazz clubs are growing in number but remain fewer than the traditional. A notable addition to this expanding scene is Zan Zeba. It was situated at 39, Gerrard St and had a house band led by trumpeter Dizzy Reece, who was West Indian by birth. They'd often play the arrangements of the big band led by Dizzy Gillespie in America. It was often a constantly changing line-up so it is definitely a gig for the top sight-readers. Sadly, the venue had a limited lifespan.

A magnificent addition to London's nightlife for some time to come is The Marquee Club, which opened in April 1958 by the National Jazz Federation. The man behind the business side of the operation? Harold Pendleton, who we've already met. It started out as a jazz club but at the same time was putting on early British blues and skiffle acts including the likes of Alexis Korner. He was beginning to get a larger interest in the music of America's 'Deep South,' and what you can do with it. The club keeps going through the 1960s and a long a way beyond, as many of us know. We've also seen his Jazz Centre Society on Greek Street in 1954. Harold divulges much more later in the book.

The following year Ronnie Scott decides to get back into the same side of the business himself, this time with friend Pete King. The first premises are in the basement of 39, Gerrard St. On 30 October 1959 Ronnie Scott's Club opens, with the Tubby Hayes Quartet and the Eddie Thompson Trio. To give you an idea of the prices clubs charged in the 1950s, membership was 10 shillings, admission (members) 1 shilling and 6 pence, 2 shillings and 6 pence for non-members. I'm sure most of you know that a shilling is 5 pence, but for a club night now in a cheaper London suburb, you're looking at £8 to £25 at the very least for the same. Given the advent of decimalisation, making comparisons are a tough ask in this day and age, but prices and times change.

Ronnie is very revealing about the form and finances of the club in his book. 'Business was generally good from the start. That first weekend we had sessions on Friday, Saturday and Sunday evening. Later we started so-called "all-nighters" on Fridays and Saturdays until 3 am. But although we got good crowds, both Pete and I soon recognised that we'd have to wait a while before retiring to palatial residences in the Bahamas.' It's fair to say an ongoing issue "Ronnie's", and all clubs whose owners had musician friends, struggled with was admitting your friends in for free, or on the cheap. If in the long run you find it difficult to make a profit, and you're in his and Pete's position then squaring that circle becomes an ever-present dilemma. The last London jazz venue to do it, where they also have a guest list, put together by the venue and the artist to a limited number, is the 606 Club on Lots Road. I do like that, show my Musicians' Union membership card and straight in, gratis. Sadly, not anymore.

The last club to mention is Klooks Kleek which opened in January 1961. It was located up in north-west London, an area called West Hampstead, and was served reasonably well by a bus from the centre of town. The evening was held at the Railway Hotel by Dick Jordan. Modern jazz is the order of things musical but, it's also a club where the punters are here to dance. As a consequence, the swing only had a limited life here, being superseded by rhythm 'n' blues by the end of 63.

By 1965 the number of jazz clubs is in decline, but since the end of the War there's been an explosion in the country's live music scene, in a way no one could have predicted. Both traditional and modern have been at the front of it, the musicians involved have been predominantly British. The other significant thing about the scene, even ten years before, is that everyone involved is resolving to use the punk 'do-it-yourself' attitude as the only way forward. This is helping to establish 'British', jazz.

What Time Are We On?

ACKNOWLEDGEMENTS:

themarqueeclub.net

A History of Jazz in Britain 1950–1970. Jim Godbolt, 1922–2013. London: Quartet, 1989 (P. 87), (P. 250), (P. 249), (P. 252)

I Play as I Please: The memoirs of an Old Etonian trumpeter. With drawings by the author. [With plates, including portraits.] Humphrey Lyttelton, 1921–2008. London: MacGibbon & Kee, 1954 – Lyttelton, Humphrey; (P. 105)

Some of My Best Friends Are Blues. Ronnie Scott; with Mike Hennessey; preface by Pete King. Ronnie Scott, 1927–1996. London: Northway, 2004 (P. 52), (P. 54)

Who's Who of British Jazz/John Chilton. John Chilton, 1932–2016. London: Cassell, 1997 (P. 65)

CHAPTER 7

The modern jazz scene is a much more confident soul as it strolls into the second half of the 1950s. Its counterpart in the States is well established, and has little to be concerned about when faced with the giants of the traditional and mainstream genres. The biggest shock to the American modern circuit is the death of alto saxophonist Charlie Parker, in March 1955 at the age of 34, from the drawn out misery of heroin addiction. The drug continues to be relatively easy to obtain legally, in both the UK and the US, for the rest of the decade, and for most of the following. The problem itself in jazz doesn't go away either. Several great virtuoso talents pass away over the same period, or have their lives blighted by it. A sad backdrop to the time we're talking about. But the good times are what always stand out and never get forgotten.

For the British musicians we're talking about, most are becoming so immersed in their talents, and the performance of them, it's no surprise they don't seize up and asphyxiate, then keel over and collapse on the deck. For Eddie Harvey and the hundreds of musicians embroiled in the life, and the live, they don't need to think twice. 'So ah, so that period of the middle 50s was "roaring" y'know. And I, well what happened in those days was that you could have a jazz band, we could have various combinations of bands with people like Ronnie Ross [baritone sax/ saxes/ flute/ clarinet], Don Rendell and all that, and Tony Kinsey. And we're all in each other's bands, and we ran little jazz clubs, and the band might last for a certain amount of time, and you either got fed up or it got stale and you, you could go into Palais which were big dance halls. But big bands like Oscar Rabin's band, they went into, The Lyceum in the Strand, and I went there for a couple of years and we used to do a broadcast a week sometimes and I had to write an arrangement.' That's far more busy than any homegrown jazz musician could possibly conceive here in the 21st century. I've had times where I could make a reasonable, regular wage but never so much that a job on the side, teaching or otherwise, wouldn't keep me out of deep waters. The trouble now is too many musicians and not enough work.' That's a fact.

Also, doing well musically and financially is a very industrious Don Rendell. By 1955/56 he has some mutually beneficial connections. Not least with some very business-like Soho gentlemen, but it doesn't always see you right. He sets the scene. 'Yeah I'll tell you what it was. I was working at the Flamingo Club with the Krugers, Jeff and Sam Kruger the Dad, and Mrs Kruger. There was a conversation I had recently with Don Lawson [resident drummer at Studio 51 and with Don from 1954], where I was telling him about Sam Kruger, and Sam would say things like this [affects a deep East End 'workmanlike' accent]. "Now Don I've helped you in the past, now it's your turn to help me". And Don Lawson said, "well what you should have said is 'don't help me no more Sam, I can't afford it' [laughs]."' There were clear thoughts being expressed.

'Why's that?' I asked. ''Cos that's how they were, it was just money, that's all they were interested in. And he [Sam] used to say to me, "you look after the music Don and we'll look after the coaches." The coach that was booked for me to do gigs under the management of the Krugers. Because he was acting like a manager and producing work. It was work I didn't want. I found it so commercial the work he was finding, so the time came when the coach company rang me up, and demanded money [smiles], and said it would be about a hundred quid.' 'Flipping heck,' I remarked.

Don carried on. 'So this idea of "don't look after the coaches" was just words. We had to pay for the coach. So to actually pay, what I did was join Ted Heath. But a couple of weeks with Ted Heath and I them paid off. I think the first week with Heath I earned 88 quid, and that was a lot of money in those days. Because we were involved in a film, that was *It's a Wonderful World* (1956), it certainly had big people in it. Sam Kruger may have been slap bang in the middle of London's entertainment scene, but his small print may have been of a slightly dubious nature in this instance, according to Don. It must be said that he was a pretty straight bloke, and I don't know anyone who would contradict that summary of him. Probably why he looked to start carving his own furrow.

At this time traditional jazz is more popular than its counterpart. In terms of attending gigs and record sales, especially amongst the young in their mid-teens through to those in their 20s. If you factor in skiffle, which is so simple to play then the two are huge in the UK. Its marketability is so straightforward because it's high energy and danceable, the way that techno and, drum and bass are now. But with the same appeal at the time, traditional is very similar in that respect. My father Chris, aged 15 here, started off listening to Lonnie Donegan and within three years was listening to Barber and Colyer. A vast number of youth are travelling down this route, but of course an American genre is arriving and is going to be more than just a distraction.

Having heard from the likes of Eddie and Don on their reminiscences of this time, what was Chris Barber doing? 'In 1956, we [Chris Barber's New Orleans Jazz Band] were doing concerts. Before that we did clubs. When the band became mine in May 54 we had six "Residents" club jobs a week, [where the band play a regular night of the week at a venue]. So we played 312 nights a year. Plus we filled in the odd night elsewhere, but we got to play concerts. Of course the concert halls here had different rules on a Sunday, and performers couldn't appear in costume. The Observance Acts.' That's foot to floor!

Thinking of my age group and younger I asked, 'what kind of concerts are we talking about, large clubs?' 'No, no, no. I'm talking about appearing at the South Parade Pier at Southsea, the Pier at Southend, it's the theatre's where people go to see shows on holiday. And local theatres too. There was a crowd of people staying in Hastings for their holidays and nowhere to go on a Sunday. So they had to put a concert on. Harry Gold's Band were stopped because they had tartan dinner jackets, so they were held to be costumed.' Strange, I thought. 'Oh, that's nonsense,' I remarked. 'It may well be nonsense but if that's the law.' 'Well yeah, makes sense,' I said. 'It's like saying I'm not speaking but my car's going a 100 miles an hour, and I'm only going 80 but the speed limit's 50,' replied Chris.

Continuing with his reflections on 1956, 'so at that time you'd have two bands on, one of which will be a dance band. Because that's what music was in those days. But suddenly you do a few of these having played dark sweaty clubs, haven't got room to play, condensation on the ceiling. And you start to think [he effects the thoughts of someone talking to themselves], "hang on a minute they're listening and they're applauding, not talking through the quiet numbers, y'know." And it's not too hot and too difficult to play, and there's even facilities, and you actually get paid a bit more as well. It's one of those things, it's a no-brainer when you get down to it. Some bands didn't like concerts, they'd get all nervous. The Alex Welsh Band did, and get chairs and sit down in the middle of the stage. We could do it 'cos we could drop from a six-piece band to four.' For jazz musicians this is a significant step forward. Not only in terms of size of venue and the better conditions of employment, but also in regard to their attitude and perspective, towards what they think is a justified reward for the performance they've given. Traditional jazz and modern jazz in the UK has grown out of the smoky, cramped basement clubs of the late 1940s, early 50s. For a section of them to now change tack and say, "yeah, I'm willing to play for Joe Public and family as well, for better terms", alters their expectations dramatically, and widens the audience for the band and music.

When it comes to it then, could you imagine Chris' band performing anywhere else? I asked him 'was he doing much TV at this point?' 'No, the only TV we did was *Six-Five Special* (started 1957). That's not doing TV, that's just wasting time [laughs], but fairly appalling. We always thought we'd do a bit but, we didn't. Mainly it's because of the BBC, ITV hadn't started then.' He's not wrong on both counts. To have a sense of humour in times like these must assist in bucket loads.

What Time Are We On?

For Don, 'domestic relations' are now colouring the professional aspect of his life, which certainly doesn't help later down the road when making the effort to reflect on it all. Of course our old friend money insists on getting in the way. 'I didn't stay with (Ted) Heath. My wife realised I was a jazz musician. There was no jazz with Heath, it was very much a "read everything" kind of band [sheet music, little improvisation, monotonous for a lot of jazz players]. I think I had to do some gigs with Tony Crombie's band before Heath, and it had Annie Ross [singer] in it. She was kind of Crombie's girlfriend. What sort of year would that be? It was definitely 55. It has to be around then because, when I had to break up my band because of this money situation, Tony Crombie took Damian Robinson [piano], Ronnie Ross and me. He didn't take the whole band, so that was that. I had to do it. I left Tony's band to get on the coach with Ted Heath, I was with Heath's band for just a short time.' It seems to have been a remarkably turbulent two seasons for Don. Life though is giving him the unique opportunity that a British virtuoso couldn't have bought.

'So, if you're doing plenty of work with Ted Heath, what brought you to knock it on the head? You can't just turn your nose up to it let's face it.' 'I was with him from October through to March 56. Heath said, "are you sure you want to leave, we're going to America?" It was going to be the first exchange of British and American musicians (after the MU and the AFM made friends again), but I said, "I'll leave". But you see that's the way it worked out, you can't buy it. Total coincidence. Within three or four weeks of leaving Heath I got that Stan Kenton job [internationally famous American jazz band leader]. So then I was with Stan all over Britain, and then across Europe. All the way through Denmark, Sweden, Germany, Switzerland, Holland, France, Italy. Like

I say you can't buy that, that's just the way things happened. That was 56. I was with him for about three months. April, May, June something like that, and then he went back to the States.' The significance of getting this seat is that Kenton's 19-piece band at this time, after a period of playing avant-garde, experimental jazz in a 39-piece set-up [yes 39!], is he's doing swing. But with some of the best, young, modern, Stateside players there are; Lee Konitz, Stan Levey, Zoot Sims and Jack Sheldon amongst others. The music, often incendiary, with arrangements by the likes of Gerry Mulligan and Johnny Richards.

Eddie Harvey meanwhile is immersing himself in the music too, and working on the odd chart with a completely different feel. 'I remember writing an arrangement of Elvis Presley's *Blue Suede Shoes* [released here in January 1956], for a big band. But also I had to transcribe big band records by Ray Antoneil, Stan Kenton (for example), so that was my university, y'know. I learnt a fantastic amount and we also played six nights a week and two afternoons, two matinees'. 'So it was in your face for a long time. It must have been,' I said. 'And that's where I actually cracked sight-reading.' The ability to read music and play it at the same time. For those of you who are new to musician's parlance, it's an invaluable skill. A lot of jazz players, not all I hasten to add (you can be just a musician with skills), possess this ability. My dad couldn't sight-read but was a professional double bass player all his life. It's like reading out loud but always trying to be at least one sentence ahead, so you know what's coming, that way you don't fall off the 'train' that you're on. It could be careering down the track depending on how quick the tune is. Others will just pick up the sheet and set fire to it in angst and despair, 'readers' too.

What Time Are We On?

Eddie told me after the interview, the only way of drilling in the discipline of sight-reading was to lock himself in his room and play three charts, three hours a day 'till I cracked it, until the skill became automatic.' I'm full of admiration of the man, he's not the first I've met like that.

The situation with Humph and his band is being taken with care and caution. His outfit has already been full-time for a while, and he has very current concerns to keep the psychological and physical demands to a minimum. He elaborates on this in his written work, published 1958. 'We were nominally semi-pro up till about 18 months ago, and even then the change to full time was almost imperceptible. It simply meant the day workers left, and those who replaced them were regular musicians who could afford to lie in after a late job instead of having to get up and go off to the office. Our routine hardly altered at all. I continued to limit the engagements to an average of just over three per week, with a trip out of town for two or three days every month or so. With the resident spot in the jazz club at 100, Oxford Street occupying Wednesdays and Saturdays, this means that for quite long periods at a time we lead a sedentary life in London. This suits me perfectly, because, although I have abandoned all full-time journalistic work, I still like to do a lot of writing.' At this time though his band is doing well-paid work when it does go out on the road. The TV and radio work is coming his way as a presenter.

There's no doubt Harold Pendleton has firmly established himself on the London scene, as both club owner and entrepreneur. He's still very much Chris Barber's manager, on the traditional/revival scene one of the most astute business leaders of the time, and keen to make sure

I'm fully informed with the frontman's significance. 'Oh, Chris led the way, and many other bands were formed, very often with silly costumes like Acker (Bilk) or Dick Charlesworth's City Gents and all those bands. There was what they called a "Trad Boom", and even the dance band musicians tried to play, even modern jazz musicians like Vic Ash tried to play, although they had no feeling for traditional jazz at all, and failed totally [laughs]. It was irritating watching people trying to play a music for which they had no feeling.' Even my generation can feel the same. Jazz or otherwise. I appreciate his thoughts of candour though.

I then put it to him, to his recollection when did traditional jazz start to appear on TV, on the BBC? 'Well over this period we knew various record producers, and we sort of, which was my job, blagged and begged to get on and to get involved. It was a slow job, I mean you'd be amazed at how hard it was to get anyone to do anything, because we were on the outer fringes of music. To a lot of people we were amateurs playing non-music, it took it a while. And we went through the whole gamut of the BBC Dance Orchestra. Jack Payne and the BBC Dance Orchestra, with Henry Hall [Harold says with a sense of exacerbation]. Rough sounding jazz bands was NOT what people wanted. So they tended to put us into little ghettos, so that you got half an hour of this. It was all hard work getting anyone to do anything I can tell you. To break through in those days you were pioneers. You were pushing and pioneering all the time, to get accepted, to get established. Luckily the Barber Band was a brilliant band and it did lead the way, and lead the way to Barber, Bilk and Ball. The Three Bs. All of which followed [talking about the late 1950s, early 1960s here].' The task involved in getting onto the only other publicly accessible media, apart from the printed press was daunting to say the least. Harold has a firm brick barrier with trench in front of him. The BBC has old traditions of its own that it's lacquered to.

One person carving more of a name out for himself, and as a result doing better and better on the contemporary scene is Tony Kinsey. It seems in the first instance he's getting an exceptional deal with Jeff Kruger, three times what Vi Hyland is paying him. I put it to him, 'do you think your band was popular because of the variety of instruments you had within it? You had vibes, you had saxophone, Ronnie Scott didn't necessarily have vibes in his quartet did he?' 'Well, I mean I think that's a general question. I think bands can be popular because they're slightly different in the front line (instruments "leading" the music, double bass and drums supplying the anchor), or whatever. On the other hand, it depends on the players really. There was Bill Le Sage on the vibraphone and piano, he was a tremendous player.' He had quite a successful recording career from what I've read, during the 1950s.

What does he think of that term? 'It makes me laugh to hear "successful recording career", makes it sound like we made some money. We didn't earn any money [laughs].' 'Oh I see, so despite the deals with Esquire and Decca Records, it wasn't a money spinner?' 'No, we never got any royalties if that's what you mean. We just got a recording fee which was probably about four quid or something, at the time. Because one wasn't aware of all these other things that you could claim [in terms of payment]. I mean if someone asked if you could do it, it'd be, "Oh great! Let's go and do it, oh yes." Play in the first place. We should have been aware of it, and I do believe that those royalties went somewhere else, yes. Where? Obviously I'm not permitted to say, they did.' He sounds rueful, hard done by. I can't blame him, it's the sorry tale musicians frequently trip up over.

'How do you resolve the issue?' I enquired. 'I made six LPs with Decca, and because I never got any royalties I used to think they couldn't be selling, but then I realised that wasn't the case! 'Cos they wouldn't have asked me to do the 1.2.3.4.5.6 if they weren't selling y'know, even to a modest amount would they?' Tony's feelings, justifiably irate. My thoughts, see above.

As time goes by Eddie is doing more and more freelancing and arranging. It's widening further the spectrum of musicians he's working with as well. Tubby is getting even further out onto the London and national live circuits under his own name. For most on the same ship as them, it's developed into an exhilarating time. 'For Tubby Hayes and all that I played with, and various other musicians. We used to take Tubby's vibraphone and didn't bother de-rigging it, we would take it from one club to another through the crowds in the West End, they [gestures avoiding and a malevolent scowl], "excuse me do you mind?" pushing this thing with the mallets [used for playing] in it, you know what I mean [laughs], through the crowds to get to the next gig. Sometimes we're working two or three gigs, and in those days we were earning a fiver a night. Well if you did two gigs in a week that was more than the average man's wages. I mean if you did three, you could go out. I remember admiring a friend of mine Alan Branscombe (piano, vibes, alto and tenor sax.) 'cos he went out on Saturday and spent a whole pound and got totally pissed [chuckles], on a quid!' The tale entertained Eddie. We need to do a little more to reassess, decimalise.

The amount of cash a freelance musician could make was quite impressive by 1956/57. Three gigs in a week was a handy occurrence in a player's diary. My dad, playing traditional, could do it on the Continent now but it would probably involve an 80 to 100 mile round trip. The pay would vary depending on the venue and the hustler behind it. The dark, heaving, shady side of Soho and Central London that you see in your mind's eye, and the film and photography of the time, is bursting with life. Adventure of the era. Little TV, no computers, what else are you going to do to entertain yourself except go out? A drink's not too pricey, especially when some places let you bring your own, the cost on the door's a bit more than shrapnel at The 51 Club.

Eddie Harvey's PR Photograph 1, early 1960s.

While in deep conversation with Eddie, I reflected to him how Tony Kinsey, had been telling me about how he really missed the café that used to be on Archer St, Soho where apparently people used to get their cups of cha, sit with a cigarette and socialise etc. 'That's right and play the [table] football game. Ronnie Scott used to be the guv'nor of that, him and Eddie Taylor that mate of mine I lived with. The pair of them, absolute experts at it.' Was it the football table at the back, the one with the handles on the side? 'Yeah that's it [both laughing]! There's a pub still there on the corner of Archer St, where people used to finish up at the end of things [business of the day], it was very good, the Harmony Inn it was called [the café].' At this time it's situated on the junction of Ham Yard and Great Windmill Street, opposite the end of Archer Street.

Jim Godbolt also provides the assertion that it was very much for dance and modern jazz musicians. He reminds us that, 'the Leaseholder of the premises was a bald-headed Czech émigré called George Siptak who opened up business in 1950.' The Traditionalists had an equivalent called The Rex Restaurant on New Compton Street. The café kept going right through the decade, becoming more and more a natural home for the modern jazz crowd, players and audience alike. As well as some of the less salubrious characters that hovered around Soho before, and after dark.

New Orleans jazz is becoming a popular music movement by itself. My father was an enthusiastic fan in his youth. He loved the music, as well as being a keen fan of skiffle. One of his forerunners, Chris Barber is becoming a 'name' along with Humphrey Lyttelton. The following remarks the trombonist makes flag up an enormous amount about how sharply in focus this genre is at the time. Unbelievably, it's much forgotten now. 'We didn't stand a chance really. If we'd known then, how powerful we were in show business in Britain at the time then we'd've done an awful lot more, but we didn't know, and they [The Industry] weren't about to tell us. And of course they didn't know either. I mean, Simon Cowell didn't exist. Simple as that! If he'd been alive and listening to them, the business my band was doing in 1956, he'd have had us playing in football stadiums, [pauses] and we'd've filled them. Wasn't done, didn't arise. We soldiered on, played where we could, and got the best deal we could for doing it [sounding exasperated].' But if that's the way business works then so be it. You have to make the best job you can of it, check destination on arrival!

Chris Barber's Jazz Band had to look out for themselves on the road because, let's face it, no one else is going to do it for you. Touring is a rough deal at times but if you're at the musical end of business, you'll need to be watching your back because it is just 'you'. 'Had to make sure we didn't get too tired. Had to make sure we didn't do two shows, can't play for four hours, got to have a local band first. Don't want to do that, want to play our stuff to our audience. So we did around five hours a week, we wanted a day off here and there, we were kind of fighting to get a day off. Otherwise you're doing all these dance halls in the north, 'cos punters weren't willing to pay the money on the door to do it.' The significant thing that's being done here is that he's continuing to get the band's name, and it's profitability, more commercial and viable. As well as the music more enjoyable.

Ken Colyer's still very much sticking to his version of an authentic New Orleans jazz, Humphrey Lyttelton's occupying the same side of the more Anglophile version with Mr Barber. In 1956, he's beginning to try out stylistic changes in his group introducing his 6th drummer, Eddie Taylor, though they aren't planned. They're markedly significant. It's fair to say Humph's moving into more mainstream territory. Players more equipped to play this style, with the suggestion of Eddie,

Ian Armit on piano who knows his traditional, and Brian Brocklehurst, a seasoned modern double bassist.

With Tony Kinsey taking his own group out on the road now, the recording and music publishing industries are welcoming him. I asked him what he thinks of the contractual, business deals he has in the mid-1950s, are they ones that he likes? Is he aware of unscrupulous, or malevolent conduct in his small print? 'Well that's perhaps later on y'know, I didn't have any problems with the producers at Decca or anything like that. But we weren't given, or offered what we should have been given. The point is every artist on a record gets a royalty. If it's his band, and my band in this case, if I get royalties then what I do with them is up to me. Divide them amongst the band or whatever. But I never had that opportunity, and I say because I wasn't aware of that um, they must've been aware I wasn't getting anything.' I think that sets out very clearly where he stands given the deal he has at this juncture. His record label is now owned by Universal Records. I was also keen to know who impressed Tony. 'Denis Rose, he was a great influence on my life.' During a period in his career like this, these must be very visceral times.

The modern jazz scene for him is very much about hanging out, as well as the opportunity to perform, listen and learn if possible. This is something jazz musicians are always looking to do. Why? No one's going to pass on the knowledge for free folks!

At the start of 1957 there's a proficient, and prolific modern jazz culture expanding across the UK, trying to catch up with traditional. It's new, vibrant, fresh and cool. Ronnie Scott is the biggest name with John Dankworth. Tubby's getting there. Tony, Eddie and Don are not so far behind. People are seeing the relevance, and significance of Mr Hayes. He's a major talent, as Ronnie convincingly expresses. 'Tubby Hayes was 22 years old and had already established himself as one of the most gifted, mature and technically accomplished musicians on the British jazz scene. He had been playing tenor saxophone since he was 12, and he had invested what he did with a terrific vitality and enthusiasm. He really made you *want* to play and I learned a tremendous amount from him. I remember our two and a half years together in the Jazz Couriers as one of the most satisfying and musically productive periods of my career.' The man has a great affection for his good mate. Ronnie's honesty about his posthumous thoughts on him are eye-opening.

This is how their two tenor ensemble got itself underway. 'The Jazz Couriers made their debut on 7 April 1957 at the opening of The New Flamingo Club in Wardour Street and thereafter worked fairly steadily. In addition to Tubby and myself, the band featured Terry Shannon on piano and Bill Eyden [later Phil Seamen] on drums, and an assortment of bass players including Malcolm Cecil, Phil Bates, Jeff Clyne, Spike Heatley [former BBC *Play Away* double bassist], Kenny Napper, Lennie Bush and Pete Blannin.' From this time on, Tubby and Ronnie are big names due to the band and are touring the UK a great deal (and under their own monikers in small-piece groups). It doesn't take long for them to start releasing four-track EPs on the Tempo record label, that same year.

Humphrey Lyttelton at the same time, is a very occupied man with many side lines on the go at once, it must be said. As he's keen to illustrate in his second autobiography. 'When I'm in London, my day is filled to overflowing with odd jobs. Apart from the regular articles [journalistic for the *NME*, then *Melody Maker*, as well as a weekly piece for *Reynolds News*], there are all sorts of things to be written – scripts for TV and broadcast shows, bits and pieces for record albums, the club bulletin which goes to our members bi-monthly and so on. There are programmes to be compiled, new numbers to be dug up, new [musical] arrangements to be timed and adjusted for TV shows, new records to be listened to for review, new books to be read, new tunes to be composed. Trumpet practice to be fitted in, too.' You can also add to that a four-hour band rehearsal every week. I can very much vouch for the regular 'get together and blow'. During the second half of the 1990s I was in a band called The King Swingers, which was based in Bath while I lived there. For a long while we carried out exactly the same task, the rewards in terms of musicality, cohesiveness and stagecraft are endless, particularly during a groups more industrious times.

Getting into other realms of work outside music, but that are music-related is very clever. You can be sure, where it makes a difference, Humph's face fits. Possibly due to being acquainted with the right people where it matters, and some 'good timing' which we all need in order to get it right. He built a media orientated career all through the 1950s and into his old age. It was spread across a whole host of areas, so when one interest waned or withered another helped to reign in the slack. To be constructing this at that time makes him a talent.

As we spoke about before, Big Bill Broonzy the American R'n'B guitar player, had been over at the keen invitation of Chris Barber in 1954. An exciting opportunity now springs to mind. 'It was 1956 and we finally realised we could almost certainly do something about this. So we arranged to get Big Bill Broonzy over here in 1957. Then we got another singer over (as well), Brother John Sellars, who'd been a gospel singer but had moved into R'n'B, had made some records which we're quite nice. First half one, second half the other. We should have only worked with Big Bill. So we worked with the pair of them, course [the] public said, "why do you want work with the band?" So it was a great experience working with them, Big Bill in particular you see.' It would be disingenuous of me not to say, we'll be returning to this topic in greater depth very soon. The changes come with the breeze of freshening times.

The effect of the collapse of the Musicians' Union ban with America is continuing to be felt right across the British jazz scene. The repercussions are enormous in terms of the player, as well as the listener and club regular. The first in that list of course is all three. Amongst many 'exchanges at', include the arrivals of Stan Kenton's Orchestra in March 1956 to play the Royal Albert Hall, and Count Basie and his Orchestra in April 1957, at the Royal Festival Hall. All complete successes.

At this period in time John Critchinson is still performing at The Icebox club in Chippenham (Wilts), with bands up from London, playing in local groups, with musicians he thinks are up to it. He's also beginning to do his first professional work, at The Regency Ballroom in Bath with Ted Carter [tenor sax] at this point. Occasionally this young player is getting down to London as well. Making the most of his growing number of contacts, he's slowly getting the impression that he's becoming part of a collective 'scene', but he's soon learning that it's a view that might be a trifle foolish. Things were not quite how they seemed on the surface. 'Tubby told me a lovely story, may have been long after that period. He told me about walking down Gloucester Place [on the north side of Marylebone, NW1] with his girlfriend then.

He was walking up, John Dankworth was on the other side walking down, and there was like a big gap between them. The John Dankworth set and the Ronnie Scott/Tubby Hayes set were two different camps, it was almost like gang warfare, it wasn't but y'know.' I put it to him that maybe there was a certain feeling of animosity there? 'Yeah, and Tubby said [puts on a slightly, gruff London accent], "well I saw 'Lord John of Wavendon' walking down the other side of the road and he looked across at me and said, 'hello Tubby, we should get together and have a jam session sometime,' and I said, 'yeah of course,' and then he used a few 'choice words' and went on". But y'know, there was that bit, that was the bit that I couldn't make when I went up to town, the divides. When these guys came down to Chippenham you became part of their world for that evening, but when you went up to town to try and see them then you were audience, that's all you were. But I wasn't looking to go up to town at that time.' I think John is a wise young man to keep things as they are. The animosity between the traditional and modern crowds runs very deep. It's very much evident in modern music now. A good example of it were those who were into Sex Pistols, and the rival grouping with The Clash. Also, Blur and Oasis.

The appeal of jazz, never mind the genre, is becoming popular with the broadcast media, radio and TV. But it's requiring a large amount of coercion and graft by the likes of Harold, and others to make it happen. Wally Houser is a little younger than some of his colleagues, his connections are solid. One of them by this time is a well-known tenor saxophone player. 'Yes I knew Tubby Hayes extremely well, great player. Tubby Hayes. Brian Edward Hayes. He came from London, an absolutely outstanding jazz talent. Almost exactly the same age as me, and I got to know him shortly after I got to know Ronnie. When he was about 17 he was coming up to Manchester, and then they formed The Jazz Couriers, probably the best modern jazz group this country's ever produced. Astounding! Tubby was an incredible musician, like Jimmy Deuchar he would write arrangements without writing a "score" [a written part of music for a musician], he'd just write the parts out [chuckles with affection, and on reflection a lot of friendship for the man]. We got very blasé at Ronnie Scott's Club because Tubby would play amazing choruses, solos of about 35 choruses, and people used to call him "Puffing Billy". But he was a great player! And at the end of his solos Ronnie would go [Wally starts clapping then quotes Ronnie], "very, very long [then laughs]."' The time and respect Wally has for him is really to be admired. It's a great example of friendship.

As proficient as jazz musicians are during the early 20th century many had serious problems with drugs. Particularly popular was heroin which required the user to mix it with water, put it in a hypodermic needle (a syringe) and inject it into a blood vessel. You could inhale it if that suited but the efficacy of the drug is diminished, either way you become what's known as a 'junkie', an addict. When it comes to this music and its history of American musicians, it's littered with addicts from the 1930s on. Charlie Parker, Miles Davis and Sonny Rollins are just a small handful of those who were tripped up in their prime, fortunately Davis and Rollins survived. Britain's Parker was sadly Tubby Hayes.

What certainly troubles many though is his tale. Eddie Harvey explains his friends' situation and dilemma. I put it to him that Tubby had become hooked on this substance. 'Oh yeah, he was a junkie. There weren't many of 'em [in London], and they were all functioning. Like Phil Seaman, wonderful drummer, he was functioning. But in those days you see they were all stabilised by the government, you could get heroin on the National Health [Service]. At 12 o'clock it was available at Boots on Piccadilly, and the number of times you'd have to drive down there with a junkie in your band to "pick up", y'know you'd be waiting round the corner while he went and got his "script" as they called it [laughs]. But they were all functioning musicians. It was "Session [recording] musicians", you can't be late on a session, no.' Well you're dead in the water if you do that, I suggested. 'They were all honest,' he returned. The point of this is that during the 1950s heroin is as readily available as sherbet in the UK. The contemporary view of drugs in the 1950s are that social perspectives of them were similar to today. For more I suggest you dig a little deeper.

Despite his rough addiction he was the kind of musician and friend you'd more than want to know, you'd highly value. You might just have to be prepared to hold on tight. John Critchinson, who knew Hayes both as a young man and an experienced professional in the early 1970s. This is how he saw the musicians from London, at the time. 'I think the essence of it as far as I'm concerned, was that when they came down [to The Icebox] most of those guys were very accessible, and they never really gave you a hard time. Also, some of the rhythm sections we must've put together must've been murder for them y'know, but they never really gave you a hard time.' I asked did he think it was because they were happy to bring the music with them and, to kind of 'spread the word'? 'To a certain extent it was that, and it was the fact that it was a gig, let's face it. That was paying as good a money, if not more money than they were getting in town at that time. I can't think that Tubby would have come down for that money, but that's what he was. Actually it was. You can have Tubby Hayes for five pounds!' But even then to take his rail fare out of that as well, y'know. Five pounds "all in", I put to him? 'I'm alright, Jack Pennington [local jazz impresario] put him up for the night, then he went back to London the next morning.' On the matter of heroin, this is what he added: 'Both Tubby and Vic Ash [clarinet, saxes and flute player] said I should go up there and try it [shakes his head in disbelief].' Critch would have been around 18. Regardless, he seems to have been a keen, talented and generous man.

Tubby's musicianship isn't doubted in modern jazz circles. Wally showed some of the deepest sentiment for him, I can only applaud him for that. 'But Tubby was a wonderful player. Good vibes player, good flute player, could do anything. Good arranger. Could do a big round of arrangements, he was an amazing musician. And he burned himself out, and he was fiddling around with drugs, and octuple vodkas, and he was dead at 38.' At times like this you can make comparisons with similar, contemporary musicians. Whether that's Paul Chambers (Miles Davis' double bass player) or Jimi Hendrix.

The hub of the London jazz scene at this time is still Archer Street. If you want a job then it's the place to put yourself up on display, keep up with the word on the scene. You don't want to be anywhere else. Tony Kinsey's vivid recollection for the time proved especially useful. 'Well Archer Street was a very important place, I mean I used to go down there every day, and see all the guys. Monday was the "Big Day", and it was full of musicians, you couldn't get a car through it.' I explained I knew it served a purpose, but was eager to expand my knowledge. He continued. 'You used to go down there and get gigs and that, 'cos the phone somehow didn't come into it. First phone gig I ever got was with the Ted Heath Band, kind of recorded when Jack Parnell was singing on *Route 66*. I recorded on that. That's where you got gigs, down there on Monday. All sorts of gigs, that's where I got the job on the boats, on the Queen Mary, through Harry Klein [baritone and tenor sax player], who recommended me for it. That was the central meeting point of a group of all the jazz musicians, particularly that was dominated really, not in a derogatory sense, but in numbers by the Club 11. Tony Crombie, Ronnie Scott, Lennie Bush, Laurie Morgan.' It's clearly a group he knows of.

His dependency on the Street, and his veracious enjoyment of the area isn't doubted at all, either. On a personal level he makes his links and ties very straightforward. 'Most of us were going down there every day, till the middle of the afternoon. Used to practice all morning and then go down there. Meet me mates. I unleashed a vibe, 'cos Soho was great. I always felt that when I got there that was when the lights came on y'know, it was in the head. It was a wonderful place, so it was exciting. It was across from the Wyndham's [Theatre], next to the stage doors. That's what we all used to do. Meet in the café, have tea and chat. People didn't drink y'know. Wasn't all about boozing. I can't remember ever meeting people, the guys in pubs used to cut to tea, and chat and have music, anything general. I mean, occasionally people used to have the odd half a pint but, it wasn't a drinking scene. In modern jazz anyway. Oh [exasperated], I wish I could remember the name of that café.' 'That was on Archer Street itself?' 'Yeah, yeah. Harmony Inn.' Tony explained there was another café for gathering on top of that one. As you can see, the social side of the music draws almost everyone in.

One matter I was keen to clear up was where live affairs stood with the traditional players in the late 1950s. Often bands have 'residencies' where they play the same night each week. So I put it to Chris Barber, 'the 100 Club, was that the main venue you played after you stopped playing the Studio 51 Club?' 'Yes we did. We played there fairly often. We had the regular booking at the 100 Club, not till the Ken Colyer Band time [when Mr Colyer had the residency at Studio 51]. We played there every now and then, y'know. I think we played Wood Green Jazz Club every now and then, 100 Club, The Ballroom at Golders Green. We had hopes you see.' I think the simple answer here is 'Yes.'

A change, an expansion in the number of clubs/bars your group gets dates for can often have many unexpected, beneficial effects. It's enlightening getting the view of those involved with their advantage of hindsight. There's no doubt Chris knows where he's coming from on numerous issues, and memories. His opinions and reflections here are succinct. 'After the 51 [Club], and some other places, the band got rather better. We got Dickie Hawdon on trumpet [flugelhorn/double bass/arranger] who was lead, and it got a bit more proficient and so on. Then Humph left the 100 Club [the Humphrey Lyttelton Club closed on 15 September 1959]. In the end he went on playing one night, but that was the Humphrey Lyttelton Club that night. But the Wilcox Brothers, who had rented the 100 Club, were renting the premises from the old lady whose restaurant it was, and run the 100 Club. Then Humph got in there and did the same thing, and in the end set it up several nights a week, as the Humphrey Lyttelton Club. In the end of course it was The London Jazz Club, the thing with Ted Morton (the proprietor). I mean they actually got the lease, from the lady with the restaurant.' The literature, books I've used refer to Mr Morton at least once or twice, but mothers? Only on a single occasion, not enough for corroboration.

Having run a weekly jazz night at The Old Farmhouse public house in Bath between 1991 and 1994, I can certainly vouch for the hard graft involved. Never mind what's put into it by a friend of mine who runs The Be-Bop Club in Bristol. Andy Hague's kept it up, putting on one night a week for around 30 years. No mean feat. Just to put the business side of 'club managing' into perspective, these are Chris' thoughts on the financial side of a 'jazz night' out in London, for proprietor and musician alike. '20 years ago [1990] I remember Ted telling me that the business rate [for the 100 Club] is 20,000 pound a year. What do think about that? And the building belongs to the Prudential [Building Society], and the rent was always going up all the time. Goodness, it's impractical. I mean, there are no punters who can go to a jazz club, wandering along Oxford St in the evenings, drinking somewhere together, course not, nowhere, you don't do that. I mean they don't live in town, and if their coming in from out of town it's so expensive, you only do it if you're going somewhere. That's it.' That maybe a view from the sunrise of the 21st century, but this trombone player couldn't be much more plugged in. Also, given the many times I've played the 100 Club, my father has and Central London, I can back up Mr Barber 100 percent.

For Harold, Chris' gent taking care of business, matters are getting a bit rough. Although he's involved in the managing and admin of the National Jazz Federation at this time, I was also keen to extract where he stood with venues and the live music scene in London, in 1956/57. He resolved my queries in his well-toned accent. 'I was embarking on my long career with Chris, which was contemporaneous with jazz concerts. Being a promoter, by then I'd become a very established promoter, and I'd lost the London Jazz Centre 'cos the people who ran it, called The Latin Quarter, didn't pay the rent and they were chucked out, and I was chucked out with them, 'cos I hung by their feet. I was club-less for a while, and I concentrated on promoting and managing the Chris Barber Band. And of course, as we brought over a long assortment of Black American singers and musicians [pauses]. 'Cos Chris typically, once he began to earn money, ploughed it straight back into importing people he felt ought to be heard.' A British musician putting unparalleled energies into that, in the late 1950s, and given the legal and immigration issues involved? A knighthood for this I think. 'Chris has always done that. Chris has never set out either to be a) a star, or b) for self-aggrandisement.' All I can do is concur with Harold on that one. I went looking for both of them. If any of you read this and come to an alternative decision, then fair play.

Humphrey Lyttelton is finding life pretty enduring, but with plenty to offer. Of his career, he says the band has gone from being semi-professional to full time. As he explains, 'even the change to full time was imperceptible. It simply meant that the day workers left, and those who replaced them were regular musicians who could afford to lie in after a late job instead of having to get up and go off the office. Our routine has hardly altered at all. I continued to limit the engagements [gigs] to an average of just over three per week, with a trip out of town for two or three days a month or so. With the resident spot in the Jazz

Club at 100, Oxford Street occupying Wednesdays and Saturdays, this means that for quite long periods at a time we lead a sedentary life in London. This suits me perfectly, because, although I have abandoned all full-time journalistic work, I still like to do a lot of writing.' It's all a very astute move. If he persists with the touring lifestyle he'll get the band 'out there' but, for some 'physically', it can take them apart and turn into a serious breakdown. This is also a band that's doing TV/ Radio, more and more, as it's public profile becomes more familiar. The 'word' continues to spread.

It's fair to say Wally Houser has known many people in jazz, but on a practical level that can be a bit of a poisoned chalice. Why? Given these acquaintances were made before the mobile and the PC/Mac, remembering all the worthwhile players for someone like me can be an arduous task. It's the very same for him. 'Alan Branscombe was the great musician who's name I couldn't think of. He was a brilliant jazz pianist. When he was in the Army he took up the saxophone so he'd have something to play on "The March". But he became a very good [alto] saxophone player. He was very good but he did himself in with drugs. He was a good fella, very nice guy. In fact he was the regular "House" pianist at The Cavern in Liverpool before he moved to London, everyone wanted to play with him. He worked with the John Dankworth Big Band. Very good player.' The man under scrutiny is a talent.

To go from the keys to a wind instrument, and reach this level, is most impressive. Most musicians usually get to one and that's good, so another's not bad at all. His description says it all. John Dankworth has been running a big band since 1953, and he will until 1964. He's certainly on the complimentary side when it comes to piano players and the matters in hand. Having been so lucky to have Bill Le Sage and Derek Smith he goes on. 'Other pianists included Dudley Moore [close colleague of Peter Cook], who stayed about nine months, until his review *Beyond the Fringe* took off, and Dudley with it, to London's West End and then on to Broadway. He was succeeded by Alan Branscombe, a gifted musician who played excellent vibes and fine alto sax. Alan, after nursing several musicians who were drug addicts through difficult periods, finally became a victim of hard drugs himself, and musical performances became a shadow of their former selves. He died needlessly in the mid-eighties, and a great talent was lost.' The drink and drug problems that prevail in music here, have a solid, small foothold in Britain long before rock 'n' roll and R'n'B arrive.

Something that does Dankworth's Big Band an enormous favour in 1958 is inclusion, in America, at the Newport Jazz Festival, Rhode Island. They're on the bill with Duke Ellington's Big Band, and that of Count Basie's. Quite an honour.

With radio a major public outlet at this time, the significant jazz acts are onto live broadcasts on a regular basis. Chris Barber paints the picture for his outfit, Chris Barber's New Orleans Jazz Band. 'In the 50s though, you did radio. Our first broadcast was with BBC *Jazz Club* in 1950. By 1959 we probably did it eight times a year. We did *Sunday Night at The London Palladium* a couple of times, [he ponders] and quite right. A band like mine isn't very visually interesting. There's not much going on and that's a difficulty. All you can do is put on a bowler hat [he says laughing].' Chris' band is a major act at this point.

Well, he's certainly getting the work. Effectively, what is happening bears a marked resemblance to the early period of the 1960s and the

Beat Generation. The group is in demand so much that every request made is met with a nod, and a firm handshake. 'Well yes. We were that popular I could say I want a concert every day. Then they'd say yes, because they'd be happy to get us. 'Cos normally it would've been five weeks ago [laughs]. It was just nobody knew the strength of what it was, and what it could be, so kept it to themselves. Or made more money out of it. They didn't, they were already making money. The promoters made more money. Within about a year we'd switched from playing Leeds Town Hall, which seats 6,000 people, to the Guild one which seats 6–3,000. We must've filled up both so they'd be full.' No mean feat at the time, and to be applauded.

I was curious to know though, whose outfits are touring with him at this time? There are a lot of traditional bands out there fighting to get up the musical ladder, who got lucky? 'It was about that time that Acker [Bilk] decided to start up his band, 1957 you see, and Kenny Ball 1959. So we had no competition, the other bands weren't trying to do anything on a big scale, they would just play, they had no idea of how to do it in a big way. But really Acker didn't either, though you've got to have hit records. You've got to get hit records in order to get big crowds. In order to get things to happen.' This is something that Acker, who started out in London with Ken Colyer's band (before returning with his Paramount Jazz Band in 1957) might just get? Chris continues, 'We played in all the bigger town halls, the main ones. The 3,000-seater ones, Newcastle, Manchester, all those sort of places, and they were all full. I could've insisted on a lot more things, but as it was I was branded as uncooperative, and unhelpful, and a nuisance, 'cos I wanted to be doing NOT what they wanted to do. Which was turn up, do your thing, and get your money.' Well, to be honest his approach and attitude seems pretty affable and business like, but I'll reiterate my 'professional interest' as a double bass, electric bass and guitar player at this point. Music manager also.

When talking about where jazz musicians get their 'knowledge' from, where they learnt their trade, the question throws up a surprising second explanation from John Critchinson. Certainly not the one I anticipated. 'It's amazing this but we all, and I've talked to Ronnie about that, when he started working with me, where we picked up the knowledge of the music depended on who you listened to. Some of them listened to the American stuff coming in, amazing that Ronnie and that lot went over and listened to Charlie Parker. They got their vocabulary from there to a certain extent, mine and Ronnie's as well. We learnt silly tunes from Donald Pearce, who was a singer. Then myself, I learnt a lot from people like Charlie Coombes, who was just a club piano player. It all comes down to how your ear is developing, the way you hear chord progressions, that's where mine came from. Then any tunes that use chord progressions you'll listen to. Charlie Coombes, he used to put them down. I used to think, "that's nice, what he played." Not so much about the technique, but the way he went about the chords.' As jazz musicians we have to listen and learn from the day we decide to take it up. If we don't we're in trouble. I worked out where I'd strayed with my errors, and what I needed to do to put the jigsaw together, thanks to my double bass teacher Dave Goodier in Bristol. Later Alec Dankworth, at Trinity College of Music in London. But the fruits of the hard musical graft that John illustrates above, are satisfying to reap.

Then Critch reveals a surprise amour. A slightly puzzled look on his face but rolling it out as calmly as his last observation. 'Another one for me wasn't so much an influence, but somebody I could listen to, in a funny sort of way, was Winifred Atwell of all things. Because she played this most horrendous, old fashioned piano, but there was something about that, the things that she played. It was the tunes! I think that's what it is. Ronnie was a bit, in fact most of us musicians were sort of the same 'cos there was no Real Books (the contemporary Trade Tune collection). There was nothing to learn anything from except records. There was no actual music.' Having spoken to my father on this issue he'd have wholeheartedly agreed with his mate. Not least because that was how he gained his own skills. From here the musicians out there can argue about how much it matters, and everyone else can debate if it does at all, if they wish.

London has a healthy number of clubs at this time as we've already seen. Wally Houser spent a generous amount of time in London during this decade, I'll let him clarify his story. 'We've moved on now though, it's 1959. When I went back to Manchester I was playing at the Club 43 one night, and Ronnie Scott was booked as the headliner. By this time I'd known him four or five years. At the end of the gig he said he wanted a cab to the station, so I drove him to the station. He said to me, "so you've just qualified as a solicitor?" "Yes," I said. "Well I'm gonna open a club, can you tell me something about leases and licenses?"' The horn-playing lawyer goes on to explain. 'Typical of Ronnie, he was getting involved in something unnecessarily complicated with the man that owned the premises in Gerrard St, where the club first opened, and I offered a bit of advice on it.' His recollections of this club lurching into life are more than a little significant.

What Time Are We On?

In Ronnie's own book he clarifies on the organisational make-up of his premises. 'The basement at 39, Gerrard Street had been various things in its time. The division of responsibilities between Pete [King] and myself presented no problems because Pete had been business manager of both the nine-piece band and the big band. So the idea was that I would play at the club on a fairly regular basis and Pete would count up the money – if any. We borrowed about £1,000 from my stepfather, took a lease on the place, bought some second-hand furniture and a few pots of paints and, with the aid of some press-ganged volunteers, started doing the place up. We built a small bandstand, bought a small grand piano, moved out the billiard tables, cunningly converted the tea bar into a coffee bar – and we were in business. The place was somewhat spartan – it didn't quite match up to the Three Deuces (New York jazz club) – but it was a start.' On 30 October 1959, came the opening night. Getting the chance to run your own club is certainly one to grab, if you feel you're the kind of character that over time can pull it off.

The tenorist expands further on the inaugural evening he put together for the Soho crowd. 'The opening night went well and I couldn't have chosen two better groups to inaugurate the club than those of Tubby Hayes and Eddie Thompson. Tubby was to play many more times at the Club and also to figure in many more UK–US band exchanges.' Ronnie clearly made a smart move in getting his close friend and colleague in, on the maiden show for the premises. The booking of the Eddie Thompson Trio stands out as well, not least because this piano player is blind. I never met him sadly but if you take into account the perspectives of my interviewees, the authors I've used for research and the man about

181

town who appeared on TV, then I'd venture to say that it takes a near inexhaustible resource of tact, diplomacy and an implicitly calm nature to succeed. Here it is from an unexpected angle, Chris. 'Ronnie wasn't a person who'd cross words at odds to anybody. No, he wouldn't [pauses]. He'd talk to anybody, because he was like he was, and OK with it.' For a traditional player, and one of the two most proficient, and well-known in the UK at the time, I think that says bucket loads.

While American jazz is starting it's 'Cool' period in 1959, the major UK event at the end of the decade that will change things permanently, concerns musical acts visiting the USA to tour. I'll leave it to Chris Barber to elaborate, and to illustrate the detail about 'the Exchange System'. 'You see, the Musicians' Union and the American Federation of Musicians in America, were convinced that the other side were going to take all the jobs, sending over their cheap work labour. The storm broke in 1937, or 38, when Teddy Hill's Band was over here, and Jack Hilton's Band used to do stage shows. I mean they used to play New York. It makes no difference if they did it now. What happened was one side or the other [the Union or Federation] pulled the plug on a show, and the other side says, "well you can't have a show here either." Tell you the bands that arrived. The band that had Bill Coleman and Dickie Wells and all that lot, that stayed behind in Paris and recorded with Django [Reinhardt] and so on, and Dizzy Gillespie was in the band as well. That's when the Union decided it didn't change after all, and people started to try and get away with it.' It's clear that by 1959 the issue has been burning for a while.

The trombonist discloses more. 'There was trouble, Festival of Britain 51, concert at the Festival Hall, opening night and they had

What Time Are We On?

Lonnie Johnson and, was it Ralph Sutton who played on it [a rhetorical question]? The bands who played with them got blacklisted by the Union, or ticked off very badly. Then of course Humph brought Sidney Bechet in, he got away just about. I mean. Unions in those days were the power of the land. We'd get Work Permits, yes. The reason we used to have to get Work Permits, was to have Unions say, "we have valid musicians, don't want you there", and that was a nonsense really if they can't compete. But the situation was of course, that we were doing so well in this country, and I said, why we want the American blues singers in was because we've got to be playing with these people.' Given the way events will turn out I think it's fair to say he's got a very valid point. Music can't develop if you don't get to hear those who came before you. Especially if they created it in the first place.

There's no doubt that in order to make things happen in the UK, he's going to have to find his own way to make things ignite. A bit of 'manoeuvring' is going to be necessary on his own part. 'The [Louis] Armstrong All Stars were touring at that time. My band, we chartered a plane and we flew from Croydon, you wouldn't be able to fly there anymore, it's not an airport y'know. This twin-engined plane flew to Bobo or somewhere, and then got the train to Paris, and got to see [18] Louis at The Olympia. I went to the Union and said, "look, y'know, it'd be nice if we could get on at Louis Armstrong again 'cos we've got this wonderful jazz scene building up here. We're playing concerts, but you gotta get more of it. People like it so much but they're not getting enough of it, and not really the best. Someone like, maybe, Louis Armstrong who's a soloist who can join in, and so on, it'll bring so much work to us all and everything else, it'll be really good." The

General Secretary of the Union, Harvey Radcliffe said to me, "why is it you always want to go to America, why don't you go to Russia?" Of course he was a Communist. It's an odd situation with the Union, I suppose the only ones that bothered to go to a meeting were the Communists. So I did. Yet I'm a Socialist, but I don't believe in being stupid, I'm realistic. They're all going and buying cheap clothes made in Japan, and not worrying about it aren't they [laughs]?' I hope that puts to rest any political queries anyone out there may have about Chris? Me? It makes no odds at all which side of the spectrum any of my interviewees may be. They're all equal in my book.

To get to the point though, on he goes. 'So, the main agent who did music concerts and so on was Harold Davison, married to Marion Ryan, singer.

Children Paul and Barry Ryan, who made all the pop records [as a duo in the 1960s]. Harold, he was "doable" in business, concerts and so forth, and everything else. He might have had Count Basie, might have interviewed him and everything you see, and he had an offer of Louis Armstrong. Louis was touring at that time. Louis Armstrong All Stars had been bought for three months by these two Australian gangsters. The Union wouldn't agree.' There's no doubt that gangland criminality is alive and well in London and the rest of the UK during the 1950s. By the end of the decade Ronnie and Reggie Kray have had their altercation with conscription, and are involved in this nocturnal line of graft themselves, according to the press and other authors. Chris is remarkably complimentary about Harold Davison. For these observations to be made by such a seasoned professional as him puts the subjects achievements, high. 'So Davison was a very clever fella. The

Union were forever bitching about politics you see, and the Americans. Saying, "they won't give Paul Robeson a passport." Well of course they wouldn't 'cos he was going straight to the World View Festival in Prague and to tell the world how bad Communism was, and how America was shit. And they said, "well if you need our passport then we're not shit." So Harold Davison had a bright idea. "Well if I offer Paul Robeson a tour in England, he's in business. I'm gonna give him a passport ain't I?" He did. So he went to the Union and said, "I've got Paul Robeson a passport you see. What about this being a sensible thing about the bands and so on?" He said, "well look if you have an exchange y'know, a P61 Exchange then it can't be harmful, to either side can it?"' He's a very 'switched on' gentleman. Harold is clearly thinking this is a problem that can be fixed. His approach to it is, people aren't talking to each other but if I help solve the problem, then maybe everybody will be happy for a variety reasons, and I'll be all the better off for it. A proactive music manager, is an excellent resource in this business. An invaluable asset. Mr Davison grabs the bull by the horns, as our trombone player informs. 'So he drew up a contract system. He drew up a, "Rules of Exchange". You know, about the music business and how it works?' 'Yes,' I reiterated. 'The rules stipulate that, the bands on exchange shall be the same size, get the same fees and play the same music. They'll only play concerts. They knew the Americans would only allow it because there are no concerts in America, and you couldn't take anyone's work by playing concerts. Not concerts, or what they called, "Resident Engagements", they couldn't. So, the Unions swallowed it.' Well things have potentially turned completely the other way. This stagnant situation whereby US bands rarely toured the UK, could be given a shot in the arm like it couldn't have dreamt of.

Then, Heaven.

He elaborates further as it appears he is very much caught in the eye of all this. 'So they got a contract drawn up, I wasn't there, but I obviously heard about it. There was this meeting, in an office somewhere. There was a legal matter raised between the Union guy and Harold Davison. And Harold said, "right this is the exchange, yes? Now I've organised this, the Louis Armstrong All Stars are going to come here," I think it was Freddy Randall who's going to go to New York. There's the exchange, their getting the same look, same money. Yes, very good. See we've put our foot down, and you've been forced to pay these bands properly. So Davison gave them a cheque for $25,000 for Louis Armstrong's services for two weeks, sounds reasonable. And went, "here we go, for Freddy Randall, [if it was Freddy Randall], here's a cheque for $25,000 for his." Outside the office he tore it up and gave it to Harold Davison. Freddy went and stayed in a hotel in New York, sent back a postcard saying how he was and came back. Free cheque!' Well, there's a city break for nowt. The gargantuan amount of mistrust and paranoia between all the parties involved leaves me speechless. I think it's also highlighting that if you want more detail, and chronology in these developments you'll need to carry out more research yourself. I'm lucky I've more than the one 'witness'.

Directly connected to the hub is Harold Pendleton. Having been promoting and managing the Chris Barber Band at this time, and given the 'Rules of Exchange' situation, he's going to the States now to 'sell' them. It's a great tale but sadly it doesn't end as well as it ought. I'll let him expand. 'Unfortunately, the very moment I arranged for them to go to America, *Petite Fleur* happened.' 'What's *Petite Fleur*?' I asked.

What Time Are We On?

'What actually happened was Monty [Sunshine] used to do feature numbers, and one of the ones he chose was a Sidney Bechet number called *Petite Fleur*. This, for some obscure reason, became a hit.' The single was in the British charts for as long as 24 weeks in 1959, getting to number No. 3, and being bought by over a million people. Thus getting a Gold Disc. That's in the charts for over half the year. You don't encounter that much in this day and age, in America it reached No. 5.

Let's put the tale back in the gentleman's hands. 'I was in New York and I walked down Broadway, every shop was playing *Petite Fleur*, which I thought, "Christ, I never thought I'd hear that." This unfortunately led to an 'overvalue' of them, and instead of modest publicity, for the tour of the Barber Band, bigger halls were booked, and a supporting group of American musicians were put on to open the show and then the Barber Band. Because they were virtually unknown, they didn't draw. So the tour, in my opinion, was not a success. It didn't make any money, because it had been overblown and overbooked. Which was a shame but, it was an interesting experience. We did several tours of America after that, but I regretted that we got overexcited by the success of the record, to book too big halls.' Hindsight is an extremely useful tool here, I'm sure it is. No matter what area of the music industry you work in, it's fair to say that you learn by experience, and your mistakes. For Harold, his work at the end of the 1950s might have provided just the bedrock an entrepreneur like him needed, for now and the rest of his professional career.

Another significant thing I'd like to highlight is a huge compliment that Harold paid Chris. It was something that he was keen to emphasise, the least I can do for him is get that across. 'He's always used whatever strength he gained from popularity, record sales whatever, to plough it back. And bringing, in Big Bill Broonzy, Sister Rosetta Tharpe, Brownie McGhee and Sonny. Of all these people it was Muddy Waters. It was that one that was the most interesting. Because in the course of my managing the band, the various things I did, I got them into America. I went to the States to stay with my friend John Lewis, who was the piano player with The Modern Jazz Quartet, we were very close friends. I went over there to try and flog the Chris Barber Band. This was 59. And I guess I toured American groups [in the UK] and put them all on. Earl Hines, Jack Teagarden All-Stars, Gerry Mulligan Quartet, The MJQ, which had a big influence on Chris, this is what I was doing promoting Chris Barber concerts.' The first group of names are old American blues artists, though at the time Muddy wasn't so young having arrived into the world back in 1913.

Harold's ambition is to be admired, as is his resolution and vigour to tackle the task at hand. He continues to recall his memories of the time. 'So while I was in America I was going into all the big agents like Joe Glaser, who managed Louis Armstrong, and the guy that managed Basie and so on, and I was getting absolutely nowhere. Because they were all going, "what, what, an English band, a Dixieland band?" 'Cos of course they always use the word "Dixieland". "What, you've got an English Dixieland band? We've got loads of them, what do we need another one for?"' Trying to sell Chris in this environment must've been an excruciating task. But nonetheless, head down and on with the business at hand.

This period seems to have been very daunting, as well as wearing, until luck suddenly turned his way. I'll let him carry on with the story, in his well-spoken tone. 'I was drawing a blank until I went to see

What Time Are We On?

Woody Herman's manager, a man called Abe Turchin. I hit it off straight away, mostly because he wanted something for Woody [clarinettist and bandleader], and we found we had a reciprocal interest. Because of the 18-year ban. Because too many British musicians went over there, Ray Noble and so on, and the American Union hated it. With the British MU we'd come up with a reciprocal deal, in which you could do "one for one".' Well, a deal is a deal, tit for tat, a handshake can mean a bond of unanimity, even a call to arms.

This appears to be a quite a tentative meeting on both sides. Each partner present wants to break the rigid lock that's been put onto the matter (now dilemma) at hand, but mutual suspicion is at maximum. The ability to entrust anything is in the dustbin it seems. 'This is what I put to Abe Turchin, I said, "look you want Woody to come to Europe, I want Chris Barber to come to America. The only way we can do it is swap six for six [the number of musicians]." He said, "Woody's got a bigger orchestra." I said, "we've got musicians too. I guarantee to you that I can put together sufficient British musicians to work with the six that Woody brings, to make an Anglo-American herd." Which I did. I said, "trust me and I'll do a tour, I'll book a tour for them. Which I'm good at doing, of England." Abe replied, "Woody can do a complete tour of England, you can book Chris." "Right." We can safely assume there is a handshake here! This might not have been resolved for another ten years, simply due to trust and "word of honour".' The music industry relies on this, managers to performers. It works to an extent, given that its annual contribution to the nation's earning is £4.5 billion last year. It's also grown faster than the country's economy in recent years. No mean feat.

Harold goes on to 'wrap up' his part of the tale. 'So that's what happened. Got the Union agreement, and we were allowed to take six plus the Barber Band, and I met them in New York, and to together with Nesuhi Ertegun, who was one of the owners of Atlantic Records. We took them down to Jimmy Ryan's to listen to Wilbur De Paris, who had a very good traditional jazz band, with his brother Sidney De Paris on trumpet, Omer Simeon on clarinet.' Jimmy Ryan's was on 53 West 52nd Street at this time. It was a big Dixieland jazz venue at the time, one of the three major traditional clubs in the city.

In his tome, Jim Godbolt is able to add more colour to this tale. After all, we've another bandleader, signed contract in hand and smart 50s flightcase. 'April 1959 saw a visit by an American band leader that had special significance. Woody Herman toured with seven Britishers and two Canadians resident in Britain. This was not a publicity stunt; not even another stratagem to comply with exchange requirements. It was a genuine musical association, a mark of respect to those local musicians who had made such progress, mostly by listening to records, that they could take their places in a crack American Orchestra. They were Bert Courtley (trumpeter), Les Condon and Kenny Wheeler (Canadian resident in Britain); Eddie Harvey and Ken Wray (trombonist); saxophonists Don Rendell, Johnny Scott and Art Ellefson (another Canadian resident in Britain).' The notable players in Woody's band are Nat Adderley on trumpet, and Charlie Byrd on guitar. Nat plays in his brother Julian's quintet at this time.

This deal was a tremendous moment in Western popular music and international management. Without it The Beatles and The Rolling Stones wouldn't have flown. The well-known American rock, R'n'B and soul acts may not have turned up until the end of the 1960s. Strangely, you rarely ever hear this agreement mentioned now. What kind of music would have developed instead?

In Chris Barber's take on affairs, how much of the Union Deal was followed through with, and what was slung on the bonfire, is debatable. Wounds can take a long time to heal. 'After that, some of the ones who went over there didn't in fact play, but the gigs they did were freebies that were in a little Sergeant's Mess of an American Air Force Base in New England, which would have been the worst gigs in the world. I mean they don't like music anyway. Get this right.' Chris is very straightforward in his thoughts here. 'People who are forced to be soldiers are probably jazz fans. People who volunteer to be soldiers, or are professional, are not. They're gun fans, or logistics fans. Until I went on in 1959, there were no British bands that went over there and did a proper tour. The Ted Heath Band did a tour, one exchange was done with them over there. The American promoter used them as a "House Band" for a show with pop artists, not present-day pop, but pretty girl pop. Doris Day, that sort of thing.' The term means you're a regular group, sometimes in the same venue each night. It may not be a good gig either. Either way, the band isn't the main attraction.

The latter part of the decade was an exciting time for all involved, musicians, management, fan and listener. Eddie Harvey had a very, 'rounded' view of jazz, he'd started off his career playing traditional, but within ten years he's playing modern jazz and left the Dankworth Seven, to become a freelance trombonist and arranger. He gave me a very resonant quote, which I feel is ideal to summarise the London scene in 1959. 'But anyway, that was a thrilling period the end of the

50s. The places we used to play, the all-nighter at The Mapleton in Leicester Square, and it was packed! And it WENT from 11 o'clock to 7 in the morning, y'know, and if you had some arrangements you'd stay up for two or three days without going to bed because of writing two, and all the rest of it.' 'Sounds fantastic,' I said. Though I don't think I'd fully absorbed the consequences of playing that late. 'A very exciting time, and on top of that we lived in town. I lived with a drummer called Eddie Taylor who was with the John Dankworth Seven, and we had a flat in Ladbroke Grove and of course it was fairly handy, being situated on the Central Line, to the West End so, parties [he smiles broadly, pauses], and Ed? He left and went to work with Humphrey Lyttelton's band and Humph was working with a lot of other people, and this like in the mid-50s. Ed was working with Eddie Condon's band, so we had all those guys round for parties y'know. They did an American tour, there was all kind of things [laughs].' I've never seen anyone talk so merrily, and with such affection about a time. That's rare and impressive.

Regardless of which side of the jazz fence you're on at this point of time, British jazz is going through a very exhilarating phase. It's certainly not over, but there's a slightly different tint to the colour of the sky, and the sun is about to slowly ascend in the distance. Hmmmmm?

What Time Are We On?

ACKNOWLEDGEMENTS:

Second Chorus. Drawings by the author. Humphrey Lyttelton, 1921–2008. London: MacGibbon & Kee, 1958 (P. 118/119), (P. 121), (P. 118)

A History of Jazz in Britain 1950–1970. Jim Godbolt, 1922–2013. London: Quartet, 1989 (P. 108–9), (P. 150–1 & SC), (P. 190/P. 231)

Who's Who of British Jazz/John Chilton. John Chilton, 1932–2016. London: Cassell, 1997 (P. 82), (P. 327)

Some of My Best Friends Are Blues. Ronnie Scott; with Mike Hennessey; preface by Pete King. Ronnie Scott, 1927–1996. London: Northway, 2004 (P. 49), (P. 49), (P. 51/52)

UK Music website; Measuring Music report 2018 (Downloaded 6.11.2018, figures used)

CHAPTER 8

SKIFFLE AND THE BRITISH BLUES

While jazz in both its genres is becoming ever-more dominant, and media profile increasingly conspicuous, in 1955 there's still plenty of scope for 'the next big thing' to come up from behind, and usurp it while attentions are focused elsewhere. Never assume you know it all, my mother used to say to me. I can safely say she was right. Changes in the melodic landscape are starting to happen that will change it greatly, and for good.

As we've already learnt, skiffle is currently a very popular form of music. The younger generation of teenagers are into it more than the grown-ups. The straightforward, simple nature of it is one of the main attractions to the listening public. A schoolboy can make/buy a tea chest bass as easily as an old-age pensioner with a dodgy leg.

We know traditional jazz musicians from a variety of groups are happily doing gigs in a similar vein across the country. All they need are six or seven chords and they've got a good slice of their musical cake covered.

Some of the musical similarities between the two I'd have thought most listeners would get to grips with, without too many stresses and strains. There's also a handful of musicians within music in general who've been spending more and more time listening to, and playing the blues. Chris Barber and Ken Colyer are doing blues/skiffle sets during their respective gigs. The modern strand is still separate and quite self-contained due to its youth and complexity.

As we've already heard, Chris Barber has made a very significant mark when it has come to bringing over the best blues talent from the States. Big Bill Broonzy in 1954 to begin with. Having recently finished his National Service his previous banjo player/guitarist Alexis Korner, is running a club right in darkest depths of Soho. In partnership with a good friend of his Cyril Davies (vocals and blues harmonica), he's running the London Skiffle Club in 1954, upstairs on the first floor, at The Roundhouse Pub, 83, Wardour Street (corner of Brewer Street). In the present day it's The O Bar. They change the name to The London Blues and Barrelhouse Club. The venue, essentially a medium-sized room above a public house, becomes a regular success and Alexis and Cyril realise they've got something on their hands. They're also running a small blues band of their own, getting gigs at folk and blues venues in London as well.

Blues is getting off the ground, but skiffle is now about to have a major national success. Having recorded it in July 1954 with Chris Barber's Blues Band, in 1956 the Lonnie Donegan and His Skiffle Group has its first big hit with *Rock Island Line* (Decca), which gets to number eight in the UK and US charts. No mean feat. I put it to Chris, was there a point at which he stopped doing the 'stripped down' blues band? 'Well we should have stopped it when Lonnie left. Unfortunately, we had some contracts. He left in March 56. He did one contract demanding he signed it in advance. That was April. What happened though was that the day Lonnie left, we played the 100 Club. The next time we were up there at Oxford St, a bloke walked in carrying a guitar looking very much like him, wearing the same clothes as he was, that was Johnny Duncan. I mean he wasn't weird, but same kind of jacket, same kind of trousers, and Johnny was a skilled performer. He was a bluegrass man from Knoxville, Tennessee, and very white [I don't know why], but good. He sang "spirituals" [a Black American form of religious music] as they do, all the white ones, and country bluegrass songs and silly ones. He was an ex-serviceman who'd been demobbed and stayed in England and got married, you see. They'd been to America and come back, and come back in a bit, his wife told us that Johnny's father of course shouldn't have let things get out of hand [I laugh]. Seriously, quite funny. We toured with him until about the end of 56, maybe 57, but he wasn't there when we did the tour with Bill Broonzy. I'm sure of that.' Quite a revolving door!

Alexis and Cyril's eagerness to get the 'blues' out to the public can't be doubted. They spend a couple of years with heads down, gigging as much as they can and taking this music to a new, younger audience, who at the same time want to see it and educate themselves.

What's helping to instigate a strong and invigorated British blues scene off the back of their efforts, are those of Chris. Finally, he's able to realise one of his personal ambitions with Big Bill Broonzy. 'We brought him over to tour with us in 57. The first time we actually brought American people in to do a thing with us [the band]. Where you had Big Bill and another guy called Brother John Sellers, a former gospel singer, of sorts, R'n'B singer more or less.' It's this sort of 'direct action', with Alexis, that will have such a dramatic and positive effect on the town halls that see them. They're far more likely to see and hear American blues for the first time. The crowd will predominantly be between late teenage and under 30. Also this year, Lonnie Donegan's *Cumberland Gap* will go to No.1 in the UK Singles Chart, so skiffle has broken through.

The genre is certainly at a high point in the UK. Because of its 'swing and simplicity' in performance. There are countless bands in the UK made up of youngsters who literally get it, and the three to six chords they need to play. The affordability of the instruments counts for a lot too. The best-known groups are The Chas McDevitt Skiffle Group, Johnny Duncan and the Blue Grass Boys, as well as The Vipers and of course Tommy Steele. It's certainly evolving into a style that's a lot more precocious. Johnny Duncan has a big hit with his rendition of the calypso tune, *Last Train to San Fernando* in June 1957.

Chris' persistence with a blues band in between sets is an integral part of his jazz groups evening show now. He has more to add on the topic of double bass players too. I have to say I've never stumbled over this scenario in the past. 'The bass player in my first band was a black guy called Bob Agen. Also Brian O' Ford. He used to work with a piano player called Errol Barrow, and there was a club in the West End somewhere called The Sunset Club, all the American servicemen went to all the time, they played there. Brian O' played with us and he was left-handed, he played a four-string guitar, a Cuatro, it's called a little one because he was a Barbadian singer. He had some dark name like Lord Invader. But he played his double bass with normal stringing, though [he was] left-handed.' The majority of bass players are right-handed and hold the strings down with their left, right pulls the strings. Brian O' hadn't changed the strings around. He'd taught himself to play back to front!

The trombonist expressed his surprise, 'how I can't THINK! I picked his bass up and I could play it because it was the right way round. I mean that's how I did the first [UK] blues single with Alexis, I could do it. I could play it. But he did it, he played good notes all the time y'know. He was a traditional player, played 'dum – dom, dum – dom.' Two-beat and things. Harder on the double bass, an electric bass you don't have to hold the strings down so hard.' In conveying this tale Chris was left absolutely dumbstruck by Brian's abilities. I'm with him on this.

The next milestone on the road in the growth of the British blues movement, is the arrival of the American singer, guitarist and songwriter about to land from the other side of the Atlantic. 'So when we did that [Big Bill Broonzy tour] we realised we've got to take this seriously. So we got Sister Rosetta Tharpe in, the first one entirely for our own band. That was entirely our own choice, 1957. She played with us for about four weeks or so in November, and that was the time when we really realised "we could do it properly", and we could play with those people, and it could be better than it was. You know from the first day we played with her we learnt a huge amount.' The last couple of sentences were said with such honest, personal candour. I really felt that this time was a turning point for him, and for British popular music. It's all about self-confidence and, finally a British player feels like they can hold their own with the originators of the music.

Someone who's been very active on the scene already is about to do more than just open another club, he's going to open one that remains in countless music biographies. At the end of the last chapter we'd left Harold Pendleton doing deals in the States. On his return? 'When we came back to London by now I'd moved the Barber Band into The Marquee on Wednesday nights. I'd opened The Marquee by now. That was 58 [1959 is the first Chris Barber Tour of the USA]. I'd opened it originally on the Saturday and Sunday, with Joe Harriott on the Saturdays, and later with John Dankworth on the Sundays. Then, I started expanding it. Manfred Mann on the Mondays, then Chris Barber on the Wednesdays, and gradually filling up the week, 'cos I rented this ballroom, the Academy cinema at 165, Oxford St. It was being designed and built as a ballroom, and Chris was there on the Wednesday. By now Donegan had gone (from the band), had become a big star. Dickie Bishop, who had replaced him had gone, and the skiffle group had been fronted by a bluegrass singer called Johnny Duncan. I hated it. There was this obligatory need to play skiffle, but the singer Johnny Duncan and bluegrass didn't fit in my opinion. In fact, later he made an album of his own called *Last Train to San Fernando* [said with disgust], which was awful, and I said to Chris, "look, this is ridiculous y'know. I can't stand this bluegrass anymore. It's not even skiffle, it's not even jazz." So Chris said, "well, let's try and do R'n'B." So I said, "where do we find the right people?" Certainly a daunting challenge.

R'n'B is effectively an amalgam of jazz and blues at this point in time. Harold goes on. 'We hunted around, we found Cyril Davies the harp player, playing in a folk club at The Roundhouse on Wardour St. That's good, so we've now got a harp player. Where do we find a guitar player? Christ knows. The truthful answer was we couldn't find a decent one. So we got Alexis Korner who loved the blues, his heart was in the right place. They [the blues band] took the stand at the interval break of the Chris Barber Band. On a Wednesday, and of course we'd already pioneered the idea of someone coming on in the intervals. Because that's how we started, by asking Humph if we could play in the interval [smiles broadly]. Most clubs played records in the interval, but we always said there's people dying to play, they may be bloody awful but they need to get experience. So let them go onto the stage while we go to the pub and refresh ourselves, and give them a bit of experience of playing to the people who stay behind at the club, who don't drink (no drinks licences at the venue). But at least they get the feeling, and it's practice, so we'd always done that, it became a principle of everything Chris and I did. Alexis and Cyril, together with two or three other people did this R'n'B set.' The, 'gain experience here' sentiment that's being promoted is priceless. It's a great way of making music accessible during the initial stages of its introduction to a new audience. It quickly helps to make this genre 'hands on'.

I put it to the trombonist, what year did you start The Marquee? '58. So we said you [Alexis] can have Thursdays. He called it Blues Incorporated, that was his first band. In fact, he was very uncertain of personnel at first. He made his first LP for Decca almost immediately, and he hadn't got a drummer yet 'cos our drummer Graham Burbidge played on it. Then Ginger Baker, some good quality drummers really. I mean it was a good band, and that was the beginning of the whole thing happening.' Good to get such high compliment, so early on. Given time on the door though, no surprise.

The next big event for the British blues movement is the visit of US guitarist Muddy Waters same year. A new sound for most over here. Chris surprised me with his thoughts and disclosures, he reflected sincerely. 'John Lewis, great, urbane, marvellous person. He said, "Rosetta Tharpe you've got alongside the band, why don't you want Muddy Waters?" I said, "I didn't think it would be possible. I mean I don't know where he is, how do you find him?"

My vision was do you send a postcard to the third cotton bush on the left at second Plantation, Mr Muddy Waters? "No," he said. "Don't be silly." "Has he got a Cadillac, has he got an agent?" I replied. So he said, "I'll find him". So he found him for me. He said, "you've got to have him, he's the real thing," which is perfectly true. So we went through our agent, in London and sure enough, booked him. The next thing was Muddy Waters and his kind of "priorities" band, came over in October 58, and that's what changed British music, again.' As mentioned before, until now most music in the UK had been played acoustically, this American plays it plugged in, amplified, electric.

So the response to this? 'Well it was then you see? The interesting part is there's an awful lot of myths about the whole thing. That, for instance, the audience didn't like Muddy Waters because he played electric guitar and it was too loud. He wasn't. Muddy Waters didn't play loud? The average blues venue in Chicago is a medium-size room with five tables with people eating at and on, and a band playing in the corner. Muddy would play one side, and we had a conversation over here. All that happened was one jazz critic, James Asbendon, a real traditional blah, blah, blah blah, blah, said the electric guitar ruined everything. He walked out anyway. On our recordings, I think you can hear it clearly on the microphones, the audience applauding. Now, the other thing was Rosetta Tharpe had a brand new Gibson Les Paul guitar. A Gold Top, a beautiful one. And she was loud as hell! And it was lovely, and no one complained. There was no complaint anywhere. She was as loud as my band with her guitar. She was perfect, wonderful!' Worth noting that he's observing the subtleties in the events at hand. Many people just get carried away by an element of the argument, the sister's the prominent feature here makes her an equal.

With rock 'n' roll having broken through in the last couple of years, the music in question is growing at a more than steady pace in the UK. It's just what British blues needs to incubate, and develop for a while. So much of this is down to Alexis and Chris and their mutual love of the blues.

At the beginning of 1959 Chris and Harold go to the USA again. They're north of New York having got to the state of Illinois, and the manager gets a question. 'I'm in Chicago with the band and Chris says, "let's go down to South Side Chicago." I said, "What for?" He said, "I want to hear Muddy Waters." So I said, "OK." We had terrible trouble finding a cab that would take us down there 'cos it's the rough area. We finally found a coloured cabbie who'd take us to South Side Chicago. This is on one of our early American tours. We go to Smitty's Corner, the café that Muddy was playing. We walk in and there's instant hostility, white faces, until they learn we're English. Once they learn we're English, not Americans they're friendly. So, we listen to Muddy, and Little Walter playing the harp, and we listen to R'n'B, and speaking as an ex-drummer I was fascinated, as was Graham Burbidge, the [Barber] Band's then-drummer, at what Francis Clay was playing *Bop-Ta-Ta, Bop-Ta-Ta*. Triplets. Whereas we always played either 2/4 or 4/4. Everything in traditional jazz was either two beat [a Stomp], or four beat [Swing]. This sound was new on us. Francis Clay said to Graham, "look, come here! Sit down and I'll show you." So he was the first [British] man to be shown, by an R'n'B drummer how to play the triplets thing. Later it took over the whole of the music. We were intrigued by all this.' For their generation this seems to have been quite a pivotal moment for British blues. Though intriguingly this isn't the only one according to Chris.

I put it to Chris, 'what are your thoughts about Alexis and his career, after he left your group?' 'Thing is, Alexis was in my first amateur band 1949/50. He carried on playing blues, and just playing in blues clubs. The blues clubs were all rather allied to the folk song movement, inasmuch as they didn't allow amplifiers. Huh! But by the time we had Muddy Waters in, we [Alexis and I] realised that was our big concern, the music. That February after the Muddy Waters Tour, the February 59 we'd been to Chicago. We'd been to the place that Muddy Waters played, all over America, and subsequently once, two times in one year. Then we got it [he clicks his fingers abruptly]. That side [of the Atlantic] you've gotta play the blues, and ultimately it was always, "hang that stuff anyway," why write it? The difficulty with blues playing, when you've got banjo and the string bass, and you don't have any amplification, is none of the instruments have any sustain. That kind of thing on the piano, it doesn't exist, all the notes go "Bong!" So it's cute, but it doesn't have that "thing" about it. So we needed that.' For the many fans of music that I'd like to think are absorbing this, sustain is caused when notes and chords are played, received by the guitars pick-up(s) but then left to 'ring', sometimes even feedback in the amplifier. An acoustic instrument can't do this. Valve devices and combos at the time have a particular propensity to do it. Transistor amps came later, around 1969/1970.

The link is abundantly clear with these two when you dig a little further. Chris told me, 'I decided to meet Alexis one day somewhere and, and maybe I met him because Big Bill Broonzy died, and we did a concert at The Dominion, Tottenham Court Road, with my band to collect money for him.' 'When was this?' I queried. '59. We did that and Alexis organised a similar concert for someone else as well, but we had that connection at that time, and he said he wasn't doing much, and we said we'll either do it amp-less or come and do it with us then. Let's just get together. He and Cyril Davies came and joined up with us, who plays harmonica, and Dave Lee Wilkins a blues player from Ealing. On the High St in the middle of Ealing.' Musicians and characters are getting together, and in their willingness to do so are bringing a British blues to a wider audience.

By this year it's fair to say skiffle is at its peak. The parallel significance of Alexis is that his playing has got around the blues much more and he's now getting Harold to bring over people like Muddy, and others from the States to play The Marquee as well.

There's hundreds of young bands out there. It's the simplicity of the music again, that's drawing them in. The tea chest's where my father started. You've got groups like John Lennon's The Quarrymen, gigging on a regular basis. Groups that include many others like Mick Jagger, Jimmy Page, Dave Gilmour and Roger Daltrey for example. Brian Jones is playing sax in traditional jazz outfits in Cheltenham. In Laura Jackson's eponymous book on him she illustrates this. 'If his time at home was a battle, outside life was different because Brian had found an outlet for his breakaway music playing with a local skiffle group. Among other things he played washboard – assuming he hadn't lost his vital thimble – but it didn't matter in any case as all the kids were just messing about. Later though, Brian tightened up his act when he became good enough to play sax with local bands belting the Trad jazz of trombone player Chris Barber and the English-born Humphrey Lyttelton, both renowned band leaders.' The seeds for the British blues and pop movements of the early 1960s are being sown.

Another young man hanging out in London at the beginning of the new decade, is singer and harmonica player Paul Jones. In an interview with me, the musician explained the scenario he found himself in at the time. 'I used to hang around with a crowd who would as regularly go to the Café des Artistes [he was 18], in Chelsea as to Ronnie's or The Alexis Korner Club in Ealing. They were my sort of more arty friends. they were into poetry and painting, music of choice was modern jazz, and that place you find you would find yourself listening to Don Rendell or Joe Harriott, Coleridge Goode. Fantastic musician. That Joe Harriott Band with Shake Keane [poet/trumpet]. Go down to the Café Des Artistes and if it wasn't Phil Seaman it would be Ginger Baker, 1960 y'know! I mean that long ago. Of course by that time Ginger was working with Alexis Korner as well.' The Café des Artistes was a bar that had live bands, based at 266, Fulham Road (it's now the K-Bar).

Not only did jazz help revive the artisan bar, but also managed to encourage the popularity of the coffee bar, like the 2i's in Old Compton Street, Soho as already covered. This is now a scene embedding itself far beyond the capital's Circular roads. In her 1992 and 2009 paperback

Brian Jones: The Untold Life and Mysterious Death of a Rock Legend, Laura Jackson had this to say on her subject, and Cheltenham would you believe. 'Back in town there had been some changes, too. The new coffee bar craze had swept westward from London in the mid-50s and, by 1960, Cheltenham was brimful of in-places to hang out. Places like the Patio, The Aztec, El Flam and, most popular of all, The Barbeque/Waikiki in Queen's Circus. To the older generation they were looked on as seedier joints, run by socially depraved misfits. To the teenagers, in the words of Brian's friend Pete Boswell, "The Barbeque/Waikiki was the place used by all the people who mattered in Cheltenham at the time."' The scene hasn't taken long to whip up the A40, the music and the fashion go hand in hand. It works the other way as well.

Alexis and Cyril joined Chris Barber's Band for six months in 1961. It's amazing who gets drawn to gigs and shows, by the need to search and discover new sounds and experiences. The trombonist has just such a tale. I'd heard Brian Jones had sung with him he said, "Yes Brian did. Brian Jones saw my band with Alexis and Cyril at Cheltenham. He asked Alexis, "how can I get to London and play blues?" you see. Alexis said, "get yourself down there and go and see The Rolling Stones." They were playing down at The Crawdaddy Club down in Richmond, 1961. Because that's where the National Jazz Festival, the Richmond Jazz Festival, that's the one where the Stones were on in the Clubhouse. As was Alexis as well. Whereas we went out on the main stage as did the other jazz people. Brian had in fact tried to join a jazz band from Cheltenham, Bill Nile's Delta Jazz Band. Bill said, "oh, you want to be in a blues band or something like that." Well he did, so that was it.' I'll leave who did what with whom with you. What I can vouch for is that my dad became the double bass player with Bill Nile's band at the end of the 1960s. What would have helped young, budding musicians get off the starting blocks in 1960/61, when they're located outside of London, is somewhere to meet 'names' from the music industry. To hear the sounds and find out the essentials required, to take them on the road to where they want to be. What did Laura discover? 'Mrs N. E. Filby whose address at 38 Priory Street would become synonymous with uproarious parties, and the place to which all jazz bands gravitated after their gigs, despite perhaps having to travel miles to get there. Big names like Lonnie Donegan, Terry Lightfoot, Acker Bilk, The Temperance 7 and Tommy Steele frequented it. It was quite unique.' As John Appleby wrote in his book, *38 Priory Street and All That Jazz*: 'It's my belief that Mrs Filby did as much as, if not more than, any organisation in town to launch Cheltenham's younger generation on the sea of life, simply by throwing open her door to hundreds of young people.' In the provincial towns and cities of the UK, given the earlier closing times and lack of draught alcohol, an establishment like this works well for all concerned. Certainly Acker, Kenny and Terry would have been familiar with it.

What matters is a proper home for British Blues and R'n'B. It finds it in West London at the Ealing Jazz Club, which opens its doors at the beginning of 1959. In March 1962 Alexis Korner starts running a regular club for the music there. Many of the future British blues and rock names were present that opening night, and more, the capacity is 200.

In 1962 The Marquee started a regular R'n'B night. I asked Harold was there anyone else of note in the Alexis Korner band, called Blues Incorporated after 1961? He put it to me, 'Dick Heckstall-Smith is the tenor player, and they could never find a drummer at this early stage. They tried out two or three drummers. In fact, when they made the first record, they couldn't find a drummer who could do it properly, so they borrowed Chris Barber's, Graham Burbidge, who had been taught how to do it properly. So in other words, the very first record in R'n'B, issued in this country, which was the beginning of the whole movement had Chris Barber's drummer on drums. I'll show you.' By the end of the year Ginger Baker is heavily involved, and Jack Bruce is the bass player. Their also taking some of their inspiration from Ornette Coleman's *Free Jazz* in the USA. The band's turnover of musicians was also intended to be regular. It included the likes of Charlie Watts and Jimmy Page.

Jack Bruce, playing traditional and mainstream jazz, has recently moved down from Birmingham. It takes the tenor player to convince him of how worthwhile the group is. 'It's rock 'n' roll. I was so ignorant about real rhythm and blues and I was such a purist snob that I didn't really get it. It took me a long time to "get" The Beatles. It was Dick [Heckstall-Smith] who introduced me to them. Dick turned me on to everything. Once I started playing that music I got so sucked in, I really loved it. Playing a slow blues in E, that double bass tucked into your groin ... such a great band.' It's clearly a momentous time for him.

In the background though, it's clear that the British blues merchant is performing an additional role here. Providing a broad spectrum with his book [of tunes], 'the important thing is that those guys were, y'know playing with Alexis when Alexis provided some gigs. Or they were playing with y'know, Don Rendell, when he was supplying some. You work for whoever calls you. But it wasn't that much of a split because at the same time as Alexis was doing Louis Jordan, Robert Johnson and whatever else it might be, he was also doing Mingus tunes, and Ellington tunes and things like that.' For any musician in the early stages of their professional career like Paul, the more they can extend their practical experience of songs, writers and styles, the better. All being well they'll develop themselves more quickly and concisely.

The group is proving a productive environment for the future Cream bass player, as illustrated in Harry Shapiro's book about him. He says, 'Playing in the octet [Blues Incorporated] was a chance for Jack to debut some of his own jazz compositions, including '*Immortal Ninth* and *HCKHH Blues*.' 'When I joined Alexis it was just two regular gigs a week,' Jack says. 'There was The Marquee on the Thursday and the Ealing Club on a Saturday. Occasionally we'd do these one-off society gigs that Alexis could get because he'd been to St. Paul's School and he was a definite "hooray."' Jazz and blues musicians can do many similar gigs these days.

Harold has something special to show me. 'So this is 'R'n'B from The Marquee.' The gentleman exhibits to me the, 'first ever R'n'B record.' British that is, released in 1962. 'And you'll notice it bangs on [in the sleeve notes] about the National Jazz Federation, which I was running [responsible for the first the Reading, then the Reading and Leeds Festival] and whose club The Marquee was originally. If you read the script [on the sleeve] it'll tell you who's there, the fact that Graham Burbidge, had to play the drums 'cos they couldn't find a drummer.' Yes, the Ealing Jazz Club it mentions and, Spike Heatley [an acquaintance of my dad's] on bass here. 'Oh, they tried all sorts of bassists here. In those days there were, wandering minstrels, almost all the musicians played with each other, early days. There are about four drummers I know of, who claim to be the original drummer.' 'That's a few,' I laughed in reply. 'It's on the Decca label, Ace of Clubs. Yeah, that was their cheap label.' Even if you look online there's not a vast quantity to say about the company. Alexis is the guitarist, the manager's right about vinyl business matters.

As the decade beds down it's an exciting time, but the ingredients are just bubbling away under the surface. Not only are a number of significant characters crossing paths for the first time, but also the musical styles and genres could produce anything. Paul? 'So the jazz, and whatever you call the other stuff was all intermingled for us. I joined this hopeful rhythm and blues group in 1962, it literally consisted of half a dozen jazz musicians, mostly out of work, and me! They were modern jazz musicians too. The bass player was a guy called Dave Richmond and you would more likely in later years find him working with Elton John, or some famous rock star. On jazz saxophone we had a guy called Tony Roberts, he turned up working with Mike Gibbs, Neil Ardley, people like that. And there was this total crossover between jazz, pop, who rock, blues. Even 60 it was going on.' This is the starting point for the Mann-Hugg Blues Brothers. After another name change they become Manfred Mann the following year. It's quite a cooking pot here, and it wants to brew in a variety of ways.

For an unusual slant on this, when I was interviewing Eddie Harvey I decided to glean from him his take on the blues, the British R'n'B scene.

Grasp/extract the perspective from someone who's thoroughly performed the three styles of jazz, big band, traditional and modern. I asked, 'It's later on, with the introduction of these blues artists that

Chris Barber brought over, that the rhythm and blues scene built up from there?' 'Yeah I did and do love the blues, but it's the juxtaposition WITH jazz [that I think] is really quite interesting, in that it's an essential part of Afro-American music, but it's a bit like mustard in a meal. If you use too much of it, it becomes a blues. In other words, in a funny kind of way, blues kind of holds the development of jazz not 'back', but 'pins it down' a bit. It's an important ingredient and if it's not present, it's not Afro-American music which is what I'm interested in. One of the reasons I came into the music for was because I love the blues.' Great to get such a heartfelt, and direct piece of thought. Very insightful, he's literally reading between the lines.

There's no doubt that when you hear the protagonists of music movements, talk about their time at the wheel, it can be intriguing and illuminating. What that pair do in the late 1950s and early 1960s on behalf of, and with British rhythm 'n' blues, Chris and Alexis shine on a very large part of people's lives when it matters. There's also an enormous future impact on all UK, non-classical music. No mean achievement.

ACKNOWLEDGEMENTS:

Brian Jones: The Untold Life and Mysterious Death of a Rock Legend. Laura Jackson, 1957 November 20; London: Piatkus, 2009. (Previous ed: published as Golden Stone. London: Smith Gryphon, 1992. (P. 1), (P. 14), (P. 15)

Jack Bruce, Composing Himself: The Authorised Biography. Harry Shapiro. London: Outline Press Ltd., 2010. (P. 61 twice).

38 Priory Street and All That Jazz. John Appleby. (Online Open Library).

CHAPTER 9

The early to mid-1960s are a golden era for jazz, and British in particular. This is where both this country's traditional and modern genres firmly plant themselves in the ground, and reach a commercial high. As a result they start to establish their own individual identities, separate from the USA or anywhere else. This decade will be tough though given the rising British blues, and rock 'n' roll scene that is developing parallel to it. But for the UK this is definitively the era of the sharp, clean-cut, Italian jazz suit.

One of our younger characters has been considering a unique offer. Should he take it up? 'So Ronnie Scott's Club opened at the end of October 1959. I actually moved to London on 1 March 1960, and on the day I got there I went to The Club. And ah, Ronnie welcomed me, and he said, "well we haven't got a solicitor, perhaps you would like to be our solicitor?" Pete [King] agreed. So I became the solicitor then, and remained the solicitor till years after Ronnie's death when the Club was sold. Therefore, I was very much involved, in every aspect of the club. I was involved in the original club in Gerrard Street, I dealt with the lease of the club when it moved to Frith Street, and when it first moved to Frith Street it was half the size it now is. After about three years of that, they acquired the premises next door and knocked it into one, into the club you now know. And I dealt with that lease as well. I also dealt with raising money to help finance these moves, and set the clubs up and money was advanced by Norman Granz [owner of jazz label Verve Records in America].' Wally Houser, our short, stocky, tailored, saxophonist has returned to London to get up and on with his life, and with some of the best connections he could have.

It's also a time where people are out there, trying very hard to be themselves. Eddie Harvey has been a very busy character for the last two years, the work of a freelance musician keeping his diary more than just a little occupied. I'll let the wind player get across where he stands at the start of the decade. '1958 was a bus strike, and I had to get around y'know, so I bought a scooter. I had it with a slide trombone on one side, valve trombone on the other and a bag of mutes on top of this rack at the back. I used to do this regular thing, Kenny Baker's Dozen [Yorkshire trumpet player's group based in the capital], every week for two years. That was another live [radio] broadcast. I used to park my scooter on the pavement, unlocked, an' y'know come out, ride it off, an' that was the day when you could do that in London in those days!' Not now. Also to the uninitiated, a valve trombone is like the slide version, except it has button valves like a trumpet and is less common.

Something that was certainly of huge appeal about the UK, to the American music contingent that had made it over to the UK so far, not to beat about the bush, was the lack of racism they'd experienced here, in comparison to their home country at the time. The great American trumpeter Dizzy Gillespie, when interviewed later in his career (BBC

What Time Are We On?

Arena – 1993) clearly described how much more relaxed and at ease he felt on this side of the Atlantic, because his colour appeared to be of such little, fractious significance. There were several other Stateside players with a similar view. Britain is a comfortable and cool place to play, and for better or worse you can buy a good Cuban cigar, if you so choose. Sadly, some racist groups have a foothold in British society, but the police and judicial system do make a reasonable effort to uphold the law, regardless of people's original lineage.

What seems to have kicked off as a potential threat, by some, to both the British jazz movements, has been the arrival of rhythm 'n' blues from America. At present jazz doesn't see that as the case though, but the winds of change are picking up. At the successful end of the traditional yard matters are still good for Barber and bands like his. Humphrey Lyttelton is on a parallel and the club and pub circuit is busy, frequented by the likes of Ken Colyer, Alex Welsh, Kenny Ball, and many other acts both in London and across the country. Of course Chris' band is still filling 3,000-seater town halls and concert venues across the country. Doing frequent, regular tours, the precursor to the popular music ones of the 1960s, and rock ones that commence at the end of the decade. Matters start to get a little difficult for our traditional trombonist. Despite his dedicated and his industrious efforts on behalf of both British and American blues music. 'Then I started to get the worst reviews of my life in the press. You know, "you can't do that muted thing if you've got a steel string [guitar] like Muddy Waters." "You can't do that thing when it's quiet." Anyway, after that various other ones came over, but within about a year of that some of the promoters here who ran all the clubs for the blues bands in those days, realised how cheap it was to hire a rhythm 'n' blues artist. You could see John Lee Hooker, Papa Arthur Brown, and pay for half-a-crown, you know, with bands that turned out to be the next Elbow later, or whatever.' It seems to be the same old story, that often occurs when you've got too much of a good thing. The price falls flat!

Another issue here is that the modern jazz fraternity aren't straining at the leash to get involved in blues, from any direction rally. Eddie's point of view is quite atypical of those I've met through my life. 'Now the blues thing. I don't like modern blues too much, I like early blues.' 'By early blues do you mean "country blues"?' I queried. Clarity seemed needed here. 'Yeah well Romeo Nelson, Lionel Hopkins, Robert Johnson, you know all of that lot. I love that period. I think the first blues musician to come over here was Josh White, who was a lovely player, I loved Josh White. Now I do treasure that side of it. Now the imitations of it and the "second generation" of blues musicians.' 'Do you mean the British blues musicians at the end of the 1950s, early 1960s?', was my reply. Keen to nail it. 'Yeah, they didn't interest me that much I must confess. They obviously had their hearts in the right place like we all did, so being a white Anglo-Saxon Jazz musician must be the most daft thing to be in the whole world. But, I do feel our generation played original music, and it's difficult to do that when your enveloped in blues because that's a little bit harder to copy in a funny kind of way.' What do you think?

Tony Kinsey was a little more direct on the same topic, and less reticent, 'Can't stand it.' In light of your experience, add this and form your opinion from there.

On his return to The Smoke our lawyer didn't think so much had changed. One element of Soho was showing signs of more serious alteration though. 'Well of course Archer St was the Labour Exchange for musicians. People would congregate there on a Monday lunchtime till middle of the afternoon, standing around smoking, talking. It became more of a social event than a business event, and then it just died away. When I first came to London it was very flourishing there, in the early 60s. I think by about 1963 it had withered away to nothing.' Given its position at the heart of the London music industry at the time, if you're a reader (of music) then you're going to be getting slightly itchy feet.

Jim Godbolt states the decline had started towards the end of the 1950s, 'the numbers to be seen in the Street declined week by week and while it seemed inconceivable to most of its denizens that such a solidly entrenched form of entertainment as the dance band [and the variety theatre] should expire, expire they did. Musicians continued to say "see you in the Street", but as the weekly listing of band calls in the musical papers shrunk, so did the once teeming throng.' Trends may literally be on the turn. But they are still pretty robust nonetheless.

What is still hitting home with the youth of the time, apart from what we've highlighted, is the 'Dance Night'. Some of the evidence for this is provided by John Critchinson, when he confirmed the music played was both mainstream and modern jazz. 'Yeah. A lot of it was big band playing pop. It was "popularised jazz", that's the word. Not actually pop, but popularised jazz with marvellous arrangements. Bloody hell! There were some great things going on.' I asked him, 'was it done by people like Ronnie Scott? Ted Heath?' 'Yeah. I mean the Ted Heath Band was brilliant. In Bath even, at The Pavilion you'd get Oscar Rabin's Band, Vic Lewis's Band, loads of 'em. Ronnie brought his band there, his nine-piece.' I know my Aunt and her future husband were big fans of these events, as well as my wife's parents. They'd go weekly to The Rink in Sunderland. I can see why, given their popularity at time, and since the 1920s. These times seem to have evaporated from modern memory, despite their high profile. They shouldn't be forgotten. Not when they only cost a shilling and six pence to attend.

The time was an exciting one for musicians. 'In these conversations I also found out that in places like Wearside, the bands would be semi-professional and playing from "the Pad" [the tunes], as performed by the Ted Heath Orchestra for example. Effectively, it was what's known now as a "covers band". Like a jump/jive, or the Oasis tribute band you might see at a wedding event, or live music club these days. You'd only really see a professional band and one that might be touring, in Newcastle. In this instance it was Ella Fitzgerald with a UK big band. Of course this is against a social background where a lot of people don't have a record deck, or even possess a TV. Given that for many there are no phones never mind mobiles, music/arts information can only be gleaned from the music press, *Melody Maker* and *New Musical Express*, or by going to dances or gigs themselves.

Arriving at the lower echelons of the traditional scene are my father's generation, sprung into this world in the early 1940s. They've been skiffling as we talked about in last chapter, and can now play a bit so their interests are broadening. Meet young banjo player and guitarist Tony Pitt. Born in Wolverhampton, grown up in Chatham, and then someone asks him to join a traditional jazz band, after depping with Kenny Ball. 'The Alex Welsh Band, for the brief time I was with them, had a residency at The Fishmongers Arms at Wood Green [London], every Sunday. That would have been from 60 to 64. The thing about Alex's band, the reason

I was in the band, let's get that straight. Alex was having a job getting work in a lot of the jazz clubs because, if he didn't have a banjo in the band, they didn't want to know. So I was in the band, I was playing the banjo, and guitar [also The White Hart at Southall with Alex Welsh]. But The Fishmongers Arms was great, because of Alex's reputation for not being in the "Bourbon Street Parade: Brigade, if you know what I mean [as discussed in relation to Ken Colyer earlier in the book]. We'd have some great guests, like George Chisholm, great trombone player, who used to play on *The Goon Show* [BBC Radio] apart from other things. Kenny Baker was also one of the guests we would have. A lot of the top players anyway, would come and play with the band.' The band had a lot going for it. I feel I should point out again that my father, Chris Haskins will play double bass as a 'dep(uty)' with them soon, he's later in Bill Nile's Delta's in 1965.

Although Tony was getting an immense sense of pleasure from a relatively new career, it didn't come without its deep frustrations. He continues. 'But of course because I was doing that, and earning lots of money, and drinking lots of that, I didn't really progress at all as a jazz guitar player. Of all the bands I played with, I played more guitar solos in The Laurie Chescoe Band than any other. With Alex of course I'd have to do a guitar "feature" [where the instrument is deliberately the most prominent] in a jazz club, and I think in those days I would do *Sweet Georgia Brown*, at equal breakneck tempo. The interesting thing about Alex's band was that they were "Condonites" [Eddie Condon, American banjoist, guitarist who'd toured the UK in 1957]. So I would do all this stuff in the jazz club, play the banjo, thrash it, solos, guitar, but the minute we got in the studio? NOTHING! I'd just sit and play rhythm [guitar]. Oh, I didn't care about it. They wanted the best of both worlds. They wanted to sound like Eddie Condon on records, but they wanted to get people in clubs y'know.' The dual need for success is not uncommon in jazz. When the lucrative element finally turns up why not try and play what's popular, and be musically diverse? Pulling that off though is a tricky business indeed.

I was keen to get the line-up here as Tony's employer did hundreds of gigs at the time. Over to our man. 'It was Lennie Hastings on drums, a guy called Bill Reid who played double bass and sousaphone, Fred Hunt on piano.' 'My father knew him,' I chipped in. The guitarist smiled and went on. 'Roy Crimmins on trombone, Archie Semple on clarinet, when I joined, and of course Alex. Fred left and we had a guy called Bert Murray on piano, for a while. He also played trombone, and then Roy Crimmins left, and Roy Williams took over but about that time I left the band, to go with Mike Cotton.' Straightforward enough I hope?

One good mate of Wally Houser's is to be a London jazz musician we've briefly met already. His reputation proceeds him. The multi-instrumentalist Denis Rose who plays piano, trumpet and tenor horn and later sax. Even the very mention of his name brings out the broadest of beaming smiles from the lawyer. It's no wonder really. 'Denis Rose, there's a character [he laughs quite hard]. Denis Rose was in prison, because he refused to make any payment to his wife, and in those days you could get imprisoned for debt. He was in prison, and Harry Morris who was the guy who'd worked on the door at the Club 11. They always used to say the Club 11 was ten musicians and Harry Morris, and he was a great pal of Ronnie's. He was a lovely little fella.' The legal position has changed there since.

What Time Are We On?

Wally carries on with his illumination about the doorman. 'He was a photographer, and came to see me [after his release], he said [Wally chuckles to himself throughout this story], "Look, Denis Rose is in prison. Go along and see him, to see if you can help him in anyway."' 'What year was this by the way?' I asked. 'Probably 60, maybe 61. So I went along to Brixton Prison [just off Brixton Hill at Jebb Ave], and I saw him in a room. As I came in he said [in a broad London accent], "Who the fuck are you?" I replied, "I'm a solicitor and I might be able to help you." He said, "I don't think you can." "Well Harry Morris told me come," was my response. "Well tell Harry Morris to f*** himself!" He walked out [bursts out laughing], and that was the end of that! [Pauses to recover but still chuckling]. After that I became very pally with Denis, he was not in a very good mood when I saw him that day, understandably he didn't want to be in prison. He was also a deserter during the war [from the Royal Army Medical Corps], and he used to walk around as a "non-person".' This last fact on the military I've reconciled [see Acknowledgements].

His importance amongst the Modernists we've covered, but this tribute from Wally is ... 'He was very, very influential on the modern music scene because he understood bebop, bebop changes and time better than anybody, also he was very influential in Ronnie Scott's development as a musician. Ronnie always remained very friendly with him. Denis was a very, an [chuckles] interesting character, a very interesting character indeed. He kind of played the piano, he kind of played the trumpet, but mostly the music went on inside his head, and he was able to impart it to other people.' That's a very rare to skill possess. 'Yeah absolutely. Hey, Ronnie and he were in a band that was run by a Belgian guy, Johnny Claes [trumpet player from Brussels], and that's where Ronnie first met Denis, that would be about 1942. Ronnie was very much a youth whereas Denis was a bit older, and a trumpet player in the Johnny Claes Band.' If you see a photo he was very much a Clerkenwell man. Experienced? Even by the early 1950s he'd toured the country with many of the 'name' groups and big bands I've already mentioned and more. He even toured Germany in 1953 with the USO (United Services Organizations). They provided entertainment to US Armed Services in Europe after the War.

The lawyer here surprised me even more with another tale concerning Denis's jail mate. 'Harry Morris is another interesting character, he was a lovely little man, he died VERY young. 33 when he went. Just had a heart attack in his car and he died. But he was always on the fringes of the jazz scene, and a great pal of Ronnie's. I mean they all came from the East End. Ronnie, Tony Crombie, Denis Rose, Harry, they were all pals as kids y'know [born in the 1920s]. I remember Tony telling me that they came up to hear somebody play in the West End, and they had to walk home during an air raid! So that's how long ago it was [he says a with a grin], dodging the bombs on the way home to the East End.' It conjures up quite an image. Making that return journey must have been no mean feat, through the damaged buildings, craters, fires, sirens and melee.

John Dankworth held the musician in exceptionally high esteem, when it came to his practical value to the cause. In his book he points out that in his early days he was, 'just about the first trumpet player in London to adopt the bebop style using the methods and chord structures of Dizzy Gillespie.' This was, 'even though his instrumental technique was not the best at the time, he became a kind of guru who represented the new musical thinking we had all adopted.' I think these reflections cover the man's significance.

Something of real significance that takes place between 26 and 27 August 1961, is the first National Jazz Festival. It happens at the Richmond Athletic Grounds, Surrey. Organised by the National Jazz Federation, if it leans any particular way it's more of a traditional and mainstream jazz event than modern. Though you'll see Chris Barber, Terry Lightfoot and Ken Colyer with their bands, John Dankworth, Don Rendell and Tubby Hayes will also perform with their outfits.

There is a grim world holding the jazz scene by the hand at this point in time. A lot of it is discreetly hidden as John Critchinson put to me. 'Never noticed it with Tubby. I never saw any one. Oh! Yeah, Bill [Le Sage] in the later days. Did see Bill Le Sage absolutely out of his brains y'know. In fact we booked him for a gig in Torquay, he turned up and he could hardly speak, much less walk. But the singer I was working with, she poured coffee into him. Anyway, but there were … [pauses], certainly drinking and drugs were a scene.' It's tough for the young player making his way at the bottom of the ladder.

He goes on, 'I can only quote direct contact with it. Ron Mathewson, the bass player with Ronnie, now he could not play unless he'd had a couple of pints and a couple of shorts. He had a, sort of a "stage fright" in a way. And then he plays end-up, and then he'd get absolutely stoned and he couldn't do anything, y'know, and he'd take anything that was going. But on the other hand he wasn't really a, he wasn't a "junkie", Ron, but he was a boozer.' I said, 'I'm sure there were plenty of those at the time?' He replied, 'there were a lot of them who couldn't play. I mean I started getting into that with The Avon Cities [jazz band – an early group working in Bath and Bristol]. A pint of beer and a whisky "chaser" before we went on the stage, y'know. And I did that for about a year, and I started getting heartburn, and God knows what, y'know? So I thought, "to hell with it!" They used to use it as a way of cooling down before they went on stage. Y'know, people do that!' I can certainly vouch for that in others. I've worked with many a talent who's needed a little more in the way of hops, or malt on a gig for the reasons given. A frustration for the players who aren't affected, but to an extent understood.

Harold Pendleton had a final story on this topic. 'I'll never forget the trombone player who Chris bought his first trombone from, called Harry Brown, could drink a bit, in fact he formed a band later called Harry Brown's Dipsomaniacs. And even worse when Mick Mulligan, when his father and brother were killed and Mick had to take over the wine business, he made Harry Brown the manager of one of his shops, who drank all the profit [both laugh] oh dear.' A sad, and expensive state of affairs indeed.

During the rise of British blues, matters start to reverse a little for Chris Barber's fortunes. The trombonist is succinct with his account of how significant the value of American blues had been over here at the time. 'It soon hit! But it soon got devalued, the value of American blues [sounds exasperated].' 'By the late 1950s?' I asked. 'By 1961. It was two years to bring them here. In a sense the "careers" in the British Musicians' Union had always been very wary of letting American musicians/bands come and play in Britain, because they thought if they weren't careful, they'd have another lot of already paid musicians, who'd come here, and work cheap, and take all the jobs. Of course the joke is that the American Musicians' Union [the AFM] thought the same thing the other way round [author bursts out laughing].' Chris grinning and querying simply states, 'neither of them thought of doing them out you see.' The rivalries between the respective trade unions was fierce, if only based on an infantile lack of trust. Which ultimately was inflammatory and unfounded.

In more musical matters, Alexis is trying to make some progress with his version of the blues. He seems to be quite idiosyncratic at the time, Paul Jones is very clear about that. 'Alexis was a whole different thing in 1962. He started that [Ealing] Club at the start of 1962, and at that point he had really turned his back on skiffle, and he was doing something far more experimental. He would basically see what it sounded like if you mixed folk/blues with Thelonious Monk, or Charles Mingus, and um, some of it looking back, wasn't so breathtakingly successful as we thought it was at the time. I mean, I just went, "yeah, this is brilliant," y'know [laughs out loud]. See people tend to think, "oh yeah, he's in that particular pigeonhole. He's in that category so we don't need to know what he thinks about something quite different."' Paul sees it from the opposite stance. I'd argue that's potentially a very healthy viewpoint in the creative arts, in music especially, regardless of the genre.

In his early days Paul was very grateful to this blues master as well, for simple, uncomplicated reasons. 'Because I mean I used to go and sit in with Alexis. He had this great reputation for encouraging youngsters, and it was totally deserved. He was really, truly very generous, and he would just point into the audience, y'know and go. "You! Your turn." And you'd get up and sit in, and sing [laughs out loud]. I mean, how many songs did I know?' In some ways he seems genuinely astonished when reflecting on it now. Who would have thought it?

When it's come to assessing the standard of the supporting players used, the singer has clearly put some thought into it. As he explains, 'All the musicians he [Alexis] had in his bands were always uniformly excellent. I guess really for me, and for those of us who congregated of a Saturday night in Ealing, in this tiny little cellar with a serious damp and condensation problem, the point was that it proved that there was some market for the music that we loved. When I had my band in Oxford [The Oxford University Jazz Band], sort of between the summer of 61, and the summer of 62 I suppose, (for the sake of argument, part of the time I was a student, and then for a while after that I wasn't), I thought that apart from folk/blues, which you could hear in places like The Troubadour and Bungee's in London, I had the only band that was playing rhythm 'n' blues. That's with a saxophone, electric guitar and harmonica which I was playing through the vocal microphone, I didn't have an amplifier.' A great line-up. It's melodic, yet abrasive and diverse.

Around the very same time though, another of my interviewees is able to shine a brighter beam on the first of Paul's capital nightspots. Now performing again, Wally? 'One thing that I did that was interesting was that I played at The Troubadour, which is a little coffee house on the Earls Court Road, and that was with another friend of mine, a long-deceased blues singer called Eric Lister, and our drummer was Charlie Watts. And I remember a bass player called Malcolm Cecil. We also had Ginger Baker working there for quite some time.' 'What year would that have been?' 'This is the early 60s. The next thing I knew Charlie

Watts was with The Rolling Stones, and the rest is history as they say. Eric Lister was my best friend.' The solicitor is very definitive in his responses. It's also to his great credit, he knows what he wants to say.

In 1961, Tubby Hayes decided to take the time to go to the USA, and try to make his name over there. This was a very prudent move on his part. A Brit who'd made the trip already was Victor Feldman, who'd gone in 1955. He'd played with the London modern crowd before his departure. Our solicitor tells the tale. 'One of the great musicians who came over [from the States] was Victor and he was one of the great vibes players of the world, as well as one of the great pianists. A Jewish boy from London. The Feldman Club, that became the 100 Club, was run by his father. Victor was a child prodigy drummer, and then he became a pianist that everybody wanted to have in their band. I mean Cannonball Adderley had him in the band, and Miles Davis. And a vibes player. He did a lot of studio work in Hollywood, making plenty of money but he died young too. He was always very, very delicate, a bad asthma sufferer. Victor was very good indeed and another nice guy. He worked in Ronnie's eight-piece band playing drums when Tony Crombie wasn't. He was another absolute natural musician.' His performances at the keyboard, on the trumpet player's album *Seven Steps to Heaven*, are excellent. A very worthwhile purchase.

With the gradual success of the first tier of jazz players, I was interested to know more about those coming up behind. What about the young crowd from the Caribbean, the Windrush Generation? Did Wally think there were there many good West Indian players on the scene in the early 1960s? 'Well, Joe Harriott of course, Sheik Heane, trumpet player. I don't know if he was West Indian or African. Eddie

Thornton, another good jazz trumpet player, don't know what's happened to Eddie. Wilton Bogey Gaynair, tenor saxophone/clarinet. Dizzy Reece, another trumpet player who went to New York, I think he's still there.' Reece's time in London was in the latter 1950s. As far as I know he's still Stateside of the Atlantic. Harriott's reputation in the UK is still good. (Names and fact checked with WW. P. 148/130/266. S.H. not an entry, cannot be verified)

While sorting his direction, Paul Jones's next step was the following. It may seem unusual? 'I'd answered an ad in the *Melody Maker*, for a singer in a dance band. You might think that's a funny thing to do, but I thought, "this is what I need to do." I need to work regularly with good musicians and just learn something about music business and, how you "do it", and all that kind of stuff. They even let me do one of my own songs. When I spoke to him the guy who ran the dance band said, "I promise you when you've been working for us for a little I'll get you an audition with Kennedy Street Enterprises," which was the big agency for pop singers. I thought that's the way to go. That was 62.' An unexpected step? Though not so astonishing.

By being made up of a variety of component parts at the same time, Paul's music was putting him in a relatively unparalleled situation. There were quite a few about in the same boat, although my father's similar interests took him towards jazz. Talking about British blues, the lead singer says, 'I literally did not think there was anyone else doing that kind of music in Britain, and one of the astonishing things that happened when Alexis opened that club was that I met all these people. People came to that club from as far away as Scotland. Just because suddenly there was a Mecca for people who liked this kind of music.

What Time Are We On?

People who liked Muddy Waters, and Howlin' Wolf, Little Walter and, all that stuff. I found there was a band in Birmingham led by Spencer Davies, there was band in Newcastle, the person I met from The Animals was the saxophone player Nigel Stanger, who'd left them by the time they became famous [laughs]. There were all people from Liverpool, and Manchester, and Scotland playing the same kind of music as I was playing, and in one sense I felt slightly disappointed that I no longer had this unique position, but of course I knew I didn't have the unique position anymore because here was Alexis doing it, and much more high profile than I was 'cos I was just doing the gigs university students get.' To find the 'like-minded' in music when you least expect it, certainly gives you a bit of a start. A slightly older, but more experienced centre point for it leaves you tearing out of the starting blocks.

The vocalist has no doubts about who he met there. He can provide the perfect analogy to describe the clubs attendees to Alexis. 'So we just used to go there [The Ealing Club], and that's the first place I met Mick Jagger, and Keith Richards and Brian Jones (of The Rolling Stones). It was like, Alexis had the big pot of honey, and we were all the teddy bears, and we wanted to get some of the honey and see what it was like. Pretty soon every singer, and every hopeful guitar player and mouth organist, with an interest in the blues we were all three deep round the bandstand. And that's when he would say, "You! Your turn. Get up!" The image of the bear and the big pot of honey is the right one.' Having fallen into this young, small, vibrant community, Paul's avenues of opportunity are wide open. In the way they are for his fellow Ealing compatriots. Brian Jones asked him to sing for the band he was starting, Paul declined.

Typical of the response I got from the musicians I met, was that of Eddie Harvey who was particularly impartial and open-minded. It was when I covered the topic of British blues at the turn of the decade. I wanted to know, did he think that the generation of British blues music of the late 1950s/early 1960s was what caused jazz its major problems, in terms of an audience and the work? It was a scenario I often heard submitted in conversation by traditional players in my early teens. 'I wasn't conscious of that at the time, they had their own audience and we had ours. Yeah, gradually y'know. When The Marquee became a blues club, we started off that club with John's [Dankworth] band when it was on Oxford St underneath the New Cinema there. I've got pictures of us playing the opening night there, in a mock marquee with stripes down the sides. After that it moved to Wardour St, and then they started featuring blues music, I don't know if it was anything to do with that? [I don't believe so, no one's mentioned anything to me] Then they started having rock bands "paying to play" there. As professional musicians we thought that was a bit much. It's like that joke of Ronnie Scott's, somebody said [to him], "do you play free jazz?" Ronnie said, "no, cheap!" [both laugh].' The 'one-liner' aside, Eddie's final point is a very fair and significant one. It's great now to have so many well-trained musicians (going to music college/conservatoire), but the 'bite back' from that is there just isn't the gig work out there to support them.

I put the original question to Tony Kinsey, as I was curious to get a second opinion here. This is the response I got. 'I agree it did tail off in popularity. I mean the only other music they had in the early 50s apart from basic dance music was trad jazz and modern jazz. When people liked modern jazz that was all they had. The rhythm 'n' blues thing came along, and the rock thing, and modern jazz suffered because of it. I mean, The Beatles are here and that. But that's what the public want. And the public will have what they want. A lot of the fringe listeners of modern jazz who would've listened to that, were drawn to that kind of music. But classical music suffers too.' Popular music, which at the beginning of the decade includes jazz, seems to have a need to diversify.

In the midst of this period, Wally Houser informs me events were busy at Ronnie Scott's Club. 'While we [Ronnie Scott's] were at Gerrard St, you know about the spat between the Musicians' Union and the American Federation of Musicians?' 'Oh yes,' I pointed out. 'Whereby American musicians couldn't work here, and English musicians couldn't work in the United States. Pete King went over to New York and had a meeting with the A F of M, which I think you'll find was a Mafia thing in those days. But they were very courteous to him, and he worked out a deal with them. The first American musician to play legitimately in a London jazz club was Zoot Sims [tenor, alto and soprano sax – 1961]. And we were all very excited about it. But that opened floodgates, because after that an incredible number of musicians came to play there. Sonny Stitt, Bill Evans, Stan Getz, Roland Kirk. Just trying to think of those who worked at Gerrard St.' Sadly, the Gerrard Street premises often get forgotten.

There is a character tying over this period, who's working with Alexis Korner and Cyril Davies and will soon go much further. I'll pass the storytelling to Paul (real name Pond) Jones, who is getting desperate for his shot at being the front man. Straining at the leash but this time there's no mucking about. As he says, 'Jack Bruce was on the first couple of albums. Jack was working with Alexis [on double bass] before it became Blues Incorporated. So the next time someone rang me up and said do you wanna join my band I said yes, and it was The Manfreds. Towards the end of 62. I remember it was late summer, the guy said, "have you ever heard of Manfred Mann? They're looking for a shouter," he said, "would you like to audition." I said, "yeah. I'll audition." And afterwards I thought, "I've been sitting in with Alexis for months now, and occasionally with other bands as well, and one or two people know who I am, who knows who Manfred Mann and Mike Hugg are? They should be auditioning for me." But that moment of pride passed and I auditioned, and to be honest I didn't see anyone else at that audition at all. So I got the job.' An occasion that must have proved more than pleasing at the end of the day. The Arts are often a place where we're made to believe 'the competition' we face is always tougher, than we are.

For our fortunate vocalist he gets a bit of a bad break. Though that's just one side of an exceptionally lucky coin. 'I stopped going to the Ealing Club so often. There was some work waiting. We immediately started working some gigs on the south coast, Southampton, Portsmouth. The Marquee. Also the National Jazz Federation [Harold Pendleton is an early secretary] was lowering its standards [jokes], by allowing the odd blues band skiffle group. Alexis had opened up this great big doorway and people started rushing through, and so all of a sudden there were clubs in London that there never had been before. I'd go to the 100 club in the 50s to catch a couple of traditional gigs when I was at school in Portsmouth, I would just go up for the weekends maybe.' The floodgates are wide open, and the waters career through. Just as the live music/pub rock scene did in the UK at the end of 1978 after punk, but before the independent music/New Romantic scene that's about to start in 1979. That features Siouxsie and the Banshees, The Buzzcocks, The Cure and Joy Division, Killing Joke, Spandau Ballet.

Whatever Paul got up to there, he certainly has very fond memories of the time. The surprise is when you get caught out, as he did unexpectedly recently. 'Somebody said to me recently, "when were you regularly attending The Moist Hoist?" I said, "I've never been to The Moist Hoist." And he said, "no, you have, The Ealing Club." I said, "oh yeah! It was NEVER called The Moist Hoist." Well it started to be called that sometime round about then, and the reason for that was, well in those days smoking was permitted in public places, and people would drink and smoke, and then sweat and shout, and speak, the air would rise to the ceiling, condensation would occur; it's not water it's sort of fluid [laughs]. It's got nicotine in it, and beer. I think people just tended to put up with it, except for the drummer because once it started dropping on his skins, it was all over, y'know he couldn't play.' He's got a fair point on the latter score. Band and audience are prepared to put up with a lot.

A difficult matter. But Paul can also illustrate what was done to resolve it. 'So what they did was put up a canvas, like a sail only on its side, and it was suspended from the corners of the room, and the problem was solved, and that's why it became known as The Moist Hoist. By that time I'd definitely stopped going. I think it must've been sometime in early 63.' Nightspots will attempt all sorts to keep the doors open. I think it's a good job they do, not least because the live music scene in the UK is fundamental, and doesn't have any room for the scalpel.

There's no doubt early 1962 proves very successful for traditional jazz. A performer of the music, Acker Bilk, makes it the biggest one to date in terms of record sales, with the release of his single *Stranger on the Shore*. A million copies sold by 2 April 1962. Another million again on top of that, in total. Its 53 weeks in the charts help to simultaneously make it No. 1 in the UK and US listings.

Working hard on the traditional side of the fence is Tony Pitt. In 1962 he's gigging at his most frequent, and still happily a member of The Alex Welsh Jazz Band. He's started to find that with the work, has also come the habits, mannerisms from spending so much time in each other's company. It's a tough life as musician. 'So we used to do a jazz club in Cambridge, at The Ritz Cinema, where they had a large restaurant, and for that night it became a jazz club. 50 yards from The Ritz Cinema in those days was a pub, that sold draught Merrydown cider. Now, it's quite strong. I used to buy it by the bottle. We would go to The Ritz, set up, go to the pub, come back, do the first set, go to the pub in the interval, by the end of the evening the band would be blitzed y'know. I mean they'd get drunk, on anything. Whatever they fancied.' Even in the early part of this decade alcohol remains a formidable opponent to the performer. Despite much wider public knowledge on the topic of drink, and its more negative issues.

Some players just want to get home. Others, once they get the booze and the music inside them, develop a desire to be fractious. 'There was often fisticuffs, and always very heated argument y'know? And it started something for me which seems to have caught on, because to my knowledge I was the first person to do it. There'd be this big thing going on in the [band] wagon [van], and I'd be sat in the front because I'm a bit, "travel sick" y'see? And there'd, literally be a punch-up going on behind me. Whether it would be Alex and Roy, or Alex and whoever else, Lennie Hastings or whatever, and then I'd be sitting there and be thinking, "oh, for God's sake," y'know? Fred Hunt, who was the driver [and pianist at this time] would pull up and let them sort it out, and then it would all quieten down. And we'd set off again, and then Lennie Hastings at the back used to say, "and another thing!" And I'd think, "oh no, it's all going to start again." And that was Lennie.' It is such a confined environment, talking from first-hand experience. Fine if life is good, if tensions are rife?

Is there more to the story? Did matters on the road ever go any further? 'Occasionally his coming out with that, "would start something else," going. I personally never got involved in any of those punch-ups except with Lennie. He was a fabulous drummer.' In his second historical tome, Jim Godbolt refers to the fact that Lennie Hastings was 'highly irascible, and often drunk.' 'If he wanted to play a certain tune and Alex wanted to play something else, he'd sulk and it'd come out in his drumming, he'd sort of play down, y'know, he wouldn't give it everything.' I can vouch for Tony's observations as I've seen him perform in a rhythm section on BBC TV's *Jazz 625* from 1964. It's difficult though if you feel awkward about your professional abilities.

One of the most standout compliments that any of my interviewees gave another, produced a drummer. My longest acquaintance John Critchinson, who I first met in 1989, said that Tony Kinsey, 'played with loads of guys. One thing that Tony had, that not anybody else had, was when he was playing he looked as though he was enjoying it [John beams broadly]. He was one of these people who played with a smile on his face, did you notice that?' I pointed out I hadn't. 'When he plays he's got his eyes closed, and a gentle smile on his face, and he's the only drummer I know, one of the few musicians I know, that has a smile on his face when he's actually playing.' That one threw me I'll have to admit. But John would spot it as on the stage, he could scour the others in his vicinity during a tune for what was up. Even engage in a chat with another player while still performing, even soloing himself.

Surprisingly, some of the interviewees had given a lot of thought to jazz musicians' jobs within the entourage/gang, the other definitions of what we do, and how we came by them. First up is Chris Barber, on the topic of 'playing in the ensemble'. 'Wally Fawkes [who left Humphrey Lyttelton's band in 1956] was more proficient in some ways than Humph sometimes. But a clarinet player has a lot more notes you see. A trumpet player is playing simple phrases, and these phrases are [pauses], you realise that's the way you play it. It isn't a question of whether you can do a personal, good interpretation of playing *Stardust* in a nice way, that's not the point. If it's wrong you'll obviously get it wrong because you're trying to play *Stardust* and you can't play it. The minute you go and play with other people there's much more to it than that, you've got to fit in and make it all work together, and that means there's a "style" question there you'll have to know about, and if you can't play that, that kind of "ensemble" playing won't work.' Chris is absolutely right here. Whether you're performing jazz, traditional or modern or blues you've got to fit within the style/genre you're performing. It starts to get interesting again when you begin to play around with that, says the Get The Blessing purchaser.

The daily task we all have though has many methods. I'll leave it to the bandleader to explain further. 'It's like having a football team with ten centre-forwards and a goalkeeper. The difficulty is you have to practise somehow. Practising playing jazz by yourself is a bit like a goalkeeper practising by himself. You need to do it with somebody else [last eight words said in unison, then laughs]. At least one [bursts out laughing]. You've got to be like David Beckham, hitting a high ball forward into the place the striker's going to be. A trombone player's job in the ensemble. You've got to work towards something where the trumpet player's going to be there too. You've got to sense what's happening. You've got to know what they play, maybe more than they know.'

At Trinity College of Music, where I studied for my Music Degree, I was encouraged to take a much more open approach to soloing and improvisation. I know my friends and contemporaries from London, Bath, Bristol and the North, who've attended a variety of universities and conservatoires like mine, were taught many alternatives but Chris' seems like the most team-orientated jazz philosophy I've come across. There's a lot to be said for it. I'm always happy to do what's asked, but it's great when a group is so inclusive.

When it comes to handing out the compliments, this is one for Eddie Harvey. It comes from Humphrey Lyttelton, and is in his second autobiography *Second Chorus*. I felt it important to highlight this, because of the high standing this trombone player had amongst his fellow musicians, then and now. 'I should like to acknowledge the assistance which we have had from arrangers. Eddie Harvey, an associate back in the days of George Webb's Dixielanders, for whom he played rip-roaring "tailgate" trombone, has done most of outside arrangements. Eddie has long since moved from the Revivalist to the Modernist camp, playing in the Johnny Dankworth Seven for many years and now a member of the Don Rendell Jazz Six. While his arrangements for us are in a contemporary style [though not 'modern' in the experimental sense], he has, through his own early associations with the Revival, a strong historic sense. And so he has been able to treat with respect and affection the old numbers which we have asked him to arrange for us.' He illustrates an enormous, yet little-acknowledged talent Eddie had outside his music, profession and generation. Andrea Vicari, the piano player, performer, teacher, friend, and other contemporary professionals are equally complimentary about the late player and arranger.

Paul Jones is leading a very urgent way of life at the start of 1963. Fronting a band playing something a bit different, a touch more abrasive, but still needing to make ends meet. As I've mentioned, and

Eddie Harvey (at the piano), freelance musician with Humphrey Lyttelton, trumpet, 1964.

he says in own words, 'The Manfred's, as we now call them, started playing at The Marquee late 62, then early 63. At that point I was determined that this would be my life. Public performance of music would be my life and that's that.' He was certainly determined about what his vocation should be.

In the early 1960s making ends meet was not an easy task. Having only recently dropped out of university, but not even earning a living yet, he resolves to get to grips with the issue. 'So I had to do something. I got a job as a travelling salesman for Esquire Records. Carlo Krahmer.' Yes, that gentleman who met earlier in the book.

He was someone that John Dankworth, and many of the more experienced faces on the UK jazz scene, knew very well indeed. In his excellent book, the altoist elaborates. 'With much of our repertoire being issued on the pioneer British jazz label Esquire (1948/52), run by the London drummer Carlo Krahmer from a primitive studio in the basement of his flat in Bedford Square, just off Tottenham Court Road.' Carlo, as we know first performed in the capital towards the end of the 1940s. Essentially he now has an 'indie jazz' label, started in 1947 with Peter Newbrook. That's commitment and foresight, given its age.

Though I think Paul should be allowed to carry on. 'Carlo was a lovely guy. He said, "you get the sales, you get the commission." I think I may have been on a really minimal salary like ten pounds a week or something. At that time he had the Prestige catalogue [American record company who to 1958 had had Miles Davis. Other artists in 1962 included the Thelonious Monk Quartet, the Modern Jazz Quartet, Yusef Lateef amongst others] just for Britain. I was working for him, so basically traipsing around London. I didn't go outside London, 'cos he had another guy who did the rest of the United Kingdom and I wasn't to tread on his territory, but I could do London from Hendon to wherever it was [ponders], Crystal Palace, I don't know [for example].' Whatever he does, the main task at hand is to be industrious. Up and at it.

He certainly needs to be diligent. 'I used to look up record shops, so I'd go up to the record shops, and I didn't do Dobell's and those things Carlo Krahmer did himself, they were right in his little parish. He was based in Bloomsbury somewhere just near the British Museum. Anyway, there I was, working for him and sitting in with anyone that would let me, and I mean it wasn't anything very much, and I added Topic Records. So I started working for them as well, which was like folk. But they had Sonny Terry, Brownie McGhee and Big Bill Broonzy, people like that. They almost overlapped 'cos Carlo had Mose Allison from whatever company he was on. So I was getting into all that side of things as well.' In 1963 that's a solid business achievement. To be able to sell their records under licence in the UK, under the Esquire brand. Especially given that the artists are playing over here since the efforts of Chris Barber, Harold Pendleton and others at the end of the 1950s.

Mr Krahmer's direction was consistent. The singer puts it clearly. 'Again, there was another incident. Carlo was putting out modern jazz, and he was putting out blues, he was making deals with Chicago record companies. Little ones like Banbera, and Loredo, and putting out some really fine records. Eddie Boyd, Dusty Brown.' Selling rare US indie blues material is a massive step forward. It seems so from the 2000s.

I put it to Paul. 'That must've very much helped the guys like yourself who had been listening, getting into blues, and going to Alexis's club?' 'Yeah. In those days major record companies weren't putting out much of that stuff at all. Pye had a deal with Chess, that was the major Chicago blues label, so you could get Howlin' Wolf, Muddy Waters, Little Walter, Sonny Boy Williamson, that type of thing but it was hard to find much else.' A hint of frustration? 'John Lee Hooker, Jimmy Reed. It was easier to get Bo Diddley and Chuck Berry, which is why The Rolling Stones went off in that direction. It's also more commercial as well.' His diversity of artists, genres and licences is exceptional given he's competing against Parlophone (EMI) for example, and Pye (International Records) who have the likes of Lonnie Donegan from 1955. Pye have Kenny Ball as well, who has a big hit in 1961 with *Samantha*, which reaches No. 2 in the Singles Chart, and in 1962 with *Midnight in Moscow*. The record even got a Gold Disc for selling a million copies.

A group of players drawing attention to their talents would be some of the younger jazz musicians who are jumping ship to perform British blues as well. 'I'm thinking of one person who spent a long time with Alexis and that was Art Themen, the saxophonist and surgeon [St Mary's Hospital, Paddington], he really is [The singer says excitedly]! Extraordinary double. He's a noted surgeon, very useful pillar of the community, and fortunately he's still working, on the tenor saxophone, in both capacities. He was with Alexis for a couple of years at least.' Still working in London and the UK at present. A little less than before but plenty of fire.

Another tenor player mentioned in connection with Mr Korner is Dick Heckstall-Smith. Similar to Themen, he likes character (he has affection for character?). This he expresses in Harry Shapiro's fine solo work on the British blues guitarist. 'The kind of jazz I like – the kind of music I like – is strong, pushy, forward, full blooded, free of self-imposed restrictions. It takes risks. It is not in the least bit afraid. It battles its way through to expression. It is full of mistakes, but couldn't care a jot about them because it knows that mistakes are its lifeblood ... It shows know mercy for half measures. It doesn't care about good taste. But this is not to say it can't be beautiful. It's beauty is that of strength triumphing over ugliness.' That's a bold, positive, descriptive statement if ever there was one. By golly!

It's not surprising that these traits and hallmarks of this new music have come from a jazz background. It's a topic that John Critchinson has memories of and more academic thoughts on. 'What I was really trying to say was the knowledge of those people actually consisted of them on the stand, the tempos they'd play – and for people like Tubby and Ronnie it's as fast as you could do it [laughs], I suppose for us in those times it was but nothing like it is now. It was quite fast. They were tunes we'd sort of heard of, some of them brought charts, but most of them [the musicians] said, "do you know 'so and so'?" To have "Real Books" [a contemporary jazz musicians collection of songs/charts they can take to jam sessions/gigs] at that time? They didn't exist. So my knowledge would have come from Jackson's record programmes [radio show] that sort of thing.' For the 'early starter' it was about being self-taught. John's good fortune was that he had the remarkable train of thought and mental agility, to keep up with those mentioned and more.

The pianist offered more on 'where' their knowledge came from, and those behind it. 'But there were no actual "arrangements", of anything so, I think that's why the Club 11 got together, and all of a sudden they realised they could do the arrangements themselves, and there were people that could write arrangements for them. So the British scene established itself that way, coming off the American thing, but being British. British changes, British chord structures and all that sort of thing. And all that was very important to establish a British scene. But the thing was it didn't have the appeal to the public in England, as the Americans did. And when you listen to Americans even playing at that time, you hear a record from the 50s of somebody playing, their whole concept of "changes" and "chord structures" is different to ours in my opinion, y'know. And that's why I still think there is still a difference between American playing, and English playing.' Knowing the who, and the what, he has clearly drawn lines in his head about where they lie, and why.

Our sideman expands further on the music. Also on the view from the other side of the Great Pond. 'We've got bands, I mean John Dankworth talked about when he went over with his band to do the Newport Jazz Festival [USA, July 1958] didn't he?' 'Yes,' I confirmed. 'And they said [American press], "oh, he's got a very American sounding band." But it didn't sound American [looks irate], if you were listening to what the American bands were sounding like. You can hear the difference, and it's good!' That's precise, on the money!

Given the direction of our chat, I put it point blank to my father's long-term friend, did he think it benefitted British modern jazz in the long run, that it was slightly different from the American? Had its own character? 'Well yeah! It had its own character only because of accessibility to the American form of things that weren't there. Then as they started to come over, so the style of actual soloing changed, and then they were bringing parts over that people had to look at and play. This is getting very technical isn't it? But it's an important side of it really.' An insightful examination of the music and chunk of its history.

To my great surprise, and delight though, in the blink of an eye Critch turned the question on himself without any prompting from me. 'And the thing that astounds me is that I don't know where I learnt mine [musical knowledge] from, but it must have come out of playing with those [London] guys. In some way learning by default, 'cos I couldn't read music and still can't. I can read "chord changes", but I wasn't very good at those even then. This is why I think there should be an advert for this programme [book], which is Ronnie with a picture of himself saying, "what the fuck am I doing here [laughs]?" Actually, I really do think that but then, you know, anyway [laughs again].' Spoken like a musician who's spent a long time on the scene, and who was a good friend and colleague of Ronnie Scott's.

Someone else who has had that good fortune has been Tubby Hayes. For many he's at the epicentre of the British modern jazz movement. A true stand-alone talent, in all the right ways, performance included (a musical tinderbox, an effusive yet controlled and polished performer). Sadly he could never get beyond his helpless addiction to heroin, available on prescription from the chemist's on Piccadilly Circus, or on your local High street. Since 1961 he'd been visiting the States regularly and playing, performing at the Half Note Club in New York, and recording. Also leading his own groups and big band here.

During the second half of the decade he struggled with a developing heart condition, culminating in surgery in 1969. In 1973 he was admitted to Hammersmith Hospital in London, and Wally Houser paid him a visit. 'I saw him the night he died, Ronnie and I went to go and see him in hospital. He had a heart-valve operation and, he was told he had to lose weight. He'd then become very underweight indeed. And then the heart-valve slipped, and he had to have it replaced.' 'When was that?' I asked. 'That was 1973, and ahh [seeming very reflective], he died on the operating table. He never came round from the anaesthetic. I remember when we left all we said, "see ya Tubbs!" He said, "see ya guys, whahhhh!" He was always "roaring". When he could get you into a justle he'd go "whahhh!" Always roaring away, with his very ebullient character, very nice guy. Generous with his music talents, he taught me a lot of stuff as well, there was a big turnout for his funeral.' 'That's good to know,' I said. 'Yeah, big turnout.' Said with a smile on his face.

For a moment Wally seemed to be slightly lost in thought, trying to find the right words, then he said to me, 'I would've almost thought that Ronnie was the leader of our generation, and Tubby was his kind of trainee. He was a good ten years younger than Ronnie.' There's a smile. 'Oh, Tubby was great!' Well, he said it like he meant it. Some people do shine that brightly.

On the traditional side of the scene, things are still busy. The 100 Club and Studio 51, like their modern counterparts continue to do a regular, excellent trade, most nights of the week in their basement premises. Continuing with their regular night at the latter is the Ken Colyer Band. Traditional's divide rolls on at the start of 1964. Given his youth, I asked Tony Pitt what he thought of the group. 'Well initially, when I first got into it, I loved it. I still think it was a fantastic rhythm section but, from where I was at that time [musically] all I got, and a lot of banjo players still do [pauses]. I wanted to play the guitar you see, so I'd sort of moved away from that [pauses] … in fact.' This is a significant musical shift within the genre. The guitar is also becoming the dominant instrument in British popular music.

Our guitarist left Alex Welsh and joined the Mike Cotton Sound at start of 1964. Change happened soon though. 'Of course once I got through that period and joined Acker Bilk [May 1964], we didn't do so many jazz clubs. All the bands still did the 100 Club, that was the main one, the rest of it was pretty much concert tours, once I got in Acker's band. So playing places like the Bristol Hippodrome, the Colston Hall. And later on of course Acker had the [Bristol] Old Granary which was fabulous. In fact, I mean we also played [pauses], the other one in Bristol was the small pubs, The Kings Head? The Cas Caswell place?' Quite possibly, Cas Caswell's a friend of Dad's. I think he means the Old Duke?

This is becoming a fortuitous period in Tony's career. You can't knock it! 'Funnily enough two of us joined the band on same day. Myself, and Tucker Finlayson on [double] bass. And at that time they had a guy called Ron Mackay on drums, who was a hell of a swinger, great guy and a good singer too. Stan Greg on piano, John Mortimer on trombone and Colin Smith on trumpet, then after that various trumpet players. Yeah, it was a good band.' So far, time has been relatively kind on Acker's band. It's well remembered, and most people over 40 know the look when they see it. No mean achievement!

The role he's performing in his opening 12 months takes a rare twist. I'll leave him to elaborate. 'But I only played the banjo with Acker's band for about the first year I was with the band. In fact, my father made a banjo. I designed one and my father made it from scratch, it was fantastic, and the thing I had in it was a 14-inch snare drum head [all jazz drummers use these, head size personal choice]. I mean, they're usually 11 ½ inches, and he'd made the whole thing from scratch, and it was incredibly nice to play and very loud. And we did a tour of Czechoslovakia, and somebody broke into the band bus and stole the banjo, and one of Acker's clarinets and various things. My father, it was hard to tell him. Anyway, I never played the banjo in the band after that, just guitar.' 'After that first year with Acker?' I asked. 'Yeah. Yeah.' That's a rough way to finish though.

At this point in time, Chris Barber is a man with a very busy diary. It's in the early part of this decade that television coverage begins to be regularly offered his way. 'Mainly because the BBC, ITV hadn't started then, was run by old codgers, and they were always known to cater for "what was known". For the "right stuff". That was it. End of subject. You certainly weren't going to get on TV playing jazz, it was very rare, very unlikely. We did very few. It wasn't until the 60s we began to get things where we'd do things like the *Today* programme with Cliff Michelmore. We'd do them several times, also with Sonny Boy Williamson [American blues musician] on harmonica. Just a couple of numbers, it was very good. They were bits of numbers, they weren't presented very strongly but they weren't talked over or anything, but they were seen. That would've been 1964.' The trombonist is one of the first to benefit from the advent of family, and music television. Great that it should be inexorably tied to blues performance as well.

A person who's often arranging these deals around this time is Harold Pendleton. During the interview he was remarkably open, and unexpecting at one point. A surprise. He feels that both Chris and he are coming at affairs in particular ways, and that is of great significance, as he explains. 'Somebody once said of me, what I've done in the whole music business was, "manure the fields, for other people to reap the crops to pioneer", which is what pioneers do, and to a large extent Chris [Barber] is the same.' There's no mistaking Harold's thoughts.

What's needed here is some refinement in the response. There's no doubting the trombonist's desire to learn. What to do with the knowledge though? Ask a close associate, Harold. 'Chris has done what he wanted to do, and he's always been interested in doing it for its own sake. Whereas the other Bs, Bilk and Ball, more or less came to it via the entertainment side, they've always wanted to be entertainers, and Kenny and his band are brilliant entertainers. And their main function was entertainment. Chris has never been quite like that. I remember once we were appearing at the London Palladium, ah (pauses) … some BBC thing and the revolve, and I remember the producer said to Chris, "Right! What I want is quick, short, sharp numbers." And what Chris said is, "What I play is long, slow blues numbers." He [the producer] says, "That's why I intended Kenny Ball to get the jobs." It's a different ethos altogether. Chris wanted to play the music that he felt and that he cared about, for its own sake.' It's a very bright part of the sky when your manager has such a positive point of view about you. I can only posthumously applaud Harold's generosity, given the mixed views and misconceptions I've come across over the years, from musicians and punters alike, since the day I was born, towards Chris Barber.

Humphrey Lyttelton is also appearing on TV, with personal success. He's doing work in the role of presenter, particularly for the BBC, and for a show that's just starting out for the state broadcaster, *Jazz*

625. It's also an excellent snapshot of live performance, collective and individual improvisation, the music's different genres, the best variety of British and Stateside musicianship and one of the channel's most highly recommended music shows if you get the chance to see it now. The show, also presented by Steve Race and John Scott, runs from April 1964 to August 1966. It features Duke Ellington, Kenny Baker, Ronnie Scott, John Dankworth, Tubby Hayes, Dizzy Gillespie and Oscar Peterson amongst others, and ran to 21 editions.

It's in steep, direct and unforeseen competition though, not least with *Ready Steady Go!* It runs with great success on ITV, from August the previous year to December 1966. There's also the BBC's own *Top of the Pops* from January 1964.

Paul Jones's career moves on in 1963. I was keen to know what kind of gigs have Manfred Mann been doing? 'There was a ring of clubs around London called the "Ricky-Tick Clubs", but they were very much sort of blues, R'n'B, that sort of stuff. Our band played in them, The Rolling Stones did. But they were definitely going, as was the Eel Pie Club. They would be clubs inspired by Alexis's venture into that territory.' So simple, straightforward.

The band's career now takes a natural progression. It helps make it more financially viable, which is all any decent, working musician wants. 'The Manfreds started to get bread and butter gigs, y'know the "residencies", and we got offered Mondays, or Tuesdays at The Marquee, so you could make a living, y'know, and that would be early 1963. I can remember it was March 1963 that I went to Carlo and I said, "I got this band and I've got about three, four, five gigs a week now, and ah, I'm leaving." And he said, "don't you think you should keep working for me, so that you've got something solid y'know [laughs]?"' Given the number of gigs I'd chance my arm as well. London rents, and general social costs weren't what they are now. That came in with the Thatcherite economics of the 1980s.

The line-up in the singer's group has a volatile turnover to boot. He paints a clearer picture. 'Jack Bruce spent a year with Manfred Mann [July 1965–66]. In fact, basically Jack and I, and a tenor player Lyn Dobson, and the trumpet player Henry Lowther all left on the same day [laughs]. Necessitating a major reshuffle [laughs again], at the palace. Basically Jack went off to do Cream, I embarked on a solo career which has been chequered in the extreme, Henry Lowther's working wonderfully. He's with the Mike Gibb Orchestra and Bill Frisell.' Jack Bruce sadly died four years ago, since the interview with Paul was carried out in 2011.

In terms of success, Acker Bilk's Paramount Jazz Band is prolific and busy at that time. Their hit is still present in people's minds, and these are Tony Pitt's thoughts when I asked him, was he on the hit *Stranger on the Shore*? 'Well Acker's Band itself, from my recollection [he pauses in thought] … the quick answer is no, because we didn't have any "hit" records while I was with the band, but the band lived on Acker's "hit" records. You see, Acker had a band of sorts in Bristol, and he wrote a tune for his daughter, Jenny, and it was picked up by someone, and used as a certain TV theme, for a certain programme and it was called *Stranger on the Shore* by the TV people. And it became a massive hit, and of course he then proceeded. At that time, when I was with Acker's Band he was recording between three and five LPs a year, with orchestras not with his band.' 'With orchestras?' I queried.

What Time Are We On?

'Oh yeah, playing all sorts of stuff, and he had all sorts of hits. *Aria* was one of them, and various other things. Of course, because of that his records became known worldwide y'know. The States, Continent, Eastern Europe. Everywhere knew about Acker.' By the early 1970s it was apparent that his success continued.

The tale of his band was as straightforward as this. 'So his band virtually lived off his success, I mean the band was good, and he was in the band, played beautifully. But when I was with the band we made a lot of records, but we never had a hit record. All Acker wanted to do was tour with his band, that's what he wanted to do, right up until the day he died. Same as Kenny [Ball]. The band virtually lived off his name. Which was great for us.' The consistent touring, and gigging, was how many of the bands ultimately made their money.

On the modern scene, I was curious to know what Don Rendell had made of the arrival of rhythm 'n' blues. But he was good enough to give me an honest and blunt answer, for which I must thank him. 'No, you see I didn't really want to change. [Laughs] I wasn't open to these changes, and I just played jazz. I didn't really ever get into a blues situation. But there's not just one blues, there's so many. The 12-bars was reckoned as the blues, but looking at books and everything there was a 10-bar blues. Basically I'm just a jazz musician playing on "standards" and blues. I wrote so much stuff it's hard to believe that I did!' It's as frank a reply as you'll get anywhere.

Our saxophonist continues to qualify his thoughts on himself. 'But you see I was NEVER a "businessman", from the point of view of, carefully looking after the stuff I'd written. I never did. Although if you look through my albums [so you look through 20 albums], that there's got to be at least 50 "originals", at least. And then I was thinking how I wrote a book for the Guildhall [School of Music and Drama, London], when I was teaching there. A saxophone book I wrote which was used in the grade exams. That's at least another six or seven compositions in that book, and with The Rendell/Carr Quintet I must've written [pauses for thought], ten of the pieces.' I don't think you can put it more succinctly than that. I'm impressed.

Having been in the trade since the war, Eddie's heard nearly every story on the vine. This is one of the best I've heard, though my heart bleeds for the poor soul who came a cropper here. 'This guy I knew learnt French horn 'cos he thought it'd be a good double for doing studio work with. And one of his famous ones was he got this jingle in [offered], and it was the "call sign" for ITN [ITV News]. It went, "Daah Da. Da. Daahh." That's all it was. He floored it! He went, "Daah Da. D'dlia Da Uhah." Something like that. Well they [ITN] put it out for years, and years and years [laughing]. You can hear him fluffing this top note. Oh! But he used to hate it y'know, hearing it every time.' Once a call sign's played and recorded, it's in the hands of the copyright holder. Guess what? You don't stand a chance. It's the other party's, the one who wrote it and asked you to play it.

In 1965, Ronnie Scott's Club moved to 47, Frith Street, Soho, also with financial help from Harold Davison. Where Stan Tracey has also become the club's house pianist. I put it to Wally Houser that it must have been a fantastic time in the early 1960s? 'Oh, it was, it was! It was very vibrant indeed musically speaking, it really was. Ah, the middle 60s as far as I was concerned was the most interesting time. When I was with Pete King a few years ago and we were looking at the old [club] diaries of who'd been playing there and it read "unbelievable!" Two weeks Stan Getz Quartet, two weeks Buddy Rich's Big Band, two weeks Modern Jazz Quartet, three weeks Count Basie's Orchestra and all the other numerous musicians were there. It just read like a *Who's Who Book of Jazz*. And really we became very blasé about it.' A

Eddie Harvey's PR Photograph 2. Music Lecturer, Royal Academy of Music, London, late 1990s

statement made with great honesty and alacrity, while grinning like a Cheshire cat. In some ways, who can blame him?

I think our solicitor/saxophonist's first couple of sentences in the last paragraph really sum up the five years of this chapter. Modern jazz, just like the traditional genre, has been through a very challenging time. Relatively speaking, at the start of the decade, they'd been the dominant forms of a rebellious new music, and rapidly found themselves under a threat from the generation behind, and a couple of musicians from their own ranks. Yet modern jazz fought back and used its advances to cast new foundations. The Traditionalists? With a little vinyl fortune, and similar tactics they did the same. Play on!

ACKNOWLEDGEMENTS:

A History of Jazz in Britain 1950–1970. Jim Godbolt, 1922–2013. London: Quartet, 1989 (P. 269), (P.127)

Jazz in Revolution. John Dankworth, 1927–2010. London: Constable, 1998 (P. 59), (P. 84), (P. 217)

Who's Who of British Jazz/John Chilton. John Chilton, 1932–2016. London: Cassell, 1997 (P. 276), (P.1 56)

P. 5. p. 4 Fact re: Rose, Denis (from the Royal Army Medical Corps) confirmed in *Who's Who* (as above); (P. 276)

Second Chorus. Drawings by the author. Humphrey Lyttelton, 1921–2008. London: MacGibbon & Kee, 1958 (P. 175)

Alexis Korner: The Biography. Harry Shapiro; discography and additional research by Mark Roster. London: Bloomsbury, 1996 (P. 106)

Jazz 625; BBC TV. London. 1964.

Ronnie Scott's detail confirmation. *Some of My Best Friends Are Blues*. Ronnie Scott; with Mike Hennessey; preface by Pete King. Ronnie Scott, 1927–1996. London: Northway, 2004 (P. 90. p. 2/WH. P. 2)

CHAPTER 10

It's 1965 and in a matter of 20 years British mainstream, and big band jazz, has gone from being the British baby on the boulevard, to the King of the Mall with three younger brothers, in traditional, modern and rhythm 'n' blues. But its shine is already in the descent. It will have future phases of popularity but regardless of the genre it will never repeat the chart success of late 1950s and 1960s. In its period of popularity it's lasted as long as the one from The Beatles, to the start of the New Romantics in 1979.

Despite its drop from the top of the tree, British jazz nonetheless is keeping a solid stance while popular music has continued to dominate since the early 1960s. One perspective that has consistently interested me amongst the interviewees, has been what the atmosphere was like between the musicians themselves. It was a question I put to John Critchinson during our spring chat. 'I think possibly the thing I remember, and maybe it's all gloss, maybe it's just me and looking at the world through rose-coloured glasses, but the whole thing seemed to me to be a very, amiable sort of "get-together" of the semi-pros and the pros. And to me that's all I really wanted to be y'know. It helped spread the word I guess didn't it? Oh yeah! To bring in those audiences, especially at The Icebox.' John paused for a little more thought.

He felt it important to point out though that, 'as I say, Tubby, all the other ones, they really were affable people, and there were certain ones that really encouraged you to do it, Bill Le Sage, Tubby, Vic Ash, Don Rendell. Who were all people that encouraged you to do it, get at it.' I've been lucky that John has been a family friend for many years. Sadly at the end of 2017, and with great surprise, John Critchinson passed away aged 82. Ronnie Scott's pianist, and house piano player from 1979, a truly great talent.

Given that Chris Barber had seen Humphrey Lyttelton right at the birth of a very bright start for him, I was keen to know what kind of influence the trumpet player had had on the trombonist. 'Well a big influence in one way really, I mean [pauses and thinks], when I came back to London from the school after being evacuated during the War, I returned to Golders Green in 1945. I discovered that I liked jazz anyway, I'd been getting records and had already had some sent over. So, I was looking for more, you could find odd records here and there. There were one or two shops in London, Dobell's and Colin Conway's shop. His at South Kensington station, and Dobell's in his father's antique bookshop in Charing Cross Road. [Since moved into Foyles Bookshop, same street] I had no idea, I had these records of Louis Armstrong, Jelly Roll Morton and that sort of thing, and so on and so forth. I knew a bit about how it came about, and the history and things. I'd also read a bit about the blues, it had been thrown away by an American airman at the American Base near Rhodes School. *Read The Blues* they called it, in a red cover. An ideal book for giving to somebody who doesn't know much about it [laughs out loud].' It was quite a moment, and proved very useful for the trombonist I was talking to.

To give your entire life over to music and performance, and for it to be an enormous success is quite unique. I think it begs a very fundamental question. One major point I was keen to ascertain from Chris Barber was simply, and how he got into this line of work in the first place we covered, what was the thinking behind your first major band? 'What Monty Sunshine, I and Lonnie Donegan, why we started my band off in 1952, we said this is absurd playing with amateurs. We're not getting any better, in point of fact with an amateur band, they've all got families and jobs and things, they've gotta do and studies and everything else which means you're lucky to get one evening a week, if you play every Friday or whatever. You play there every Friday, and each week after you finish you realise you made the same mistakes again, and haven't got any better at all. And you weren't going to get any better. Now, this doesn't bother some people. But the ones that, began to try and play, you know seriously, and thought the music was valid, was worth it, most of those still wouldn't give anything up for it. The point is that we said well y'know, the people that started up creating jazz in the first place probably did nothing else at all! Played every bloody night all the time! In fact, trying to earn a living at it, you had to play every night because there wasn't much money in it you see. So that's what we did.' As straightforward and candid as ever!

As the son of a professional jazz double bass player, I was very pleased when my father Chris Haskins said he was happy to pass on a couple of telephone numbers for my use. Also, to act as a reference point for the traditional, and blues sides of the music. Very good of him. During the 1970s he was the electric bass player for The Rod Mason Jazz Band, completely made up of thirty-something 'Tony Pitts'. They'd done their time on the London scene during the 1960s, in various outfits. He was very keen I get this written. In the 1980s he moved to mainland Europe where he played with The Piccadilly Six, who were based in Zurich, Switzerland. He died in May 2016.

The book's been a hobby while I've been unwell. I'm surprised my interviewees all said yes and it's done. Along the way Eddie, Don, Harold, John, Chris and Tony Pitt all passed away. This may well be your last chance to read their thoughts on the music they played, and managed in Harold's case. The rest of them are 70 or more as I write now.

The modern British popular music scene originally starts at the end of the Second World War with British traditional jazz and big band dance music. It's following on from the dance music of the 1930s. It soon develops British modern jazz with the help of the Americans. But these 'British' forms of the music are ours, and significantly so, according to some of my interviewees. To what degree that might be, is entirely up to you. Some of my contemporaries see that argument from both sides of the boundary fence as well. Me? The British genres exist, and we have our own swing, no doubt about it! But the music (all varieties) needs handling with care.

In 2018, there aren't the number of live venues there were back in the 1950s, a lot of them don't even pay musicians the going 'Musicians' Union rate' for a gig (so the band is effectively underpaid). They pass round a jug amongst the audience, thus devolving themselves of the responsibility of paying them. Declare it to the Inland Revenue? I don't think so. Put the cost on the crowd.

What Time Are We On?

Gentrification is sadly the other new enemy of live music. Developers, and other people grouping together, forcing venues to shut or put the performance on early. There is nothing wrong with 11 o'clock closing (just needs stricter law enforcement, from ALL angles), and if you're moving into an area with a music pub in the next two streets, maybe you should know about it beforehand. The Internet and Telephone Directory both make this easy.

As I said early on, many of the familiar characters have long gone, thus making this kind of literary task that much more tricky. When I started writing it, I was surprised to find how limited my options were. Every time I typed in a name on my iMac, it came back with the first sentence in the past tense. The famous, household names in jazz, apart from Chris Barber, are no longer with us. Acker Bilk went in 2014. Their fellow band members have been going at a steady pace as well, though some are still around. To see a traditional jazz band is more of a rare event these days.

Over time there's one thing we should never forget. How we created our own popular music. I've heard TV commentators put it entirely down to The Beatles, or the blues, nonsense. In the 1920s and 1930s our jazz, and its groups, was ostensibly influenced by the traditional and mainstream jazz of America. Later, by the big band music of Woody Herman, Duke Ellington and Count Basie, and any shellac records we could get our hands on. The country was encompassed by ballrooms, so plenty of room to dance. After the Second World War we were soon presented with our own British traditional revivalism. By 1958 we'd firmly established British modern jazz. Around that a broad and solid live nightclub scene grew, not only in London's capacious West End, but also for the first time late bars started to appear in some of the UK's other major cities. Leeds, Bradford, Bristol, Manchester, Birmingham, Liverpool and Sheffield. By the advent of the British blues scene at the end of the 1950s, those places had been joined by Coventry, Plymouth, Southampton, Newcastle, Sunderland and Wolverhampton.

I hope this book, with its many thoughts and contributions from those on the front line at the time, has a broad enough horizon to set the record straight on some of it. My interviewees and contacts were very keen for me to do that. We can't let the 1950s disappear, because that way nobody gets any credit except Lonnie Donegan and Elvis Presley. Without the formal contracting of original US blues greats to perform over here, by Chris and Harold, would you have the listened to The Beatles or The Rolling Stones? Regardless of your age. (THE END)

WHAT TIME ARE WE ON?

BY MATT HASKINS

SPOTIFY LISTENING LIST

Band Title/Album/Track Title

1945–1949 (First-Time 'Rounders):
Louis Armstrong, King Oliver – King Oliver's Creole Jazz Band; *Canal Street Blues*

Bunk Johnson – *Rare and Unissued Masters 1943–46 Vol. 2; I Wish I Could Shimmy Like My Sister Kate*

Duke Ellington – *The Essential Duke Ellington* – Disc 2; *Take the A Train*

Louis Jordan & His Tympany Five – *Compilation Disc D; 1947–49; Barnyard Boogie*

George Webb's Dixielanders – *Bluein' the Blues/South* (listed under track title only)

Freddy Randall and His Band – *Before and After; Dr Jazz*

1950–1955:

Humphrey Lyttelton and His Band – *On Call*; *Apex Blues*

The Ronnie Scott Quartet – *Not So Fast, The Complete Esquire Recordings 1951*; *September Song*

Chris Barber's Jazz Band – *Chris Barber 1954–1955*; *The Girls Go Crazy About The Way I Walk*

Ken Colyer's Jazzmen – *Colyer's Pleasure*; *La Harpe Street Blues* **N.B.** The track is potentially a Decca single from 1954

John Dankworth & Cleo Laine – *Archive '53–'58*; *Somebody Loves Me*

Victor Feldman – *Golden Selection* (Recorded August 1955, Remastered); *Brawl For All*

1956–1960:

Humphrey Lyttelton – *On Call*; *Bad Penny Blues* (1956)

Alex Welsh and his Band – *Vintage Alex Welsh (1955–1956)*; *All of Me* (1956)

Tubby Hayes and 'The Jazz Couriers' feat. Ronnie Scott – *After Lights Out*; *Oh, My!* (*The Swinging Giant Vol. 2* – Jasmine Records 1957)

Don Rendell Jazz 6 – *Playtime*; *Dolly Mixture* (1958)

Chris Barber – *This is Chris Barber's Jazz Band*; *Petite Fleur* (1st UK Group to sell 1 million copies, 1959 UK Chart Pos. No. 3, US No. 5)

Jimmy Deuchar – *The Complete Tempo Recordings 1955–58*, Disc 2; *Milestones* (1958)

What Time Are We On?

1960–1965:

The Joe Harriott Quintet – *Free Form*; *Formation* (1961)

Ottilie Patterson, The Chris Barber Jazz Band – *Blues Book And Beyond*; *Mama, He Treats Your Daughter Mean* (originally released 1961)

Kenny Ball and His Jazzmen – *Midnight in Moscow*; *Midnight in Moscow* (UK Chart Pos. No. 2, 1962)

Mr Acker Bilk & His Paramount Jazz Band, with The Leon Young String Chorale – *Stranger on the Shore*; *Stranger on the Shore* (UK Chart Pos. No. 1, 1962)

Alexis Korner's Blues Incorporated – *R & B From The Marquee*; *Rain Is Such A Lonesome Sound* (1962)

Manfred Mann – *The Five Faces Of Manfred Mann*; *Smokestack Lightning* (1964)

The Stan Tracey Quartet – *Under Milk Wood*; *Cockle Row* (1965)

The Tubby Hayes Orchestra – *100% Proof*; *Nutty* (1967)

For further information about the author please go to www.matthaskins.net

Printed and bound by CPI Group (UK) Ltd, Croydon, CR0 4YY

21/05/2026

02115617-0001